D1486016

GENETICS FOR CAT BREEDERS

THIRD EDITION

Titles of related interest from Pergamon Press

ROBINSON
Genetics for Dog Breeders, 2nd edition

EDNEY
The Waltham Book of Dog and Cat Nutrition, 2nd edition

LANE
Jones's Animal Nursing, 5th edition

The Waltham Book of Dog and Cat Behaviour

ANDERSON & EDNEY
Practical Animal Handling

EMILY & PENMAN
Handbook of Small Animal Dentistry

GENETICS FOR CAT BREEDERS

THIRD EDITION

BY

ROY ROBINSON, F.I.Biol.

PERGAMON PRESS

Member of Maxwell Macmillan Pergamon Publishing Corporation

OXFORD · NEW YORK · BEIJING · FRANKFURT
SEOUL · SYDNEY · TOKYO

U.K.	Pergamon Press plc, Headington Hill Hall, Oxford OX3 0BW, England
U.S.A.	Pergamon Press Inc., Maxwell House, Fairview Park, Elmsford, New York 10523, U.S.A.
PEOPLE'S REPUBLIC OF CHINA	Maxwell Pergamon China, Beijing Exhibition Centre, Xizhimenwai Dajie, Beijing 100044, People's Republic of China
GERMANY	Pergamon Press GmbH, Hammerweg 6, D-6242 Kronberg, Germany
KOREA	Pergamon Press Korea, KPO Box 315, Seoul 110-603, Korea
AUSTRALIA	Maxwell Macmillan Pergamon Publishing Australia Pty Ltd, Lakes Business Park, 2 Lord Street, Botany, NSW 2019, Australia
JAPAN	Pergamon Press, 8th Floor, Matsuoka Central Building, 1-7-1 Nishi-Shinjuku, Shinjuku-ku, Tokyo 160, Japan

First edition 1971
Reprinted 1973, 1975
Second edition 1977
Reprinted 1978, 1983, 1987
Reprinted with corrections 1988, 1989
Third edition 1991

Library of Congress Cataloging in Publication Data
Robinson, Roy.
Genetics for cat breeders/by Roy Robinson. — 3rd ed.
p. cm.
Includes bibliographical references and index.
1. Cats—Breeding. 2. Cats—Genetics. I. Title.
SF447.5.R6 1991 636.8'0821—dc20 91–7995

British Library Cataloguing in Publication Data
Robinson, Roy *1922—*
Genetics for cat breeders. – 3rd ed.
1. Cats
I. Title
636.80821

ISBN 0-08-037506-5

Printed in Great Britain by B.P.C.C. Wheatons Ltd, Exeter

Contents

Preface to the Third Edition

INTEREST IN THE genetics of the cat has continued to increase. Indeed, more than ever, breeders are coming to appreciate the value of genetic principles in the creation of ever more beautiful pedigree cats. The text of several chapters has been thoroughly revised for the third edition to encompass the latest developments and descriptions of new breeds and colour varieties.

ROY ROBINSON
November 1990

Preface to the Second Edition

THE LAST 5 years have seen a remarkable upsurge of interest in cat genetics and a corresponding increase in our knowledge. This is most heartening, although one must acknowledge that certain problems still remain unsolved and new ones have arisen. However, that's animal breeding! The incorporation of new information has meant that the text of the first edition has had to be carefully revised. In particular, Chapters V and VII have been expanded and Chapter VI rewritten in its entirety. I am indebted to many cat fanciers and especially to Miss Patricia Turner for fruitful discussions.

ROY ROBINSON

Preface to the First Edition

THE WRITING of this book springs from the belief that the continued advancement of cat breeding relies upon an acknowledgement of modern trends in animal breeding. It should be recognized that the world of small animal breeding is discarding "rule of thumb" methods for a more balanced programme of scientific method and skilful breeding. The science of genetics has much to offer both to the theory and the practice of cat breeding. The thoughtful breeder should ponder on the fact that once his or her cats are provided with a good home, properly fed and receiving expert veterinary care, the sole hope of producing the superlative animal lies in the art of breeding.

In the preliminary chapters an endeavour is made to outline the elementary principles of heredity. The theory has been subdued to a large extent in deference to the more practical considerations. Quite considerable advances have been achieved in the practical application of genetics to the larger, economically regarded, livestock and these techniques may, with profit, be adapted to cat breeding. The cat may be thought of as "different", especially in its psychological make-up, but its heredity differs little from other animals.

An account of proven heredity of the cat is of considerable interest in itself, and of immense value for the complete understanding of the animal. A fair amount of information on the genetics of the cat has been published, in the main, in relatively inaccessible scientific journals. A simplified summary of this work is given with special regard to the constitution of breeds which, so far as the author is aware, has not previously been attempted in a comprehensive manner. Research into feline genetics has been carried out in many different countries, for the cat is truly cosmopolitan, and the benefits to be derived are similarly universal. It is hoped that this book will be of service to breeders wheresoever in the world they may reside.

A special chapter is given on those abnormalities which are either suspected or known to be genetically determined. Some abnormalities are due entirely to genetic causes and some result from a genetically determined constitution interacting with a dietary deficiency or developmental defect which would not necessarily upset a normal cat. It is hoped that this chapter will be of service to veterinary surgeons in the pursuit of their profession.

I am indebted to the many breeders who have discussed various problems with me and for their interest. Discussions with Alison Ashford, Peter Dyte, Roy and Maureen Silson and Patricia Turner, knowledgeable breeders all, have been particularly valuable. My thanks are due to Animal Photography Ltd., Anne Cumbers, Cat Information Centre, Will Green and Hugh Smith for permission to reproduce photographs.

ROY ROBINSON

1

Introduction

A FEW words may not be out of place on the sort of information a cat breeder might be expected to obtain from genetics. Three aspects will probably be of special interest. Firstly, there is genetics itself, especially that part of it which is concerned with coat colour in mammals. No breeder should confine himself to cats alone in his reading. Studies on variation in other species of animals could give valuable insight into similar variation in cats. This is an aspect which makes Searle's (1968) interesting book on colour variation so useful, dealing as it does with the whole spectrum of mammalian species.

Secondly, a detailed account of the known genetics of the cat. The various mutant genes which have been reported and the effects they produce. The variation of colour and coat types which result from combinations of the genes. How these have been seized upon by breeders and skilfully woven into established breeds. An account of variation both within and outside the breeds which is of intrinsic interest and which might be useful for creating new breeds. All of these aspects will be discussed in succeeding sections. Some can be covered in depth but others can only be lightly touched upon because of sketchy information or lack of reliable knowledge.

Finally, there are the methods of animal improvement which could be used in cat breeding. What constitutes inbreeding and if or when to employ it. What is selection, when to apply it and which traits should be concentrated upon. A discussion of these problems is undoubtedly called for and should be satisfied. In dealing with methods of animal improvement, it is rarely possible to go beyond a general discussion because only the breeder has the data from which to make correct judgements. In a sense, animal improvement at an elementary level remains an art rather than an exact science. It is a question of gauging the worth of the individual by inspection, rather than by measurement, and of making decisions based on shrewd judgement, rather than on a set number of matings or on the passage of a certain number of generations.

When all has been said and done, the occasion may arise when certain observations appear "odd" and do not fit into the scheme of things. One possibility which should be looked into at the onset is that a mistake has not been made. A mistaken identification, an error in the breeding records or an accidental mis-mating. Only saints are perfect—the rest of us make all sorts of errors. If mistakes can be ruled out, then it may be that the genetic explanation is not as accurate or as complete as it could be. Alternatively, something new has been discovered, such as the discovery of two genes for rex coat of some years back or the folded eared mutant of recent years. In this event, it is wise to seek competent advice. Whenever unexpected results occur, it is always advisable to consult other people. The chances of discovering something novel are slim but the possibility is always there.

Mendelism and Genetics

The first accurate description of the principles of heredity was enunciated in 1866 by Gregor Mendel. Alas for the inspired reasoning of this remarkable man, the scientific climate was not ripe for ready acceptance of his simple, almost blunt, account and Mendel's discovery languished until 1900. Round about this time, the prevailing ideas on heredity and evolution were being critically appraised by inquiring minds and, in particular, biology was beginning to emerge as an experimental, as opposed to an observational, science. About 1900, Mendel's work was acclaimed by three biologists, independently and more or less simultaneously. This fact should demonstrate perhaps more than any other how biological thought had changed in the intervening 34 years.

It is common knowledge that Mendel carried out his experiments with the ordinary garden pea. Once the basic principles were grasped, there were many people who were eager to discover if his ideas applied to other plants and to animals. It was soon found that they did, in most cases with astonishing similarity and, in others, with subtle variations which served to strengthen and to extend the principles he had formulated.

Mendel's laws of heredity, as his principles are known, stood up to the test of repeatable experiment. Their generality for all species of plants and animals implied that they were fundamental. In the early days, the study of heredity was known as "Mendelism" until W. Bateson in 1906 coined the word "genetics" for the new biological discipline. Thus, heredity became a science, with principles which can be checked and with laws of real predictive value. From the humble beginning of a man pottering around in a spare corner of his garden, genetics has grown to such an extent that research establishments are devoted to the subject and no corner of biology or medicine can escape its impact. For those who find pleasure in learning a subject by reading of its historical development, Dunn's (1965) book is recommended.

There is no grand design in science. This means that the growth of fundamental ideas and their application can be very uneven. In some respects, genetics has had more than its fair share of opposition from established practice. Possibly this is understandable since heredity has often been thought of as something intangible and difficult to pin down. Thus, it became shrouded in mystery and bedeviled with mystical ideas. Unfortunately, animal breeding has a very rich quota of legend based on all sorts of queer prejudices. This has delayed the practical application of genetics to some forms of animal breeding; particularly, it would seem, in those branches less exposed to economic pressures. However, there are encouraging signs of increasing awareness that genetics has something worthwhile to offer the person who is willing to make the effort.

It required several decades for the foundations of genetics to be laid. In the meantime, animal breeding carried on more or less as usual. There was indeed more emphasis placed on selection but this was merely an intensification of current practice. That selection was the key to animal breeding had been known since Darwin focused attention upon how effective the process can be. On the other hand, a rational genetic theory of animal improvement had to wait upon an understanding of the effects of inbreeding, cross-breeding and the relative effectiveness of various methods of selection. The work of Lush (1945) is monumental in this respect. There is now a very considerable and impressive amount of theoretical and experience on the genetic aspects of animal improvement.

Once the mechanism of heredity had been satisfactorily settled, it became obvious that concepts based on the "percentage of blood" and the overestimated influence of remote ancestors had to be revised. Even the use of pedigrees in breeding became suspect unless one is very familiar with the ancestors listed and could recall their apparent worth. A tabulation of names, devoid of accurate description, is scarcely any value at all except for intimating that the individual is derived from a well-known stock. If the ancestors have high-sounding names, but are unknown: how can the worth of the animal or its potential breeding be assessed?

Nomenclature

The domestic cat is often referred to as *Felis domesticus*. The word *Felis* indicating that the animal belongs to the main genus of cats and the word *domesticus* indicating that it is a domesticated form. This is fair enough. However, Carl Linne, the founder of scientific classification, named the domestic cat as *Felis catus*. This designation is also often employed. Everything would still be straightforward but for the fact that Linne singled out the blotched type of tabby as *catus*, apparently neglectful or oblivious to the equally common mackerel type. In some people's eyes, the omission needed rectifying, so the mackerel has come to receive the designation of *torquata*.

The name of *domesticus* is seemingly the most appropriate even if, in strict nomenclative terms, it is not correct. As a designation, it certainly describes the present status of the cat. It is unfortunate that the origin of the cat is so obscure, for the animal must obviously be a domesticated form of a wild species. If the wild ancestor was definitely known, the use of the species may seem preferable, even if *domesticus* is added. However, at present, the presumptive wild ancestor is not known with certainty although there seems to be excellent grounds for suggesting that it belongs to the *silvestris-lybica* species complex. The typical tabby pattern of these species is the mackerel type. For this reason it is customary to refer to the mackerel form as the "wild type", from which the blotched sprang as a mutant.

Origin and Species Hybridity

Few writers on the domestic cat can resist speculation on the origin of the animal. It is well known that the ancient Egyptians revered the cat and worshipped a cat-goddess. Egypt is commonly regarded as being a major centre of origin but whether it is the only centre is perhaps open to question. There is nothing to prevent anyone attempting to domesticate the cat anywhere and at different times. Certain Asiatic peoples may have had a hand in the domestication. It is doubtful if the problem will ever be definitely solved. Like the dog, cats of wild origin but of slightly less fearful disposition than the average, may have acted as food stealers or scavengers and eventually may have been accepted or, at least, tolerated. The animal's adeptness in keeping down rats and mice may have been appreciated, who knows?

Presumably, the acceptance of the cat would occur at the hutment or village level. Also, there must have been sufficient genetic variation for docility of tameness within the species for the cat to become trusting of men and to breed either close to or within the village. Barter of animals probably occurred and cats may have become part of the paraphernalia of traders. In this manner, cats would have reached the towns and cities and probably would have acquired status as exotic pets (witness the Ocelot of today). There would be selection against the wilder individuals and possibly in favour of colour variation. Once accepted, the spread of the cat is more or less assured. Though not a prolific breeder, the animal is a persistent producer of litters and has a long span of reproductive life.

Zeuner (1963) provides a good general account of the domestication of the cat. Some of the very early finds (molars and jaw fragments) could be those of a domestic cat although it seems more likely that they are from the wild cat. It seems possible, as is claimed by some archaeologists, that the cat was domesticated by the Egyptians as early as 3000 B.C., but Zeuner considers that the evidence is ambiguous. Yet, by 1900 B.C., it is possible that the cat was in the process of semi-domestication. The swamp scenes of this period could depict a wild cat just as well as a domestic. However, by 1600 B.C., the cat was clearly domesticated and was regarded as a sacred animal. Outside Egypt, for instance in Greece and Palestine, the cat was known but was relatively uncommon because the Egyptians did not allow them to be taken from the country. The Egyptians were also apparently not adverse to carrying off every cat they saw to Egypt. This could be a factor in the belief that Egypt is the centre of origin.

The rise of Christianity caused the cat to lose its sacred position.

The Romans carried the cat back to their home-land and throughout their empire. It was soon to be found in central Europe and even in Britain. The remains of several cats have been discovered in a Roman villa at Silchester and thought to be domestics. The cat also travelled eastward, probably via Babylonia, into India where it is known to have been domesticated for some 2000 years.

On the assumption that the Egyptians domesticated the cat, the problem becomes: from which wild species did the animal descend? The Egyptians apparently kept a number of cats, among which the Jungle cat *(Felis chaus)* and the African wild cat *(Felis lybica)* may be mentioned. Morrison-Scott (1952), in his study of Egyptian mummified cats, suggests that *chaus* may not have been domesticated in any true sense of the word since these are poorly represented. The majority of skulls which he examined belonged to a form smaller than *chaus*, yet larger than *lybica* or the present-day domestic cat. This form is named *Felis lybica bubastis* and is thought to be derived from, or to be a race of, the widely distributed African wild cat *lybica*. Apart from size, the skulls of mummified cats and of *lybica* were closely similar. Curiously, there does not seem to be any existing known wild form which matches *bubastis* exactly. On present showing, the above is likely to be the extent of direct evidence for the origin of the cat.

However, another approach may be made and this is by a consideration of the number and distribution of wild species. The two most likely ancestral forms are *Felis silvestris* and *F. lybica*, the European and African wild cats, respectively, on account of their size, characteristics and coloration. The former occurs in Britain, throughout Europe (except for Scandinavia), South-West Russia, Caucasia and Asia Minor. The latter occurs in most of the larger Mediterranean Islands, much of Africa, Arabia, Turkestan and northern India. It is of interest that while some taxonomists are prepared to accept *silvestris* and *lybica* as two distinct species, each one is divided into a large number of geographical subspecies and races, based mainly on differences of background colour; intensity and distribution of striping; whether or not the striping is breaking up into spots; and the evanescence of the striping or spotting.

Thus, there is the diversity to be expected of a widely distributed species. In general, there is a north to south gradation of coat thickness, intensity of ground colour and amount of tabby markings.

Of the two, *lybica* displays the greater variation. If one examines these species complexes as a whole, it does not seem incongruous to merge *silvestris* and *lybrica* into one species, with geographical groups. A recent study by Weigel (1961) has done this, giving *silvestris* as the embracive species name. That indefatigable student of the Felidae, R. I. Pocock, is on record as stating that the two species possess a similar tabby pattern which is not possessed by any other of the felids.

The results of inter-species hybridization affords another approach and, from a genetic viewpoint, the most interesting. Much of the literature on hybridization is very old and, unless a critical stance is taken, it is easy to believe that the domestic cat will produce hybrids with practically any wild species (e.g. Hamilton, 1896). This could be so but too many of the early claims are based on breeders' reminiscences and travellers' observations to be reliable. On the other hand, of course, if two species so different as the lion and tiger can be crossed reciprocally—tigron from the union of a male tiger and lioness and liger from a male lion and a tigress—then it is conceivable that a large number of the smaller cats might be capable of producing hybrids. The above cross is fairly easily obtained, but the disparity between the two species is revealed by partial sterility. The male hybrids are thought to be completely infertile while the female hybrids are only partially fertile. These facts reveal the genetic remoteness of the lion and tiger.

Several sources of error have to be heeded if claims of hybridity are to be taken seriously. Simple observation is not sufficient. Feral domestic cats abound in many parts of the world and many resemble wild species in colour and temperament. The domestic cat is a variable creature and no variation of colour or bodily proportions should be construed as positive evidence of alleged current or past hybridity. Only if a person has intimate knowledge of the animals concerned can a claim be entertained; yet this is not conclusive. To be conclusive, it is necessary for the parents to be confined and the matings controlled. This can be managed by zoos and a certain amount of information is available from this source.

Authentic hybrids between the domestic cat and various races (Scottish and European) of *silvestris* have been obtained on several occasions. In the majority of cases, the offspring are mackerel tabby in colour and wild in temperament. In one instance, however, a male hybrid was observed to be "as tame as a fire-side cat, so that after a while he was allowed out of his cage to wander about" (Gillespie, 1954). This is interesting because it denotes genetic variation for "tameness", one of the prerequisites for domestication. The hybrids seem to be regularly fertile. This could be significant since it is usually indicative of not too distant genetic relationship. Several of the domestic females carried mutant genes and these can be expressed by the hybrid genotype. Self black (the wild male was evidently a heterozygote!), piebald with white spotting and Manx taillessness have been transmitted (the last two genes being dominant). Though the transmission and expression of mutant genes (the numbers were too few and the variation of expression was not closely studied), are not of great weight, again there is indication of some degree of genetic identicalness. Most of the hybrids possessed the bushy tail of *silvestris*, but this was not always the case, and, in one instance, the second generation showed variation in the amount of hair on the tail.

Alleged hybrids between the domestic cat and various races of *lybica* (both African and Indian) are claimed on several occasions in the older literature. More recently, fertile hybrids have been obtained between the domestic cat and the Steppe cat *(lybica caudata)* under controlled conditions. Furthermore, Pocock (1907) was able to produce hybrids between *silvestris* and an African race of *lybica*. These were typical mackerel tabby, similar to the parents. Two were eaten by the *lybica* mother shortly after birth while the surviving kitten at nine weeks was showing signs of having the well-covered hairy tail of *silvestris*. Thus, there is direct, as well as circumstantial, evidence that hybrids can be secured with *lybica*. If credence is given to these early accounts, there may be found stories of fertility and variable degrees of tameness for the hybrids.

Hybrids between the domestic cat and the Jungle Cat *(Felis chaus)* have been obtained. The hybrids are tabby in colour and with somewhat more tabby striping than is apparent in *chaus*. Morphologically, the resemblance is closer to *chaus*, for the hybrid is larger, longer legged and shorter tailed than the domestic. The hybrid is apparently fertile, for daughter hybrids have been mated back to the *chaus* father and have reared litters. The hybrids appear to be well cared for and are said to be tame. Piebald white spotting, introduced by the domestic cat, showed the usual dominant expression on the hybrids (Jackson and Jackson, 1967).

Two further crosses may be noted because of the implication that they can be productive of hybrids. The crosses were between the domestic cat and the bobcat *(Lynx rufus)* and Oncilla or Little Spotted Cat *(Felis tigrina)*; two species from the new world. In both instances, the hybrids tend to resemble the wild species, rather than the cat and were of wild disposition. Nothing is known whether or not the hybrids were fertile. The intriguing aspect is that hybrids could be produced at all since the point of departure for the old and new world species must have been a vast number of years ago. Yet, despite this, the three forms can come together to produce viable offspring. The implication is that the production of offspring, *per se*, from the domestic cat and either *silvestris* or *lybica* loses some of its significance. Only the probability, if not certainty, that these offspring are fertile may turn out to be important for demonstrating genetic kinship.

No matter how much time is spent on detailed systematic examination of species appearance or how supposedly diagnostic features are compared, the crucial test of genetic relationship is that of crosses. The fact that the wild species and the hybrids are fearful and barely manageable is an unfortunate complication but one which can possibly be overcome. Already, certain European zoos are making determined attempts to breed and rear *silvestris* in captivity. The lack of kinship between the domestic cat and a wild species may show itself in one of two ways. Firstly, there is the obvious one that the animals may copulate but no viable young are forthcoming. Or, secondly, young may be born but these are sterile either in one or both sexes. These various possibilities are sometimes taken to represent different degrees of relationship. The former implying a more distant relationship than the latter.

However, the important item is that the putative wild ancestor of the domestic cat should be capable of producing fertile hybrids. Perhaps a clearcut answer may not emerge; for it is possible that the ancestral species may have become extinct or that the cat may be capable of producing fertile hybrids with more than one wild species. The latter seems possible because of the apparently fertile hybrids with *chaus* in addition to *silvestris* and *lybica*. This need not necessarily indicate that the cat descended from initial crosses between more than one wild species. In this context, *silvestris* and *lybica* are not to be regarded as true species, but rather as geographical races, since they will produce young when paired together.

Suppose that the Egyptians did confine more than one wild species together and that hybrids did occur under these artificial conditions. Subsequent events would be determined by the degree of control exercised by the Egyptians, and the viability and fertility of the hybrids. It would be doubtful if any real control was exercised or, if so, it would be largely that of allowing the best and more vigorous cats to reproduce. The outcome could be that a genetic constitution will emerge which rapidly shed itself of any weaknesses, which, in general, would be the hybrid genotype. There will, in fact, be a selective return to the species genotype. Hybrid animals are often exceptionally hardy and vigorous, but these features often fail to recur in subsequent generations (indeed there can be a decline) and the species combinations of genes finally reappear as the best means of breeding the animals with a semblance of normal health. In other words, a viable type could be evolved which had incorporated the best features of more than one species but, nevertheless, likely to resemble one species more than the other. Phenotypically, this seems to be the *silvestris-lybica* complex.

There seems little doubt that the present-day cat population of the world is a single genetic entity. By that, it is meant that cats brought together from the remotest localities will inter-breed and produce fertile young. Even cats brought from Asiatic countries are fertile with European cats, in spite of the possibility that these have been separated since the early days of domestication. One final point will be made: no matter how diverse the modern cat may be in coat colour or body conformity, all of the variability can be interpreted in terms of gene mutation and recombination which has occurred after domestication.

Discredited Beliefs

Several discarded ideas will now be briefly discussed. One or two have some inherent interest but they are essentially false trails despite the fact that they were widely accepted by breeders prior to the turn of the 19th century or even more recently. Their unfounded speciousness is exposed by failure to pass the tests of repeatable experiment.

Telegony is the alleged influence of one sire upon the offspring of another when mated to the same female. In its most common form, the fear is expressed that a pedigree queen, accidentally mated by a mongrel cat, will now be useless for pedigree breeding because all of the subsequent kittens will be mongrels however she is mated. This fear is groundless. The use of one male has no means of influencing the young of another. Telegony also fails in another respect. If true, a mating with a first-class sire should guarantee the production of superior kittens however the queen is subsequently mated. Alas, this will not work, as anyone can prove to himself if he wishes to take the trouble.

Maternal impressions is another belief which would make breeding so much easier if it was true. This term is given to the alleged influence of the surroundings on the offspring while these are still in the uterus. A pregnant female kept in close proximity of outstanding animals might be induced to produce kittens of above average merit. Or, a certain colour might be induced by keeping a pregnant female in company with other cats of the desired colour. Unfortunately, neither of these artifices has any hope of success, except by chance which has no connection with the principle involved.

Acquired inheritance is a general term to denote an environmental influence which, working on the body, is able to allegedly modify the germ-cells so that the influence may be seen in subsequent generations. Now, the environment encroaches upon the development of the individual from the moment of conception. Firstly, there is the pre-natal maternal environment and, later, there is the pressures of the post-natal world. Thus, there is ample opportunity for the environment to buffer or modify the body. In fact, it does so in a myriad of ways but the contents of the germ-cells which constitute the hereditary material escape the influence. On occasion, the germ-cells can be reached but the effect is usually so damaging that procreativity is out of the question.

The cruder aspects of acquired inheritance have long been disproved (such as the breeding of tailless mice by chopping off their tails), but ever so often more subtle versions of the myth appear to gain credence. Eventually these, too, are shown to have little validity. In general, any bodily experience or mutilation is extremely unlikely to be inherited. A disease affecting the mother during pregnancy could produce diseased or deformed offspring but, even so, neither the germ-cells of the mother nor of the offspring are affected.

The only environmental factors which are known to affect the germ-cells are X-rays, atomic emanations and a variety of chemical mutagens. These agents do so by inducing chromosome aberrations and gene mutation. Furthermore, the mutation is entirely at random and occurs at a very low frequency. The possibility of increasing the mutation rate of certain kinds of mutants to bring about a desired change has been discussed among scientists, but the likelihood of this is remote.

2

Reproduction and Development

REPRODUCTION in the cat is a fascinating topic in its own right and it is presumed that most breeders are familiar with the general outline, even if they have not troubled themselves overmuch with details. The majority of cats will reproduce quite happily; if in good condition and are not interfered with more than absolutely necessary. In any case, except for trivial complaints, if certain aspects are not all they should be, it is always advisable to call in a vet. His skill and experience is invariably greater than that of most breeders and this should be drawn upon without hesitation. The more valuable the animal, the greater the need for expert advice and attention.

Practical Aspects of Reproduction

This section makes no pretence at being exhaustive, but constitutes a summary of the more practical aspects of the subject. The summary will form a preamble, so to speak, to a more detailed discussion of what is actually transmitted from one generation to the next at the act of coitus.

Under optional conditions of husbandry and diet, sexual maturity or puberty in the female normally occurs between the ages of 7 to 12 months, depending on a variety of factors, such as month of birth and growth. Exceptionally, a rapidly growing female may reach puberty as early as 6 months. Size is probably the governing factor since one report gives the female as being able to commence breeding when weighing about 2·5 kg (5·5 lb). However, regardless of the actual onset of puberty, it is usually judged prudent not to breed from a queen until she is about 12 months of age.

The attainment of puberty is less obvious in the male but is usually

13

taken to be a month or two later than in the female. A weight level of about 3·5 kg (7·7 lb) is thought to be a convenient point. Queens will continue to produce litters until they are many years of age. The actual cessation of breeding is a gradual affair, usually accompanied by a rise of sterile copulations and decline in litter size, although a figure of between 8 and 10 years has been mentioned as not untypical. It is rare for a female to reproduce beyond the age of 14 years. If males attain puberty a month or so after females, they are also capable of breeding for a number of years beyond the latest age for the female.

Oestrus or heat is the period in which the female is receptive of the attentions of the male. The duration is normally from 3 to 6 days although persisting as long as 10 days if the queen is denied access to the male. The period is marked by relatively distinctive behaviour which enables an experienced breeder to judge the most propitious time for the two animals to meet. For a day or two (the pre-oestrus stage) the female becomes very affectionate, demanding unusual attention and rubbing herself against objects and indulging in playful rolling. There is usually much howling and "calling" although there are differences between breeds in this respect.

The second stage is characterized by treading and the adoption of the coital crouch (flattening of the back and raising of the hind quarters) to gentle stroking or a nudging of the genital region or the presence of a male. The cat is now fully receptive and coitus (mating) will occur. Successful intromission is accompanied by a loud cry or growl. After the two cats have parted, the female usually engages in quite vigorous rolling, rubbing and licking which subsides into a short period of inactivity. Mating may be resumed within an interval of 15 or 30 minutes. Several matings per day for all but the last day of oestrus may occur if allowed.

Litters may be born at any time of the year although less frequently during the winter months. The typical breeding period is from January to July or even somewhat longer. The winter pause, however, can be effectively reduced by the provision of artificial illumination to counteract the lack of day-light. Two, or even three, litters are normally produced per year, the peak months being March to April and July to August. In the absence of coitus, the female usually shows recurrent oestrus at intervals of 14 days although it is reported that some animals may have irregular cycles. An infertile mating is usually followed by a pseudo-pregnancy which lasts about 30 to 40 days, whence the female comes into oestrus.

The cat is one of the few mammals in which the eggs are released by the ovary as a result of nervous stimuli provided by coitus. The gestation period is about 65 days although the extraordinary variation of between 58 and 71 days have been recorded. Some latitude must be given, however, to imprecise information on the actual day of the release of the eggs, especially for matings spread over several days. The number of eggs is probably always in excess of the number of kittens born, due to intra-uterine mortality of foetuses. Unfortunately, precise data on the extent of the mortality is lacking.

A survey to determine weaned litter size revealed that the average litter consists of 3·9 kittens, with an extreme range of 1 to 10, based upon 5073 litters (19,813 cats). Size of litter varies with weight of mother, heavier females tending to have larger litters than the lighter females. Probably as a result of this but not necessarily, because average gestation period should be taken into account, kittens born to smaller females are heavier than those born to larger mothers. The sex ratio has been found to be 104 males: 100 females, based on 16,820 kittens.

The lactation period may vary from 50 to 60 days although partial weaning may commence before this. Complete weaning leads to a rapid cessation of the milk flow. There is no oestrus immediately following paturition (post-partum oestrus) but the oestrus cycle usually recommences between 2 to 4 weeks after weaning.

The ideal litter for a queen seems to be about 4 to 5 kittens. Few females seem capable of nursing more than this number unaided if rapid growth of the kittens is to be expected. Kittens from large litters can be transferred to queens with small litters or kittens may be supplementarily fed with milk in a doll's bottle or special cat feeding bottle. It must not be overlooked, of course, that the ability to suckle a complement of four young is inherited and to assist an incapable queen is not good policy in the long-term. It is beneficial for the young, no doubt, but the young themselves could inherit the incapacity and this is something to guard against. Breeding stock should only be chosen (as far as possible, after other aspects are taken into account) from queens who have reared kittens with a good record of growth.

Stories abound of cats reaching a ripe old age, but people interested in geriatrics are loath to accept undocumented statements. A report on authenticated cases of cats living beyond 20 years brought to light a range of longevity from 19 to 27 years, with an average of 22 to 23 years. Unsubstantiated claims have gone higher, the figure of 31 years being the highest recorded. Unfortunately, the errors involved in recalling past events and establishing the age of an animal are notorious. It is of interest that aged cats reach a well-preserved senility as regards retention of teeth, condition of coat and activity. This is in contrast to dogs (a comparable domestic carnivore) where senility is said not to be so kind to the individual.

It should be appreciated that genetic factors may influence most of the features discussed above. This means that strain and breed differences may exist. The Siamese is often singled out in this respect although not always with substantiating statistics. The Manx, for instance, will usually have smaller litters than the average due to the intra-uterine mortality which is associated with the tailless condition.

TABLE 1. BASIC DATA ON REPRODUCTION AND THE LIFE CYCLE OF THE DOMESTIC CAT

Item	Average	Typical variation
Puberty, males	12 months	10–14 months
Puberty, females	9 months	7–12 months
Oestrus cycle	14 days	Irregular
Oestrus	3–6 days	3–10 days
Gestation period	65 days	58–71 days
Weaned litter size	3–9	1–10
Sex ratio	104: 100	75–130: 100
Breeding period	Jan.–July	Jan.–Oct.
Lactation period	50 days	48–60 days
Cessation of breeding	8–10 years	To 14 years
Longevity	22–23 years	To 27 years

Germ-cell Lineage

The cat as an entity commences life as the union of two germ-cells. This occurs in the oviduct, a thin tube of tissue which conveys the egg (female germ-cell) to the uterus upon its release by the ovary. Though the act of coitus provides the stimulus, the eggs are not liberated until many hours have elapsed. The delay allows the sperms (male germ-cells), which have been deposited in the vagina, to make their way to the site of fertilization either to meet or to be on hand for the arrival of the eggs. Fertilization accomplished, the egg undergoes cleavage, passing through the morulae and early blastodermic stages. Implantation is said to occur about the 14th day. From this point onward, growth and development is rapid and the tiny blob of protoplasm becomes transformed into a recognizable foetus. After about 65 days, the cat is ejected into the world as a young kitten, not fully able to fend for itself but equipped with a suckling reflex to obtain nourishment from its mother.

Since a new individual is created by the union of germ-cells, it follows that their contents must form the material link between successive generations. The male and female germ-cells differ greatly in size and structure as befitting their different functions. The egg is relatively large and spherical, being rich in nutriment to carry it over the developmental period from fertilization to implantation. On the other hand, the sperm is a fragile thing, microscopic in size and possessive of a long tail, with just about sufficient energy for it to reach and enter the egg for fertilization. The function of the egg and sperm is to house a nucleus and to ensure that two nuclei (one from the egg and one from the sperm) can come together and fuse. Genetically, the important constituents of the two nuclei are the chromosomes. These are extremely small bodies, but visible under the microscope, and are bearers of the hereditary material. Their joining up to form a common nucleus enables the egg to commence development as an independent entity.

In biological terms, the body of an individual is known as the "soma". It consists of myriads of cells, all of which are concerned with either the structure or the innumerable physiological functions which are necessary for sustaining life. The greater bulk of the somatic cells are not involved in reproduction although some are indirectly. The reason for this is that, as the fertilized egg gradually changes into an embryo and then into a foetus, the various path-ways of development become sorted out and diverge at a progressive rate. A fundamental divergence is between those cells which are destined to produce the soma and those which are destined to form the germ-cells. Developmentally, once separation has occurred, growth can then be semiautonomous, subject only to the restriction, if growth is proceeding normally, that the various processes must not become out of step with one another.

It is possible, therefore, to postulate a continuum of cells directly concerned with reproduction: the "germ-cell lineage". The reproductive organs (testes and ovary) for the production of germ-cells are known collectively as "gonads" and the rudiments of these are laid down at an early stage. The germ-cell lineage may be envisaged to be semi-independent of the soma and to alternate as gonads-germ-cells-gonads-germ-cells on an unbroken line, bridging generations via the germ-cells. Figure 1 is an attempt to show this concept. The germ-cell lineage is depicted as immortal while the soma is built up anew in each generation for the sole purpose of nurturing and facilitating the passage of the germ-cells. This does not mean that the germ-cell lineage is unvarying. Far from it, the genes on the chromosomes within the nucleus are subject to mutation and recombination, and the genetic constitution as a whole is responsive to the forces of artificial and natural selection.

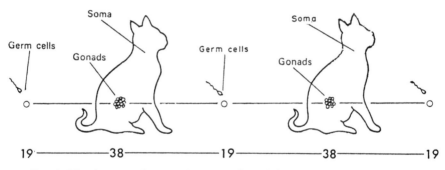

FIG. 1. The distinction between the germ-cells and the soma or body. The former is the bridge linking generations and enabling the germ line to continue indefinitely. The germ-cells have only 19 chromosomes but, by fusion, the number is doubled to produce 38 chromosomes in the somatic cells.

Hereditary versus Environment in the Shaping of the Individual

A careful distinction should be made between the genetic endowment and subsequent development. The former is completed at fertilization and is heredity in the strict sense. In other words, this represents the extent of the parental contribution. True, development has yet to proceed and this is where the genetic inspired growth processes and the effects of environment can interact. Now, in genetics, the environment has a wider, yet more technical, meaning than just that of the surroundings. All tangible non-genetic influences constitute the environment. At first, the developing individual has to contend with the maternal environment (pre-natally, as provided by the uterus, and post-natally, as provided by the level of maternal care) and later by the impact of the physical world.

As development proceeds, it is buffered on every side by environmental influences. The picture is complicated by the fact that the various characteristics which make up the individual are affected to different degrees by the innate genetic constitution. For instance, at one extreme, it could be held that post-natal growth is largely governed by the diet. If this is inadequate, a poorly developed and stunted animal will result. The animal may even languish, become susceptible to disease and die. Somewhat similar results could follow if the individual is reared in cold, damp, surroundings. These two items are singled out because the two main environmental factors are the diet and temperature. The former is obviously of great importance since growth is dependent on nourishing food. Yet, it should not escape notice that the dietary effect is almost entirely negative. Given adequate food, the growth is then largely governed by the genetic constitution.

At the other extreme, some characteristics are scarcely affected by the environment. To cat breeders, coat colour and hair type are important attributes and these are almost completely controlled by heredity. True, the Siamese pattern is modifiable to some extent since the amount of pigment deposited in the hairs is influenced by the temperature. Yet, this is the exception which tends to emphasize the rule, for only one particular series of genes (of which Siamese is a member) is affected in this way. In general, it is next door to impossible to modify the colour by manipulation of the diet.

A third item is worth mentioning for completeness. This is developmental error and it arises from accidental quirks and irregularities of development peculiar to the individual which cannot be easily attributed either to genetic or environmental causes. This source of variation is possibly of little concern for practical cat breeding, though it is advisable to be aware of its existence. In general, variation of this nature is relatively small but the odd occasion may occur where this is not the case. A good example is provided by the variation of piebald white spotting. Though the variation can be described in broad terms, no two white marked cats are exactly alike. In part, this is due to erratic development of the white areas during embryonic growth and is a feature of the particular individual.

The Chromosomes

Since the chromosomes within the germ-cells are the hereditary material which is passed on from generation to generation, the mechanism by which this is achieved deserves to be discussed in more detail. Two sorts of cell division will be described: ordinary cell division ("mitosis") and two special divisions which lead up to the formation of the germ-cells. These divisions are known as "meiosis". The treatment will be admittedly oversimplified in order to bring out the essential similarity and to show that meiosis is a subtlety modified form of mitosis.

In ordinary mitotic cell division, which takes place during growth or to replace worn-out or damaged tissue, the membrane containing the nucleus dissolves away and the chromosomes (38 in the cat) orientate themselves so as to form an ordered line-up in a plane across the centre of the cell. This is a period of intense activity within the cell and presently it can be seen that each chromosome has given rise to a partner, alike to it in all respects, by a process of self-copying. The chromosomes lie in close proximity for a while and then commence to move away, as if by mutual repellence. Each of the 38 chromosomes behaves in the same manner and the two groups tend to move in unison and eventually huddled together at each end of the cell. A nuclear membrane forms around each group, to bring into being two nuclei, and the cell may constrict between the nuclei or simply throw up a cell wall. The nuclei are now contained in separate cells and these increase in size until they are identical to the previous single cell.

The mitotic divisions are responsible for the growth of the soma, cell by cell, until the tissues, bones and various organs are built up. They are also responsible for the formation of the gonads, these being formed at the appropriate stage of embryonic development.

The fact that the gonads are formed so early in life does not mean that they are functional. This does not occur until many months later, when somatic growth is completed, or almost completed, and the animal attains puberty. It does mean, however, that the gonads are semi-independent of the soma, remaining quiescent until, under the influence of hormones, they become active and commence to produce germ-cells. It is at this stage that the mitotic divisions are transformed into the slightly more complicated meiotic.

As in mitosis, meiosis begins by dissolution of the nuclear membrane and the orderly line-up of the chromosomes. However, instead of the chromosomes behaving as separate bodies, they come together in pairs. The pairs of chromosomes do not join up but the pairing, none-the-less, is very intimate. Careful examination has revealed that the pairing is not at random but only involves those chromosomes of similar size and shape. It is clear that the 38 chromosomes are in reality 19 pairs of chromosomes (i.e., two of each kind). This explains why pairing can occur since different chromosomes as a rule behave independently of each other. Whatever is the attraction which brings the similar chromosomes together, it soon wanes, and the repellent phase sets in. The chromosomes move apart towards opposite ends of the cell and the 19 chromosomes remain bunched together while a nucleus forms around them. A cellular wall divides the cell and the two new cells are engendered. This is the first meiotic division. A second follows which is essentially a mitosis. The chromosomes line up but do not pair. Instead, a partner chromosome is formed by self-copying and the chromosomes fall apart to form a separate nuclei. The appearance of a cellular wall results in two new cells. Note that this division only involves 19 chromosomes.

The important meiotic division is the first and the above account merely skims the surface of the processes involved. The important aspect is the reduction in number which takes place. There are 19 different chromosomes in the somatic cells of the cat but, since each one is present twice, this gives a total of 38. This number is known as the diploid, the reduced number of 19 being denoted as the "basic" or "haploid". The products of meiosis are transformed into germ-cells, each containing 19 chromosomes. The transformation is more or less direct for the male, the meiotic divisions leading to the production of sperms. The transformation is less direct for the female, though the end result is the same, the production of a fertilizable egg nucleus

GENETICS FOR CAT BREEDERS

containing 19 chromosomes. The union of two germ-cells, each with 19 chromosomes, restores the diploid number of 38. The necessity of reducing the somatic chromosome by half should now be apparent. If this did not occur, the number of chromosomes would double in each generation, which would be absurd. However, the substitution of meiotic divisions just prior to the production of the germ-cells is an elegant mechanism for maintaining the constant number of chromosomes. True, there is alternation of $38 \to 19 \to 38 \to 19 \to 38$, but this is in fact the fundamental mechanism.

TABLE 2. THE HAPLOID NUMBER OF CHROMOSOMES FOR CAT SPECIES

Common name	Zoological name	Haploid number
African golden cat	Felis aurata	19
African wild cat	Felis libyca	19
Black footed cat	Felis nigripes	19
Bob cat	Felis rufa	19
Caffer cat	Felis ornata	19
Caracal lynx	Felis caracal	19
Cheetah	Acinonyx jubatus	19
Clouded leopard	Neofelis nebulosa	19
Domestic cat	Felis catus	19
European wild cat	Felis silvestris	19
Fishing cat	Felis viverrina	19
Flat-headed cat	Felis planiceps	19
Geoffroy's cat	Felis geoffroyi	18
Jaguar	Panthera onca	19
Jaguarundi	Felis jaguarondi	19
Jungle cat	Felis chaus	19
Leopard	Panthera pardus	19
Leopardcat	Felis bengalensis	19
Lion	Panthera leo	19
Margay cat	Felis wiedi	18
Northern lynx	Felis lynx	19
Ocelot	Felis pardalis	18
Pallas's cat	Felis manul	19
Pampas cat	Felis colocolo	18
Puma	Felis concolor	19
Rusty spotted cat	Felis rubiginosa	19
Sand cat	Felis margarita	19
Serval	Felis serval	19
Snow leopard	Panthera uncia	19
Temminch's golden cat	Felis temmincki	19
Tiger	Panthera tigris	19
Tiger cat	Felis tigrina	18

The arrangement of the chromosomes in pairs is also part of the mechanism. It is not sufficient that the germ-cells should receive any random collection of 19 chromosomes but the same basic 19 in every cell. The line-up ensures that this occurs by sending one of each pair to opposite ends of the cell. However, the chromosomes may be jumbled up in the cell before a division, the meiotic line-up effectively sorts out the pairs. The diploid-haploid alternation, of course, is confined to the germ-cell lineage, the soma invariably containing 38 chromosomes except for accidents of division. These accidents tend to be rare but, when they do, they can lead to abnormalities. The production of the tortoiseshell male cat, to be discussed anon, is one such instance.

The latest information on the haploid number of chromosomes for both the small and large cats is given by Table 2. It may be seen that the number of 19 for the domestic cat is by no means exceptional. Indeed, detailed studies by karyologists (people who study chromosomes) have shown that not only do the majority of felids possess a similar number but the sizes and shapes of the individual chromosomes do not differ a great deal between species. This explains why it is possible to obtain hybrids between many of the species, even if the hybrid may be sterile. Note that those species inhabiting Central and South America have 18 instead of 19 chromosomes as possessed by the Old World species. The cause of this is a fusion between two of the smaller chromosomes to form a larger chromosome during the course of evolution. This has effectively reduced the chromosome number by one.

Sex Chromosomes and Sex Determination

The normal complement of 19 pairs of chromosomes of the cat differ among themselves. Some pairs are larger than others and so forth. In general, the pairs of chromosomes are identical in size and shape. The reason for this, of course, is that each chromosome is represented twice in the somatic cells, hence their identicalness is no cause for surprise. According to the latest examinations, there are nine pairs of large chromosomes and nine pairs of medium to small chromosomes.

What is interesting, however, is that in addition to the above, one pair of chromosomes are not identical. Their most obvious difference is in size. One is a medium sized chromosome while the other is quite small. Why should this be? A clue may be found in the fact that the unequalness is confined to the male. Observations have shown that the female has ten pairs of medium to small chromosomes while the male has nine pairs plus the unequal sized pair. It may be deduced that the latter are associated with sex. In point of fact, they are sex chromosomes. This makes the pair rather novel and to distinguish the other chromosomes from them, all of the ordinary chromosomes are called "autosomes". The sex chromosomes themselves are further distinguished by calling the medium sized chromosome the X and the smaller chromosome the Y. Since the Y chromosome is carried only by the male, it is commonly referred to as the "male" chromosome. Therefore, the male is XY and the female is XX, the symbols indicating the sex chromosome constitution of the two sexes.

A check that the unequally sized sex chromosomes are a true pair is provided by a study of meiosis in the male. In the line-up of chromosomes, the sex chromosomes can be seen to pair up and migrate to opposite ends of the cell. This means that the two cells formed by the division are not fully identical. Each cell contains a set of identical autosomes but one cell contains an X chromosome while the other has the Y. These cells are transformed into sperms and it follows that there are two sorts of sperm, those carrying an X and those carrying a Y. Furthermore, since the cell divisions are proceeding continuously, the two sorts of sperm are produced in equal numbers.

In the female, on the other hand, this differentiation of the germ-cells cannot occur since the sex chromosomes in this sex are an identical pair. At meiosis, the XX sex chromosomes come together at the line-up, and separate in the usual manner, but it does not matter which member of the pair ends up in the fertilizable egg nucleus. The result is always the same, the egg will contain one X chromosome. When the egg and sperm unite at fertilization, the sex chromosome constitute of the individual will depend upon the sperm. The egg will contribute one X but the sperm will contribute either an X or a Y. The two sorts of sperm occur in equal numbers, hence two sorts of individual are formed at fertilization. Namely, those with XX and those with XY chromosome. The former will develop into females and the latter into males. The cycle of sex chromosome reduction and reconstitution is mediated in the male. It

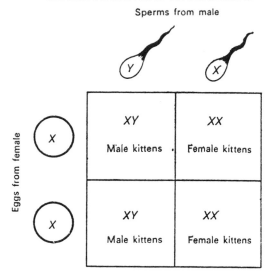

FIG. 2. Sex is determined by the X and Y chromosomes. The male is of constitution XY and the female is XX. The male produces two sets of sperms (X and Y) while the female produces only one (X). These uniting at random give an expected 1:1 sex ratio among the offspring.

follows, therefore, that the sex of the individual is determined by the male (Fig. 2). It is also determined at the moment of fertilization and the XY and XX chromosome constitution of the embryo will see to it that the developing sex organs will be appropriately male or female.

Sex Development

Sex is initially determined by XY and XX constitution of the individual and in most instances subsequent development is perfectly normal. However, in some cases, the normal development is upset and one of a variety of anomalies may arise. Most cases of anomaly tend to be rare and this is an indication that the cause is an exceptional event.

In some instances, the abnormality will be independent of the sex chromosome constitution. It will either be due to accidents of developments or be caused by genes on the autosomes. For example, a not infrequent anomaly is unilateral or bilateral cryptorchidism. A male with one testis fully descended is usually fertile and will sire both male and female kittens, indicating that his XY constitution is unimpaired. The defect is clearly one of development. The cause of the anomaly is not known with certainty but the problem is discussed in a subsequent chapter.

On the other hand, some sex anomalies are known to be due to unusual sex chromosome constitutions. These cases are of particular genetic interest. Whereas the Y chromosome may carry very few genes, the X may carry a fair number. It is not possible to say how many because their discovery is dependent upon the rare event of mutation. Yet, one X borne mutant has been known in the cat for a very long time. This is sex-linked orange, the gene responsible for the tortoiseshell pattern. The reason why this pattern ordinarily occurs only in the female is due to sex-linkage. The genetic situation is fully discussed anon but one aspect is of relevance at this point. Tortoiseshell males occur as a rare event and one of the explanations for their appearance postulates an abnormal XY constitution. This suggestion can be checked by examination of the chromosomes and this has been done for a number of cases.

The simplest case is the presence of an extra X to produce XXY. This curious and anomalous constitution could occur as mistakes during meiosis or in the mitotic divisions which occur after fertilization. Whatever the cause, the cells of the individual have gained an extra X chromosome. While a XXY constitution can produce an externally normal male, the animal is usually sterile. Other unusual constitutions which have been found are cats with mixtures of XX and XY cells, of XX and XXY cells, and of XY and XXY cells, together with yet more complex combinations involving a Y with several X chromosomes. Individuals with mixtures of different cell types are known as mosaics (Centerwall and Benirschke, 1973). In summary, the Y chromosome is so strongly male-inducing that the individual develops as a male despite the number of X chromosomes which also may be present. However, the price to pay is that these males are sterile.

Opposed, so to speak, to the above are individuals with only one X chromosome, a constitution which is written as XO. These are able to live and are females but sterile. They typically fail to come into oestrus, a feature which is the most obvious external sign of the anomaly (Johnston *et al.*, 1983). It is worthwhile having an examination made of the chromosome content for any cat, male or female, which is sterile.

Almost all of the anomalous constitutions involving the *Y* chromosome were discovered because they produced the rare tortoiseshell male. The reason is the chance occurrence of the orange gene *O* on one of the *X* chromosomes. The fact of being male and tortoiseshell is an inducement to study the chromosome constitution. Without the presence of an *O* gene, these cats would be simply infertile males.

Some tortoiseshell males are fertile and there are two mechanisms by which these can be produced. A frequently recurring mosaic is a mixture of *XX* and *XY* cells, a type which is represented as *XY/XX*. This constitution is easily understood because the cat is a mixture of male and female chromosome constitutions. However, it is possible to have a mosaic of the type *XY/XY*, a mixture of two male chromosome constitutions. Such a cat can be a tortoiseshell should one of the *X* chromosomes carry the *O* gene. Whereas the *XX/XY* mosaic is sterile, the *XY/XY* mosaic is fertile (Moran *et al.*, 1984; Robinson, 1985).

The second mechanism draws upon the concept of somatic mutation. A body cell can mutate in a similar manner to a germinal cell. A mutation on the *X* chromosome of a male cat to produce an orange gene *O* will result in a tortoiseshell. The form most commonly encountered is a red tabby with variably sized patches of black pigmentation. These have been produced by a mutation from *O* to *o* in the body cells of the red tabby. These males are fertile and they usually breed as a red tabby (Robinson, 1985). An account of the sex-linked inheritance of the orange gene *O* is given in a later chapter.

3

Principles of Heredity

THE BASIC laws of heredity are relatively simple. Indeed, stripped of all detail, these can be reduced to two: (1) the law of separation of the genes in the germ-cells and (2) the law of independent assortment of the genes in various crosses. If, to these, is added the phenomenon of linkage (which itself is a more precise definition of the second law), then much of elementary genetics is easily covered.

It may be wondered if the very simplicity of the bare bones of heredity may be a factor operating in their disfavour. Some people may feel that the notion of genes cannot explain everything in the development of a complex mammal such as the cat. This adversion is understandable but mistaken. The cat is indeed a complex organism and it must be admitted that a detailed understanding of the animal's genetics can certainly lead into deep waters. Yet, a start has to be made somewhere, and where can this be but a consideration of the basic principles no matter how divorced they may seem at first sight from the living animal?

A step-by-step approach, proceeding from the simple to the more profound, is basic for most sciences and has certainly proved itself in genetics. No matter how complex an organism may be, it can always be broken down into simple attributes for expository purposes. In genetics, these are conveniently referred to as inherited "characters" or "traits". It may be felt that this approach will introduce some degree of over-simplification, but this need not necessarily be so. As the exposition unfolds successive attributes are added until the overall concept is as complex as may be felt desirable. In this way, it is possible to gain insight into the general picture. To clothe the bare bones of heredity, so to speak.

The principles of heredity can be explained to a large extent without

28

reference to the chromosomes, but it is doubtful if this is altogether wise. It should never be forgotten that the chromosomes constitute the material basis of heredity. However, such references as are made will be kept to a minimum. In the early days of genetics the hereditary determinants present in the cells were known as "factors". In modern terms, the factor is now the "gene". In essence, genetics is concerned with the comings and goings of the genes as these are transmitted from parent to offspring and the effects of genes on the growth and appearance of the individual. Just about everything, in fact, in the life of the cat.

Genes and Alleles

The gene may be visualized as a minute portion of a chromosome and each chromosome consists of some thousands of genes. The genes are highly complex chemical structures, each neatly dove-tailing into one another to build up the chromosome (the genetic code and its development). However, a little dated, though apt, simile of the chromosome is that of a string of beads; each bead representing a gene and, the whole string, the chromosome. At an elementary level, this concept is still useful in conjuring up a mental picture of the relationship between the gene and chromosome.

The genes multiply during cell division by a remarkable process of self-copying which is of a high order of exactitude. The duplication is so good that many hundreds of thousands of daughter genes are produced before a mistake occurs and an inexact copy is made. The creation of the inexact copy is known as mutation and, the altered gene, as a mutant. The original gene and its mutant form are referred to as "alleles". The two genes are said to be "allelic" because one has originated from the other and, therefore, must occupy the same position in the chromosome. This position is the "locus" of the gene on the chromosome. The locus concept is important in genetics because each chromosome contains some thousands of loci; especially, as it is possible to represent each locus as capable of producing a characteristic mutation or series of mutations.

The occurrence of mutation is so uncommon that, for most practical purposes, the event can be ignored. Nevertheless, all of the existing colours and coat types of the cat have come into existence as a result of mutation. It is an indication of the rarity of the event that the number of varieties are so few in spite of the millions of cats bred all over the world. Only about two dozen, or so, mutant genes are definitely known. One reason for this is that a cat displaying a new mutant may not be particularly attractive at first sight. Instead of being carefully nurtured and developed, it may be destroyed out of hand as a "freak". This sort of behaviour certainly results in a loss to science and probably to the fancy.

The inherited colours of the cat provide excellent illustrations of the principles of heredity. It should not be imagined, however, that genetics is concerned merely with colour or coat types; nothing is further from the truth. The growth of the animal, its behaviour, proneness to certain afflictions and disease, and its reproductive ability, are all controlled to a greater or lesser extent by the genetic constitution. It happens that the simpler aspects of genetics may be explained more clearly, using coat colours as examples, than if less sharply defined traits are considered.

Simple Inheritance

The wild type coloration of the cat is the ubiquitous tabby pattern and it has been established that the pattern consists of two components. These are: (1) areas in which the hair fibres are banded or ticked with yellow pigment and (2) areas in which all-black hairs predominate and the yellow ticking is reduced in amount. The former comprise the drab yellowish-brown agouti coat to be found in a wide range of animals apart from the cat. The latter represent the melanistic overlay (bars, spots, rosettes or reticulation) which is a feature of the cat family. Tabby pattern, therefore, consists of two co-existing systems of pigmentation or, seemingly more likely, a background of agouti, with a superimposed system of black pigmentation.

One of the first mutants to be found in the cat was probably that of self black. This was so long ago that it is now futile to speculate just when the event occurred. It is of greater practical importance to know how the mutant colour is inherited. This was determined about the year 1918 and this knowledge may be utilized to demonstrate the transmission of a single gene. The self black colour comes into existence by a change in one of the genes controlling the agouti background. In the black individual, none of the hairs display yellow pigment. The hair fibres are mainly black, the colour fading to a blue for the lower regions of the hair shaft.

A pure breeding strain of tabby cats will, by definition, produce only tabby kittens. Similarly, a pure strain of black cats will produce only black kittens. If now, animals of the two strains are crossed, it will be found that the offspring are all tabbies. Despite their tabby appearance, these offspring are carriers of black (as indicated by parentage) and the black colour would be expected to reappear in subsequent generations. This is so, for should the tabbies be mated among themselves, the next generation will consist of tabby and black offspring in the ratio 3 : 1. Alternatively, the tabby offspring may be mated to the black strain, in which case, the expected ratio of tabby: black will be 1 : 1. A mating could also be made to the pure tabby strain, but little would be gained thereby (as far as appearance goes) for all of the kittens would be tabby.

For purposes of discussion, the three generations and the different matings are precisely defined. The initial generation, prior to crossing, is symbolised as P (namely, the parental), the first cross generation as F_1 (namely, the first filial generation), and the generation descended from the F_1 as F_2 (namely, the second filial generation). The two other matings are known as backcrosses (BC) and it is usual to indicate to which parent or strain the backcross is made. Of the four crosses, the F_1 and F_2 are the most informative from a genetic viewpoint although the backcross has its uses.

In a preceding chapter, it is stated that the chromosomes are represented in pairs in the somatic or body cells, but only once in the germ-cells. Since the chromosomes are composed of genes, it follows that the genes must be present twice in the individual (one gene in each chromosome), but singly in the germ cells. This fact can explain the expected ratios of tabby and black kittens. The ratios are engendered by the fusion at random of germ-cells carrying different alleles. At this stage, it is convenient to introduce symbols for the various genes, since these greatly facilitate the discussion. It is usual to choose as symbols the capital and small letters of the Latin alphabet.

The symbol adopted for agouti is A and that for black (non-agouti) is a. It is mandatory to represent genes and their mutant alleles by the same letter (one by the capital and the other by the small for a reason which will become apparent anon). As each individual contains two of each gene, the pure breeding tabby will be *AA* and the pure breeding black will be *aa*. The germ-cells contain only one gene and this will be either *A* or *a*, according to strain. The F_1 tabby offspring must be of constitution *Aa* since it is the outcome of fusion of *A* and *a* bearing germ-cells.

The F_1 animals of constitution *Aa* will produce two kinds of germ-cells, those carrying *A* and those carrying *a*. The cell divisions which lead up to the formation of germ-cells are essentially impartial and any particular germ-cell is as likely to receive gene *A* as to receive *a*. The result is that the F_1 animal will form *A* and *a* bearing germ-cells in equal numbers. When two F_1 individuals are mated together, the germ-cells will unite at random. The chances of fusion of an *A* sperm with an *A* egg (to produce an offspring of *AA*) is as likely as that of fusion with an *a* egg (to produce an offspring of *Aa*). Similarly, the chances of fusion of an *a* sperm with an *A* egg (to produce an offspring of *Aa*) is as likely as that of fusion with an *a* egg (to produce an offspring of *aa*). These four unions can be depicted by the simple diagram of Fig. 3.

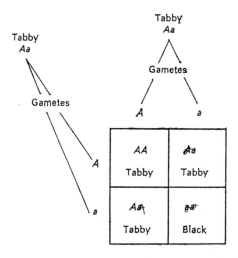

FIG. 3. The expectation from mating two F_1 heterozygous tabbies; to illustrate the 3 : 1 ratio of tabby: black for the F_2. Note that among the tabby offspring, one-third will be homozygous *AA* and two thirds will be heterozygous *Aa*.

Summing the results shows that the following offspring are produced: one *AA*, two *Aa* and one *aa*. The first type is a pure breeding tabby, while the second type is an impure tabby, and the last is a black. So far, so good; just one more step is required. The *AA* and *Aa* tabbies, though different in gene constitution, are of identical appearance, hence they should be grouped together. When this is done, a ratio of 3 tabbies to 1 black is obtained. This ratio, therefore, has a sound rational basis and, furthermore, has been confirmed by experimental breeding. It may indeed be verified by any breeder who is willing to make the necessary effort. The 3 : 1 ratio has been rightly described as the fundamental ratio of heredity. Other F_2 ratios occur but the 3 : 1 ratio can be discerned in each one of these.

The results so far call for the definition of several important ideas. The recovery of black individuals in the F_2 is said to be due to the "random assortment" of the genes *A* and *a*; or, rewording, to the "segregation" of gene *a* in the F_2. In genetics, the germ-cells are termed "gametes". The individual which results from the fusion of two gametes is termed a "zygote". Two types of zygotes exist. There is the true breeding or "homozygote" of constitution *AA* or *aa* and the impure or "heterozygote" of constitution *Aa*. This designation is general and is used in regard to any pair of alleles.

The fact that tabby cats homozygous or heterozygous for *A*, respectively, cannot be distinguished by sight, indicates that the influence of gene *A* predominates over *a*. When this occurs gene *A* is said to "dominant" to *a* or that gene *a* is "recessive" to *A*. The dominance/recessive phenomenon is indicated by the choice of symbols. When one of two alternative alleles is dominant to the other, the dominant allele is given the capital letter. In the present case, the agouti gene is symbolized by *A* while recessive non-agouti allele takes the symbol *a*. By adhering to this rule, it is easy to remember which is the dominant or recessive allele.

The phenomenon of dominance heralds an important distinction. The two tabbies *AA* and *Aa* are of identical appearance but of different genetic constitution. The outward appearance is referred to as the "phenotype" and the genetic constitution as the "genotype". Even for the simple case of homozygous versus heterozygous tabby, it will be appreciated how important is the distinction. For, although the two tabbies have a similar phenotype, their genotypes infer quite different breeding ability. The first will produce only tabby offspring while the second is capable of not only producing tabby but black kittens as well.

The backcross of the F_1 to the black parent is an interesting mating. The black parent can only produce one type of gamete, namely, a, whereas the F_1 individual will produce two, namely A and a. The offspring, therefore, will consist of tabbies (Aa) and blacks (aa) in a 1 : 1 ratio. Figure 4 shows how the expectations from the backcross can be worked out. These results lead to two deductions. Firstly, the 1:1 ratio indicates in a more direct manner than the F_2, that the F_1 is producing A and a gametes in equal numbers. Secondly, all of the BC tabbies will be carriers of black by virtue of their parentage. In this respect, they can be viewed as heterozygotes on par to the F_1 individual.

The existence of both homozygous and heterozygous tabbies in F_2 means that it is impossible to write down the genotype by mere inspection of the phenotype. The most that can be inferred is that the least one A gene must be present. It is customary to indicate the ambiguities of this nature by inserting a dash sign (–) in the genotype. That is, to write A- to denote that the individual may be either AA or Aa. In other words, to generalize, parentage is a helpful guide to the determination of the genotype. Where one parent is of the recessive form, those offspring displaying a dominant character must be heterozygotes.

The situation is different for a recessive character. A recessive trait cannot be expressed unless the responsible gene is homozygous. The fact has two general implications: (1) that, when an individual exhibits a recessive trait, the genotype relating to it can be written

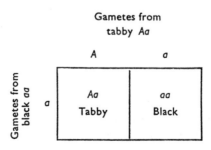

FIG. 4. The expectation from mating F_1 heterozygous tabby to a black; to illustrate the 1 : 1 ratio of tabby: black.

down without more ado, and (2) where two such individuals are bred together, they will breed true for the character. In the present example, the black individuals produced either by the F_2 or the backcross, can only have the genotype *aa*. Therefore, should they be mated together, they will only produce black offspring.

The inheritance of non-agouti is quite straightforward and raises no special problems. The gene "disappeared", as it might be put, in the F_1 but reappeared in the F_2 and BC in its original form. Neither the agouti, nor the non-agouti, gene "contaminated" each other as a consequence of being in close juxtaposition in the F_1. On the contrary, the transmission was in a thoroughly wholesome manner. The various tabby or black offspring remained clearly tabby or black in appearance, displaying no evidence of a "blend" of characteristics. This aspect may be generalized to include all cases of simple gene inheritance, not only non-agouti but all those subsequently to be described in this book.

Checkerboard Diagrams

The previous section has described the inheritance of two alleles of the same locus (the agouti). In fact, the symbol A, used to represent the agouti gene, may also be used to denote the agouti locus. However, the cat has nineteen pairs of chromosomes, each one of which is composed of some thousands of gene loci. Consequently, it is important to know what will happen when animals are bred together which are heterozygous for two or more mutant genes carried by different chromosomes.

For example, one such gene could be that known as blue dilution (or dilution for short), a common mutant in the cat. The gene causes a modification of the arrangement of pigment granules in the hair fibres, with the result that the coat appears slate-grey or bluish. Dilution is inherited as a simple recessive (symbol d) to the gene producing dense pigmentation (symbol D). A black is a dense coloured animal of genotype DD and a blue is a dilute form of genotype dd. The F_1 of a cross between these is black, with the genotype Dd. In the F_2, the blue colour will recur in the ratio of 3 black and 1 blue. In other words, the mode of inheritance is similar to that of agouti versus non-agouti. This may be verified by substituting the symbols D and d for A and a, respectively, in Figs.

3 and 4, and deriving the expectations of black and blue kittens. In essence, another gene locus has been defined with the symbol D.

Since the a and d genes do not belong to the same locus, it is possible for the two genes to be present on the same individual. When this occurs, the outcome is the non-agouti blue (self blue). The animal is clearly non-agouti (because of the absence of agouti ticking) and is clearly blue (because of the colour). The genotype, therefore is $aadd$. Now, the question to consider is what will happen when the blue is crossed with tabby having the genotype $AADD$? Since the a and d genes are independent, both will be present singly in the gametes as ad. Similarly, the gametes produced by the tabby will be AD. Note that the gametes can only transmit one of each pair of genes. The F_1 from crossing the above will have the genotype $ad + AD = AaDd$. It will be a tabby in appearance since the A and D genes are dominant to a and d, respectively. In the F_2, the genes will assort from each other and recombine at random to produce ratios of 9 tabby, 3 blue tabby, 3 black and 1 blue.

The easiest method of deriving the expectations for crosses involving two or more mutant genes is by the aid of checkerboard diagrams. The diagrams of Figs. 3 and 4 are checkerboards of a sort, but these fail to demonstrate the power of the method. Checkerboards are simple to construct and faithfully reproduce the random assortment of the genes and the complete range of expected genotypes. The rules for the construction of a checkerboard are as follows. All the possible types of gametes are written along two sides of a square; those from one parent along the top and those from the other down the left side. Vertical and horizontal lines are added to divide the square into as many columns and rows as there are different gametes. Within each cell are now written the gene symbols at the head of the column and at the side of the row in which the cell resides. To complete the diagram, it is merely necessary to examine the genotype of each cell and to write in the phenotype. Summing the various phenotypes will give the expected ratios. Checkerboards are so useful that there should be no hesitation in their use. Indeed, they provide valuable exercise in the manipulation of genes and for grasping the essence of the heredity mechanism.

There is one aspect to be carefully observed and this is that the gene content of the gametes is correct. Each gamete can carry only one of each pair of alleles. On the other hand, it must be ensured that one gene of each pair is included when the combinations are made up. An example should clarify matters. The cross of tabby ($AADD$) × blue ($aadd$) gives the F_1 of $AaDd$; an animal doubly heterozygous for a and d. The number of different gametes produced by this genotype will be four, made up as follows: $AD + Ad + aD + ad$. It should be noted that each one contains two genes, either A or a, combined with either D or d. The essential principle is that all possible combinations of A versus a in respect to D versus d must be formed.

Once the number and composition of the gametes are found, the procedure is straightforward, as shown by Fig. 5. It remains now to establish the phenotypes and this is achieved by a consideration of the dominance relationships of the pairs of genes. Genes A and D are dominant to a and d, respectively, and produce their effects independently. This means that the genotypes $AADD$, $AaDD$, $AADd$

Gametes from tabby $AaDd$

	AD	Ad	aD	ad
AD	AADD Tabby	AADd Tabby	AaDD Tabby	AaDd Tabby
Ad	AADd Tabby	AAdd Blue tabby	AaDd Tabby	Aadd Blue tabby
aD	AaDD Tabby	AaDd Tabby	aaDD Black	aaDd Black
ad	AaDd Tabby	Aadd Blue tabby	aaDd Black	aadd Blue

Gametes from tabby $AaDd$ (vertical axis label)

FIG. 5. The construction of a checkerboard diagram for two pairs of assorting mutant genes. The expected ratio is $9:3:3:1$ for the four classes of offspring. Note the various homozygous and heterozygous genotypes within each class.

and *AaDd* are tabby, that the genotypes *AAdd* and *Aadd* are blue tabby, that the geno types *aaDD* and *aaDd* are black and the single genotype of *aadd* is blue. The $9 : 3 : 3 : 1$ ratio arises from the fact that some genotypes occur more than once. Indeed, if the frequencies of the various genotypes are examined, it will be seen that these, too, bear definite ratios to one another. For instance, the number of heterozygotes and homozygotes, with respect to any dominant gene, will be in the ratio of $2 : 1$ for an F_2 generation precisely as noted earlier for the segregation of one gene.

It must follow that any individual which displays one or more recessive characters will be homozygous. Therefore, all of the non-agoutis must be *aa* and all of the dilutes must be *dd*. This is true whether or not the individual is blue-agouti (*A-dd*) or a blue (*aadd*). The latter, moreover, shows two recessive characters and must be homozygous for both *a* and *d*. This is so. It is not possible to be equally explicit for individuals displaying one or more dominant characters. In the present case, for example, the blue-agouti may have either of the genotypes *AAdd* or *Aadd*. Following the remarks of the previous section, these ambiguities are represented by dashes in the genotype. Thus, the genotypes corresponding to the above F_2 would be written as: 9 *A-D-*, 3 *A-dd*, 3 *aaD-* and 1 *aadd*.

An instructive checkerboard is that representing the expectations from backcrossing the F_1 of *AaDd* to the self blue. The same four colours will be produced but in the ratios of $1 : 1 : 1 : 1$ as shown by Fig. 6. The perceptive reader will no doubt observe that this result is a direct extension of the $1 : 1$ ratio of the backcross with one gene. The reason for the ratio is that the four classes of offspring

Gametes from tabby AaDd

		AD	Ad	aD	ad
Gametes from blue aadd	ad	AaDd Tabby	Aadd Blue tabby	aaDd Black	aadd Blue

FIG. 6. Expectations for backcrossing a double heterozygote to the double recessive; to illustrate the $1 : 1 : 1 : 1$ ratio.

accurately reflect the random combination of genes which form the gametes produced by the F_1. This is so because the self blue is homozygous for two recessive genes. The blue can only produce the gametes ad and any F_1 gamete carrying one or more dominant genes will immediately reveal this fact by the colour of the expected offspring. It may be noted in passing that the genotypes of all these BC colours can be written out in full.

It is possible to have another type of backcross when two genes are involved. This arises where one gene is heterozygous in one parent but homozygous in the other. Such a cross will be of the type $AaDd$ (tabby) X $Aadd$ (blue-tabby). The offspring will be expected to occur in the ratio of 3 tabby, 3 blue-tabby, 1 black and 1 blue, as shown by Fig. 7. In effect, the $3:3:1:1$ is a combination of the $3:1$ and $1:1$ ratios, as will be readily seen by those with an eye for such relationships.

Gametes from tabby AaDd

		AD	Ad	aD	ad
Gametes from blue tabby Aadd	**Ad**	AADd Tabby	AAdd Blue tabby	AaDd Tabby	Aadd Blue tabby
	ad	AaDd Tabby	Aadd Blue tabby	aaDd Black	aadd Blue

FIG. 7. Expectations for a cross in which one gene is assorting in a $3:1$ and another in $1:1$; to illustrate the $3:1:3:1$ ratio.

A more extensive checkerboard is that of Fig. 8 which depicts the expectations for an F_2 generation involving the simultaneous assortment of three recessive genes. The third gene is l, a mutant allele which produces long hair and may be assumed to be inherited independently of a and d. The F_1 could be that of a cross between a tabby of genotype $AADDLL$ and a blue long hair of genotype $aaddll$.

Gametes from tabby *AaDdLl*

	ADL	ADl	AdL	Adl	aDL	aDl	adL	adl
ADL	AADDLL Tabby	AADDLl Tabby	AADdLL Tabby	AADdLl Tabby	AaDDLL Tabby	AaDDLl Tabby	AaDdLL Tabby	AaDdLl Tabby
ADl	AADDLl Tabby	AADDll Tabby LH	AADdLl Tabby	AADdll Tabby LH	AaDDLl Tabby	AaDDll Tabby LH	AaDdLl Tabby	AaDdll Tabby LH
AdL	AADdLL Tabby	AADdLl Tabby	AAddLL Blue Tabby	AAddLl Blue Tabby	AaDdLL Tabby	AaDdLl Tabby	AaddLL Blue Tabby	AaddLl Blue Tabby
Adl	AADdLl Tabby	AADdll Tabby LH	AAddLl Blue Tabby	AAddll Blue Tab. LH	AaDdLl Tabby	AaDdll Tabby LH	AaddLl Blue Tabby	Aaddll Blue Tab. LH
aDL	AaDDLL Tabby	AaDDLl Tabby	AaDdLL Tabby	AaDdLl Tabby	aaDDLL Black	aaDDLl Black	aaDdLL Black	aaDdLl Black
aDl	AaDDLl Tabby	AaDDll Tabby LH	AaDdLl Tabby	AaDdll Tabby LH	aaDDLl Black	aaDDll Black LH	aaDdLl Black	aaDdll Black LH
adL	AaDdLL Tabby	AaDdLl Tabby	AaddLL Blue Tabby	AaddLl Blue Tabby	aaDdLL Black	aaDdLl Black	aaddLL Blue	aaddLl Blue
adl	AaDdLl Tabby	AaDdll Tabby LH	AaddLl Blue Tabby	Aaddll Blue Tab. LH	aaDdLl Black	aaDdll Black LH	aaddLl Blue	aaddll Blue LH

Gametes from tabby AaDdLl (left vertical label)

FIG. 8. A complex checkerboard to illustrate the assortment of three genes. Despite the size of the diagram, it is built up in exactly the manner as that of simpler checkerboards.

The F_1 will be triply heterozygous ($AaDdLl$) and the F_2 offspring will be that shown by the body of the checkerboard. The eight classes will be expected to occur in the ratios of $27 : 9 : 9 : 9 : 3 : 3 : 3 : 1$. The interesting aspect is that, while the diagram may appear formidable at first sight, inspection should reveal that this is not altogether so. Each sequence of genotypes and phenotypes are built up by simple duplication of the steps described for previous checkerboards.

The ratios discussed in this and other sections represent, of course, the theoretical expectations for the various matings. This does not mean that in a litter of four kittens, for example, three will be of the dominant type and one will be of the recessive. Or, after a total of sixteen kittens have been bred, exact $9 : 3 : 3 : 1$ ratios will be obtained. Unfortunately, the factor of chance will intervene of the same nature as that which prevents an exact $50 : 50$ ratio of head : tails for 100 tosses of a perfectly balanced coin. However, the ratios are approximated if a large number of young are bred. This is admittedly difficult for the cat but, in more prolifically breeding animals (e.g. mice or hamsters), the theoretical ratios can be closely realised. The fact that exact ratios cannot always be obtained with small numbers does not invalidate the usefulness of the expected ratios. Most events occur in this world as a matter of relative probabilities and animal breeding is no exception. The usefulness of the expectations resides in their value for planning experimental crosses and, in a wider sense, as a guide to breeding programmes.

As a check on the working out of checkerboards, it is helpful to know the maximum number of different gametes which are produced by an individual heterozygous for a given number of genes. An individual heterozygous for one gene will produce two different gametes; for two genes, the number is 4; for three genes, the number is 8; for four genes, the number is 16; for five genes, the number is 32; the number of different gametes doubling for each additional gene. The number of progeny which make up the expected ratio for an F_2 generation is the number found above multiplied by itself. The respective numbers for the five cases enumerated are 4, 16, 64, 256 and 1024, respectively. This series of figures should be sufficient to indicate how the sizes of the successive F_2s would have to escalate in order to breed all of the expected animals. For more than a few genes, the task rapidly becomes impractical. This aspect, as a matter of fact, constitutes a serious problem in animal breeding, for it frequently means that it is not possible to obtain all of the results to be anticipated from particular crosses.

Dominant and Recessive Mutants

The majority of mutants of the cat are inherited as recessive alleles to the wild type gene. That is, to the gene normally present at the locus in the wild coloured animal. However, exceptions do occur and no account would be complete without a mention of the possibility of dominant mutant alleles.

The most clear-cut instance of dominant inheritance is provided by a gene which is responsible for the yellow-eyed white (often blue or odd eyed as well but this is another story). Typically, the coat is fully white or white but for a few small patches of colour. The symbol for the allele is W; the wild type gene being represented by w. The white cat may have either of the genotypes WW or Ww. If two of the latter animals are mated together, a ratio of three white to one coloured is obtained, regardless of any other coloured genes which may be assorting at the same time. This is shown by the checkerboard of Fig. 12.

Detection of the Homozygous Dominant

A practical problem of breeding which sometimes has to be solved is that of deciding whether or not a reputedly homozygous cat may be heterozygous for a recessive gene. In principle, the solution is clear. Suppose it is desirous to discover if a black animal is heterozygous for blue dilution. The procedure would be to mate the animal to a blue. If only black kittens are produced, the animal may be assumed to be a homozygote but if a single blue kitten is produced (regardless of how many black siblings) the animal is a heterozygote.

In practice, the problem is that a heterozygous animal may produce a number of black kittens by chance. The situation is analogous to that of tossing a coin and obtaining a run of heads. It is obvious that equal numbers of heads and tails are expected but this does not prevent a series of either heads or tails to occur occasionally. Similarly, with the breeding of only black offspring when equal numbers of black and blue are expected. The difficulty can be overcome, however, by stipulating that more than a certain number of black kittens are bred before it is accepted that the animal is homozygous. In this way, the risk of being wrong (the error as it is called) can be made as small as desired. Should 5 offspring be bred, and none are blue, the risk of error is 3 per cent. This is reasonable but not as stringent as might be wished if the establishment of homozygosity is held to be important. The breeding of 7 black offspring is better since the error is reduced to about one in a hundred. This is equivalent to mating 100 known heterozygous black cats, rearing 7 kittens from each, and finding that one individual has produced entirely black offspring. Column A of Table 11 gives the probabilities of being wrong for various numbers of black kittens per tested individual.

The black-blue example is purely illustrative. The same problem would arise if it is necessary to test a tabby for positive heterozygosity for black, or a normal coated animal for either long hair or one of the rex coats and so on. In each case, it is convenient to testmate the cat with the form which it is suspected of carrying. A test could be carried out by mating the animal with another, known to be heterozygous for the recessive gene in question, but this procedure is not very efficient and is not recommended for those cases where the direct test can be performed. Many more kittens have to be bred to reduce the error to minor proportions. Column B of the above mentioned table will exemplify this point.

Incomplete Dominance

All of the mutant alleles so far described share a common property. All of them are inherited as complete recessives or as complete dominants. This is certainly the usual situation but a small number of mutant genes exhibit incomplete dominance. In these cases, the usual 3 : 1 ratio is modified to a 1 : 2 : 1 because the heterozygous class comes into its own instead of being indistinguishable from the homozygous dominant.

The most frequently quoted case of incomplete dominance in the cat involves the piebald form of white spotting, as found in the Tortoiseshell and white or a large proportion of mongrel cats. The piebald allele is symbolized by S, as opposed to s for non-spotted. The heterozygote, Ss, is usually mildly or moderately spotted of grades 1 to 4 of Fig. 21, mainly on the stomach and fore parts of the body, while the homozygote is much more extensively marked with white (grades 4 to 7). When two cats of genotype Ss are mated together, the offspring will segregate into one extensively spotted, two moderately spotted and one non-spotted in accord with the production of offspring having the genotypes SS, Ss and ss, respectively.

Unfortunately, the inheritance of white spotting is not the best of examples of incomplete dominance. At least, not the best in the sense that the two phenotypes of Ss and SS are always readily distinguished. The expression of white is very irregular and this fact makes it difficult on occasion to decide if a white spotted individual is Ss or SS. Nevertheless, the principle should be clear. A somewhat better example is given in the succeeding section on multiple allelism, where the $1 : 2 : 1$ breeding behaviour of the dark phase Burmese, light phase Burmese and the Siamese is discussed (see Fig. 10).

Multiple Allelism

A gene locus may mutate to produce a new allele on more than one occasion. Each separate event could give rise to the same mutant but this need not be so. Although each mutation would only arise rarely, if each one produces a distinctive phenotype, it would be possible for a succession of alleles at one locus to be brought together over a period of time. The number of alleles which may occur for a locus is almost unlimited but geneticists are chary in recognizing new mutants as distinctive alleles unless sound evidence is forthcoming.

Each series of alleles is given an appropriate name. For example, one important series in mammalian genetics is known as the albino for the reason that the most commonly known allele is the pink-eyed albino. It is not unusual for one or more alleles of a series to be incompletely dominant to each other, especially those at the bottom of the scale of dominance. Yet another property is that the series often affect one particular feature in a progressively severe manner.

The number of alleles which have been reasonably established for the albino series in the cat are four and these may be listed as follows:

Name	Symbol
Full colour	C
Burmese	c^b
Siamese	c^s
Blue-eyed albino	c^a
Albino	c

The symbols used to denote members of an allelic series consist of the same base letter (to denote that all of the alleles belong to the same locus) with suitable superscripts for each allele. In this case, the base symbol is c. The names of the alleles are taken from those breeds for which each one is primarily responsible. The normal (unmutated) gene is C and the four other genes represent mutant forms.

No matter how many alleles may be known for a locus, only two may be carried by a particular individual. This follows from the discussions of previous sections. For example, a black heterozygous for Burmese or for Siamese will have the genotypes Cc^b and Cc^s, respectively. It cannot be heterozygous for Burmese and Siamese simultaneously, since this would imply a genotype of Cc^bc^s. However, circumstances may conspire to suggest that this could be so and the situation deserves to be explained. A Burmese may be heterozygous for Siamese, with the genotype c^bc^s. If this cat is crossed with a tabby heterozygous for c^s, the following offspring are to be expected: 2 tabby, 1 Burmese and 1 Siamese. Full details are shown by Fig. 9. The explanation for the three colours resides in the random assortment of the genes c^b and c^s versus C and c^s, and the dominance relationships between the genes. This example illustrates the care which has to be exercised at times in the interpretation of breeding results.

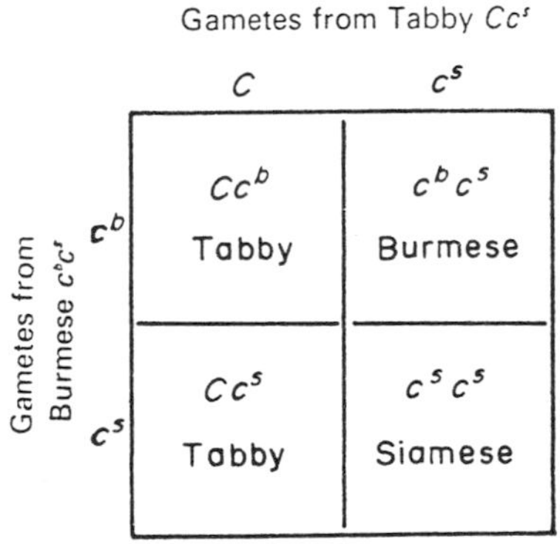

Gametes from Tabby Cc^s

	C	c^s
c^b	Cc^b Tabby	c^bc^s Burmese
c^s	Cc^s Tabby	c^sc^s Siamese

Gametes from Burmese c^bc^s

FIG. 9. Expectations for a cross involving three alleles assorting independently. Note that only two alleles can be present in one individual. The result is the breeding of three colours in the ratio of 2 : 1 : 1.

The dominance relationships between the various alleles are summarized by Table 3. The gene C for full colour is dominant to all of the mutant alleles but these, in general, are not fully dominant to each other. The allele showing this most clearly is c^b, for $c^b c^b$ is often noticeably darker than $c^b c^s$. Thus, two phases of Burmese are recognized by most Burmese breeders. It is sometimes stated that there is a small amount of overlapping of phenotypes, such that a light-coloured $c^b c^b$ may be very similar to a dark $c^b c^s$. This may be true but this does not overturn the principle. It must be admitted that the effects of the c^a and c alleles have not been investigated in all combinations but c^s, c^a and c are so close that it is doubtful if a radical phenotypical difference is produced by the substitution of c^s by c^a or c. If there is a difference, it will be in the direction of a slightly paler phenotype than the corresponding c^s combination. Preliminary observations indicate that $c^s c^a$ is somewhat lighter than $c^s c^s$ but that the difference is small. It did not seem worthwhile to stress this point in the table by separating $c^s c^a$ from $c^s c^s$.

TABLE 3. PHENOTYPES PRODUCED BY COMBINATIONS OF THE ABINISTIC SERIES OF ALLELES

Genotype	Appearance	
	With agouti	With non-agouti
CC, Cc^b, Cc^s, Cc^a, Cc	Tabby	Black
$c^b c^b$	Sepia tabby (dark)	Burmese (dark)
$c^b c^s$, $c^b c^a$, $c^b c$	Sepia tabby (light)	Burmese (light)
$c^s c^s$, $c^s c^a$, $c^s c$	Tabby Siamese	Seal Siamese
$c^a c^a$, $c^a c$	Blue-eyed albino	Blue-eyed albino
cc	Pink-eyed albino	Pink-eyed albino

Another cross between members of the series is worthy of attention. This is between two Burmese of the light phase. The genotype of this colour is $aac^b c^s$ and, when bred together, the form will produce dark phase Burmese, light phase Burmese and Siamese in the ratio of 1 : 2 : 1. Fuller details are shown by the checkerboard of Fig. 10. The light phase, therefore, is a perpetual heterozygote and nothing can be done to alter this fact. Despite this, there is no reason why the colour should not be bred by those who find it of interest. The

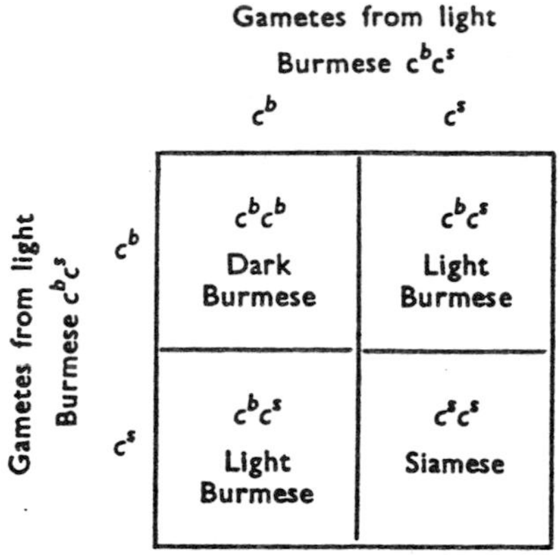

Gametes from light

Burmese $c^b c^s$

c^b c^s

	c^b	c^s
c^b	$c^b c^b$ Dark Burmese	$c^b c^s$ Light Burmese
c^s	$c^b c^s$ Light Burmese	$c^s c^s$ Siamese

Gametes from light Burmese $c^b c^s$

FIG. 10. The expectations from mating two light phase Burmese; to illustrate the 1 : 2 : 1 ratio of an incompletely dominant gene.

dark and light phases, in fact, are an excellent example of incomplete dominance.

A second series of alleles is known in the cat. These are concerned with the production of various forms of tabby striping. Three forms are recognized as under:

Name	Symbol
Abyssinian	T^a
Mackerel	T
Blotched	t^b

The order of dominance is usually taken to be as shown. In other words, T^a is dominant to T and to t^b, while T is dominant to t^b. However, the dominance of T^a is incomplete. The series is of unusual interest because the T gene produces the mackerel type of tabby which is closely akin to, if not identical with, the *silvestris* pattern of the wild cat. This is the probable ancestral type and forms a convenient "wild type" designation for the species. The other two alleles have probably arisen from T by mutation. This is intriguing because, while t^b is inherited as a recessive to T, the T^a gene is inherited as a dominant. Mutations at the same locus, therefore, may be due to alleles which are either recessive or dominant to the wild type. There is no restriction in this respect. It may be noted that a dominant allele in this case is represented by a capital letter with a superscript to indicate that it is not the wild type.

A third series of alleles is of recent discovery; so recent indeed that their existence ought to be qualified as subject to confirmation. These are the prime determinants of the black and brown pigments and are as follows:

Name	Symbol
Black	B
Brown	b
Light brown	b^l

The allele present in the ordinary tabby or "non-agouti" animal is B for black pigmentation. This has mutated to brown (b) or light brown $(b)^1$. The b allele is responsible for the ordinary brown or chocolate colour as found in the Havana or chocolate Siamese. The colour is a rich deep chocolate. The second allele is of recent discovery and produces a light chocolate brown or "milk chocolate". The colour is distinctly lighter than Havana. The order of dominance is that of B to both b and b^1, and that of b to b^1.

Masking of Genes

An important phenomenon of gene behaviour must now be described. The term dominance has a special meaning in genetics. Its use is restricted to those cases where one of two alleles at the same locus predominates over the other in the heterozygote. However, the effects of some genes are so over-riding that they are able to conceal the presence of genes at other loci. This "masking" effect is known as "epistasis" and it is not the same as dominance. The distinction should be carefully noted since it is easy to confuse the two.

Easily one of the most remarkable cases of the effects of one gene masking those of another is that of non-agouti over the various tabby alleles. The masking is virtually complete, so that while a black cat must carry tabby alleles, one would scarcely think so to judge from the uniformly black coat. The reason why the tabby striping cannot be seen is because the striping occurs as a pattern of solid black hairs against a background of agouti. However, the non-agouti gene eliminates the agouti ticking to produce a black background. Hence the tabby striping is completely swamped and cannot express itself. Rather, it would be surprising if it could! Yet, the alert reader may object that this statement is not wholly true. A "ghost" pattern of tabby striping can often be seen in the coat of the young kitten and sometimes in the young adult under certain conditions of lighting. Sometimes, the type of tabby can even be distinguished. This implies that the masking need not necessarily be complete at all stages of growth or at all times. It also confirms the statement that the black cat does indeed carry one or two tabby alleles although their presence may not be obvious.

The masking of the effects of one pair of genes by another produces a characteristic ratio in the F_2. This ratio may be exemplified by the interaction of non-agouti and the tabby alleles. Suppose that a blotched tabby (AAt^bt^b) is mated to a black of genotype $aaTT$. The F_1 will be tabby (because of the dominance of A to a) and be of the mackerel form (because of the dominance of T to t^b). The genotype is $AaTt^b$ and four types of gametes will be produced, viz., $AT + At^b + aT + at^b$. It is necessary to compile a checkerboard of sixteen squares to show the full expectation in the F_2 as per Fig. 11. The expected offspring are 9 mackerel tabby, 3 blotched tabby and 4 black. This ratio follows from the necessity of having an agouti background for the type of tabby striping to be discerned. Unless it is possible to determine the nature of the tabby carried by the black kittens, these will have to be lumped together into a single group.

Unless one is aware of the existence of genes masking the effects of others, certain results may seem mystifying. For example, in the cross of $AAt^bt^b \times aaTT$, the F_1 are mackerel striped ($AaTt^b$). It might be wondered how this result could be, since the only apparent tabby animal is blotched and this is recessive to mackerel. The difficulty is cleared up once it is realised that the black could carry the mackerel allele. The confusion may arise because of an erroneous belief that tabby is dominant to black. This is not strictly true and it could be a dangerously misleading half-truth at the best of times. It may be reiterated that it is the dominance of the agouti gene A to non-agouti a which could bring this belief into being. This is only part of the story

Gametes from mackerel tabby $AaTt^b$

		AT	At^b	aT	at^b
Gametes from mackerel tabby $AaTt^b$	AT	$AATT$ Mackerel tabby	$AATt^b$ Mackerel tabby	$AaTT$ Mackerel tabby	$AaTt^b$ Mackerel tabby
	At^b	$AATt^b$ Mackerel tabby	AAt^bt^b Blotched tabby	$AaTt^b$ Mackerel tabby	Aat^bt^b Blotched tabby
	aT	$AaTT$ Mackerel tabby	$AaTt^b$ Mackerel tabby	$aaTT$ Black	$aaTt^b$ Black
	at^b	$AaTt^b$ Mackerel tabby	Aat^bt^b Blotched tabby	$aaTt^b$ Black	aat^bt^b Black

FIG. 11. The $9:3:4$ ratio which results from the simultaneous assortment of two mutant genes, one of which masks the expression of the other.

and the complete situation is not obtained until the type of tabby is concurrently examined.

Crosses with the W form of dominant white can also produce some apparently baffling results unless one is alert to the fact that whites are not all genetically alike. Suppose a blue ($aaddww$) is paired with a white of genotype ($AADDWw$). The F_1 will be expected to consist of half tabby ($AaDdww$) and half white ($AaDdWw$). It might be wondered whence came the tabbies since the blue does not carry the agouti gene nor the gene for dense coloration. The answer, of course, is that both genes are introduced by the white parent. The white coat colour might produce the impression that the animal lacks the ability to carry any colour genes at all but this is entirely misleading. The animal is white because it carries a gene which prevents the expression of pigment (of any colour) on the coat although the genes themselves are present.

This aspect can be further understood by contemplation of the expectations from crossing *AaDdww* X *AaDdWw*. The expectations are: 9 tabby, 3 blue-tabby, 3 black, 1 blue and 16 whites. The reader should work out the expectations for himself; particularly to verify that, for every one of the 16 coloured individuals, there is a corresponding white individual of the same genotype but for the presence of a *W* gene. This should emphasize that white animals may have almost any genotype.

Should two heterozygous white cats, which are also heterozygous for another gene, be mated together, the 12 : 3 : 1 ratio of Fig. 12 will be obtained. In this example, the two cats are shown as heterozygous for non-agouti. Because of the epistatic nature of *W*, the assortment of the *A* and *a* genes can only be seen in the one quarter of offspring with coloured coats. The other three-quarters will be white animals except

Gametes from white *AaWw*

	AW	aW	Aw	aw
AW	AAWW White	AaWW White	AAWw White	AaWw White
aW	AaWW White	aaWW White	AaWw White	aaWw White
Aw	AAWw White	AaWw White	AAww Tabby	Aaww Tabby
aw	AaWw White	aaWw White	Aaww Tabby	aaww Black

Gametes from white *AaWw*

FIG. 12. The 12 : 3 : 1 ratio which comes into being from the masking effect of the dominant *W* gene.

possibly for an occasional spot or two of coloured fur. As a matter of practical interest, it is often possible to determine from these spots which genes are carried. Those with tabby spots will be of genotype *AA* or *Aa* and those with black spots will be *aa*. This minor point is mentioned because it is wise to be continuously on the look-out for clues which can establish the genotype.

The phenomenon of the over-riding influence of some genes brings into focus a point made earlier in respect to dominance, namely, the importance of making a distinction between the genotype and phenotype. The animal's appearance is one thing but its breeding ability is something different. Appearance is often the only guide to the worth of an individual and full use should be made of it but, on the other hand, it is not entirely trustworthy. The genetic calibre of the individual lies not so much on appearance but on the quality of the offspring. For this reason, it is advisable to supplement appearance by consideration of parentage and the adoption of a breeding system. It is well to recall the aphorism that animal breeding would be a greatly simplified pastime but for the existence of dominance and epistatis.

Mimic Genes

It is not uncommon for two or more independent mutant genes to have identical or closely resembling phenotypes. This sort of parallel behaviour is not due to coincidence but is connected with the fact that each character is governed by numerous genes. Any one of which may mutate to an allele bringing about a similar change in phenotype. Such genes are rather loosely called "mimics".

That such genes can occur in the cat is shown by the occurrence of at least two rex mutants. These are the Cornish and Devon rexes, each of which are inherited as recessives. The test for similarity or independency of the recessive genes with the same phenotype is to inter-cross the two forms. If they are genetically identical, the offspring will resemble the parents but, if they are independent, the offspring will be normal. Crosses between the two rexes have produced normal coated kittens; hence, the two genes are genetically distinct. The symbols for the Cornish and Devon rex mutant alleles are *r* and *re*, respectively.

The cross between the two rex mutants deserves to be discussed in more detail. Symbolically, the cross will be *rrReRe* X *RRrere* to give the F_1 of genotype *RrRere*. Each parent has contributed a wild type gene (viz., *R* and *Re*) and this is the explanation for the abrupt disappearance of the rex coat. Should the F_1 be inbred to produce an F_2, the ratio of normal: rex will be 9 : 7. This curious ratio will occur because the two rexes are of similar appearance and it may be difficult at times to distinguish one form from the other. The double rex combination (*rrrere*) will be a rex and probably identical to one of the other rexes. The reader may like to work through the appropriate checkerboard (Fig. 13) to assure himself that the expected ratio is indeed that of 9 : 7 of normal and rex kittens.

Mimic genes are of interest to geneticists because meticulous examination often reveals subtle differences which are valuable in understanding how characters develop. In practical breeding, however, they can be a nuisance. For instance, unless careful breeding records are kept, it is possible for the mutant forms to

Gametes from normal *RrRere*

	RRe	Rre	rRe	rre
RRe	RRReRe Normal	RRRere Normal	RrReRe Normal	RrRere Normal
Rre	RRRere Normal	RRrere Devon rex	RrRere Normal	Rrrere Devon rex
rRe	RrReRe Normal	RrRere Normal	rrRere Cornish rex	rrRere Cornish rex
rre	RrRere Normal	Rrrere Devon rex	rrRere Cornish rex	rrrere Devon-Cornish rex

(Gametes from normal *RrRere*)

FIG. 13. The expectation for the F_2 generation from animals heterozygous for the two rex genes: to illustrate the 9 : 7 ratio of normal: rex.

become mixed up. Furthermore, it could be a serious mistake to cross the two forms and expect to recover each type at a later date. Their similarity may be conducive to errors which would be costly to rectify. If the descendents of such crosses are recklessly distributed, the occasion may arise when two animals of the recessive form are bred together, only to give offspring of the dominant phenotype. This is likely to cause dismay and even to cast doubt on the validity of the rule that recessive traits always breed true.

The rule is not contradicted, of course; it only seemed to be so because of the similar phenotype possessed by each gene. Actually, the genes belong to different loci, hence the reversion to normal is to be expected. Other cases of mimicking genes may wait to be discovered and an obvious candidate is blue dilution. In the mouse, several distinct diluting genes are known which, when inter-bred, produce wild type offspring. Some of these mimic blue dilution closely and could be easily confused. Suppose such a situation existed in the cat. The occasion will eventually arise when two apparently blue individuals are mated, only to produce black kittens. This could mean that one parent was homozygous blue dilution, but the other carries a different diluting gene. It must be emphasized very strongly, however, that few people may be willing to accept the existence of two independent diluting genes unless it can be convincingly shown that a mis-mating (or double mating) can be precluded. This is not always so easy to establish as one might think.

The Multiple Recessive

One of the features of genetics which intrigues some people is whether there is a limit to the number of mutant genes which can be combined together. Simply answered: not as a rule. There are perhaps two qualifications to be made in regard to this statement. Both involve practical considerations of what is possible and what is not. Some mutant genes confer a slight inviability on the individual which, while not being particularly noticeable in isolation, may reveal itself more obviously when in combination. Sooner or later, this reinforcement effect could bring the process of combination to a halt. However, no effects of this kind have yet been observed for the cat.

The second qualification has to do with the problem of lack of recognition of the combinations because of epistatis. This is especially true for colour mutants. In general, each additional gene will result in a reduction in colour until a nearly white or white animal is engendered. The cat with the greatest number of recessive genes is the lilac Siamese of genotype $aabbc^sc^sdd$. If to this is added the gene for long hair, the Lilac Colourpoint will result, of genotype $aabbc^sc^sssddll$. Or, a Cornish rex version could be produced, of genotype $aabbc^sc^sddrr$. From crosses between these, the Lilac Siamese long haired Cornish rex of $aabbc^sc^sddllrr$ could be derived. Phenotypically, this animal is of Lilac Siamese coloration, with the fine hair and curved whiskers of the long hair rex.

Expressivity and Impenetrance

One of the delights or nuisances of animal breeding, depending upon one's point of view, is that no two individuals are exactly alike. This variation affects both the wild type and the mutant form but, seemingly, more especially the latter. The existence of this variability has led to the concept of "expressivity" as a means of describing the situation. Some mutant phenotypes are relatively stable while others vary considerably. A character which shows wide variability is that of piebald white spotting as illustrated by Fig. 21.

Now, the interesting feature of the variation is that, while more than one gene may be involved, there is reason to believe that most of the variation is due to a single gene. The S gene is semi-dominant which means that the heterozygotes and homozygotes are different on the average age and this fact will be contributory. Yet, even when this is taken into consideration, the variation in expression of the spotting is variable, particularly for the heterozygote Ss. This variation can be assessed by plotting the number of individual successive grades of spotting as a curve on a graph. This could be termed the "expressivity profile". A curve for one strain of cats could be different for another and, thus, be indicative that the expression of the character may vary not only between individual cats but also between stains.

If a character is extremely variable, then it is conceivable that some individuals could fail to express the character at all and appear as normal. This curious phenomenon could even occur for a character which is not exceptionally variable. The special terms "penetrance" or "partial manifestation" are used to denote this situation and it means that the character has failed to manifest although the genotype would indicate that it should. Fortunately, impenetrance is not an important factor for the colour genes known at present. All of these manifest regularly and to expectation. As an example of impenetrance, however, mention may be made of the probable existence of a minor spotting gene which produces a small white spot or clump of hairs on the breast or lower belly. The size of the spot is variable and it is possible that some animals, which ought to exhibit the spot, do not. These are solid in colour. Such animals are called "normal overlaps" because, though of normal coloration, they have a mutant genotype and will indeed breed as a mutant.

Though coat colour genes, as a rule, exhibit regular penetrance, this is not true for genetic anomalies. It is not unusual for these to display impenetrance. The inheritance of tail kinks or nodulation could be an example and doubtless other instances will come to mind. A possible reason for this is that the body of an animal shows surprising powers of self-repair. This is particularly true when a defect makes an appearance early in development, before the tissues are too well formed that timely and self-regulating growth cannot swing into action to rectify the defect. That is to say, to put the matter simply, the genetic disruption may persist and eventually produce a defective individual. In another individual, however, the disruption can be overcome with the result that an outwardly normal individual is produced. The varying severity of many anomalies is due to the same process, only in these cases, the self-rectification has only been partial. In both cases, the gene causing the disruption is present and, particularly in the case of the spuriously normal individual, this should not be overlooked.

Manifold Effects of Genes

Some genes seem to modify only one character while others appear to influence the expression of several characters simultaneously. In this latter case, it is said that the gene has "pleiotropic" action. The concept of pleiotropism is intimately bound up with the depth of analysis of gene action. To a superficial appraisal, many genes will exhibit pleiotropic effects to a lesser or greater degree. For example, if eye colour and coat colour are treated as separate characters, then the Siamese gene could be regarded as pleiotropic because of its effect on both eye colour and coat colour. Yet, if the pigmentation of the animal is treated as a whole, there is no pleiotropism, since the blue eye and whitish sepia coat are both due to the same cause. Namely, the severe impairment of pigment formation brought about by the gene.

A better example of pleiotropism is shown by the dominant white gene. The most obvious effect of the gene is to produce the white coat colour. This it does in 100 per cent of cases, i.e. all cats with the gene have white fur. However, the gene also produces blue eyes and deafness. This it does in about 70 per cent and 45 per cent of cases. Thus, it may be said that the gene is "pleiotropic" in that it effects three diverse characters, coat colour, eye colour and the hearing organs. The gene is completely "penetrant" for coat colour but "impenetrant" for eye colour and deafness. It is probable that no gene is truly pleiotropic. A gene may appear pleiotropic because the analysis of the effects have not been taken far enough to reveal the fundamental action of the gene. In the example, all three effects could stem from a common cause, as yet unknown.

Linkage

The cat has nineteen pairs of chromosomes and it is probable that each one contains some thousands of genes. While the number of known mutants are small, the chances are that these will be borne by different chromosomes. The inference for practical breeding is that the various mutants will be inherited independently of each other.

However, the situation is changed if two mutant genes happen to occur in the same chromosome. The inference of independent assortment will no longer hold and, in crosses, the two genes will tend to stay together as these are transmitted from one generation to the next. This "staying together" is termed "linkage" and the two genes are said to be "linked". Linkage is an attribute which cannot be forecast but only discovered by experimental breeding.

None of the mutants of the cat are known to be linked. Regrettably, this is not due to experimental tests for linkage which have proved to be negative but rather to a complete absence of tests. It is traditional to assume that genes are inherited independently until such time that evidence for linkage becomes unmistakable. As more mutants are discovered (such as, the recent addition of the folded-ears gene) and progress is made with cat genetics, the chances of finding a linkage will increase until the event becomes an almost certainty. For this reason, apart from general knowledge, it is wise to be aware of the possibility of linkage and to be on the look-out for possible instances.

Two phases of linkage may be recognised. In one, two genes may be located in the same chromosome, whence they are said to be "coupled". When the two genes are present in the same parent, they will be transmitted together far more often than they are separated. This is the criterion for this phase of linkage. In the other phase, the two genes are in different members of the pair of chromosomes. When the genes are present in the same parent, they will be transmitted separately far more often than they are together. The criterion in this case is that the genes are not recombining as freely as they would if they are inherited independently. The two genes are then said to be in "repulsion". It may be seen that the names given to the two phases indicate clearly what is to be expected in breeding operations. In the first, the two genes are behaving as if coupled while, in the second, they behave as if they are repelling one another.

It may be queried: what exactly is linkage and do linked genes remain permanently linked? The special cell divisions which lead to the formation of gametes require that the pairs of homologous chromosomes come to lie in extremely close proximity and to form intimate contact at certain points along their length. During this process, internal stresses are induced which are relieved by spontaneous breakage and rejoining. In a proportion of cases, the rejoining is between constituents of partner chromosomes, rather than between those of the same chromosome. The result is that the chromosomes have exchange segments of themselves with each other. In effect, the changes are a means of ensuring that the pairs of chromosomes have a common unity but this aspect is beyond the scope of this book.

The exchange of material between homologous chromosomes means that blocks of genes have been conveyed from one chromosome to the other; or, to use the appropriate term, have "crossed over". The separation of linked genes is known as "crossingover" and the term means that (1), for coupling, the mutant genes have been separated from each other and (2) for repulsion, the formerly separated genes are now combined in the same chromosome. Now, the chance of separation will depend upon the relative distance between the two genes. The greater the distances, the greater the chance of crossingover. Therefore, it is possible for two genes to be "loosely" or "closely" linked. When two genes are closely linked, the absence of random assortment is particularly noticeable.

The whole topic of linkage is of some import for both pure and applied genetics and most genetic textbooks discuss the subject in depth. However, in applied genetics, the event of linkage may be received with mixed feelings. For example, the intrusion of linkage is annoying when a breeder is endeavouring to create a new colour variety by the recombination of genes only to find that this is proving to be more difficult than anticipated.

Sex-linked Heredity

It may be remarked with some pride that the cat is one of the few mammals to boast of a case of sex-linked inheritance which dates from the dawn of genetics. The curious situation of the tortoiseshell pattern of the female and the great scarcity of tortoiseshell males has been cited in most books on animal genetics.

It is stated in a preceding chapter that the sex of the individual is determined by a pair of special chromosomes: the X and the Y. These chromosomes carry gene loci which can mutate, just as those borne by the ordinary chromosomes. However, there is a vital difference. A mutant allele carried by a sex chromosome will be associated with sex and display "sex-linkage". This is the situation for the mutant which produces "ginger" or red pigmentation and which is indirectly responsible for the mosaic pattern of the tortoiseshell.

The gene responsible for the ginger cat is known as orange and is symbolized by O. The colour is produced by an alteration in the animal's pigment physiology so that entirely yellow pigment is produced instead of a mixture of yellow/tabby for the tabby and yellow/black for the non-agouti. The word yellow, it may be interposed at this juncture, is used in a general sense to include all cream, yellow and red pigmentation. Yellow is the technical term for the pigment granule which produces all of these colours. The black tabby striping emerges as red striping of the same pattern and the intervening agouti areas become yellow or rich beige.

The sex linkage of O becomes apparent when the segregation of the gene is considered for the various matings. The O gene is borne by the X chromosome. Now, the male has but one X chromosome; consequently, they can only be either O (yellow) or o (non-yellow). On the other hand, the female has two X chromosomes; consequently, they may be one of three genotypes. These are: OO (yellow, Oo (tortoiseshell) or oo (non-yellow). The tortoiseshell, therefore, is the heterozygote and is unique in that its coat reflects the influence of both the O and o genes in different parts of the animal at the same time. The yellow areas corresponding to O and the non-yellow areas to o.

To predict the results of matings with sex-linked genes, it is necessary to know which colour is the male or vice versa. For convenience, all of the possible matings with the orange mutant are arranged in Table 4. The expectation for the table can be found by the aid of checkerboard diagrams, as shown by the examples of Figs. 14 and 15. The reader may find valuable exercise in working out the expectations for all of the crosses of the table. The point to remember with sex-linked genes is that the male can only transmit one gene (O or o) in 50 per cent of gametes; the other 50 per cent carrying a Y chromosome which does not possess a O locus.

Gametes from tortoiseshell
Female Oo

		O	o
Gametes from yellow male OY	O	OO Yellow female	Oo Tortoiseshell female
	Y	OY Yellow male	oY Black male

FIG. 14. The assortment of the sex-linked O gene. Note that O can only be transmitted in half of the male gametes.

Gametes from tortoiseshell
female *Oo*

		O	o
Gametes from black male *oY*	o	*Oo* Tortoiseshell Female	*oo* Black Female
	Y	*OY* Yellow male	*oY* Black male

FIG. 15. A second example of the assortment of the sex-linked *O* gene. Note that the wild type gene *o* can only be transmitted in half of the male gametes.

In the table, the word black has been used to denote non-yellow, this usage being common practice. This policy is acceptable, provided it does not blind one to the fact that "black" can mean tabby, blue, chocolate and other colours; the common denominator of which is that they are "non-yellow". The mutant genes producing these colours will be inherited independently of *O* and the assortment of these may have to be taken into account for working out the full expectation for

TABLE 4. EXPECTATIONS FOR THE POSSIBLE MATINGS OF YELLOW AND TORTOISESHELL CATS

Mating		Expected offspring	
Dam	Sire	Males	Females
Yellow	Yellow	Yellow	Yellow
Black	Yellow	Black	Tortoiseshell
Tortoiseshell	Yellow	Yellow Black	Yellow Tortoiseshell
Tortoiseshell	Black	Yellow Black	Tortoiseshell Black
Yellow	Black	Yellow	Tortoiseshell
Black	Black	Black	Black

Note: In the above table, black is used as a euphemism for non-yellow (e.g. black, tabby, blue, etc.).

any cross or series of crosses. The procedures to follow are those for ordinary inheritance, as shown by the checkerboards described earlier, in combination with those for sex-linkage.

The conversion of black pigment to yellow is so effective that the non-agouti yellow of genotype *aaO* or *aaOO* is identical in appearance to that of *A-O* or *A-OO*. That is, gene *O* masks the expression of the *A* and *a* genes. This fact can be verified by crossing a yellow male of genotype *AAO* to a black female of genotype *aaoo*. The offspring will consist of tabby males and tabby tortoiseshell females. Since the black female cannot carry agouti, the offspring must have gained the gene from the yellow parent. As it happens, the patchwork colouring of the tortoiseshell provides direct visual evidence that the yellow gene can mask the expression of non-agouti. It is possible to have both tabby and black tortoiseshells of genotypes *A-Oo* and *aaOo*, respectively, yet the yellow areas in the two cats are exactly the same. One could not ask for a better demonstration of the epistatic nature of *O*.

Sex-limited Expression

There is another form of sex associated heredity which, unfortunately, is sometimes mistaken for sex-linkage. This is where the expression of a gene is confined to one sex although the gene, itself, is carried by one of the ordinary chromosomes. No clear-cut instance of sex-limited expression of a gene affecting coat colour has been reported for the cat although examples are afforded by those characteristics which are clearly either paternal or maternal.

If it is supposed that cryptorchidism is due to one or more genes, this would be a character which is sex-limited to the male (at least, that aspect of the deformity which results in undescended testes). This defect is cited mainly as an example since, at this time, little is known of the extent to which it might be genetically determined. If the defect is due to a recessive gene (possibly with impenetrance), it would be a fine example. The lesson to be learnt from sex-limited inheritance is that while the trait will be inherited through both sexes, the trait will manifest only in one. This means that the breeding potential of the non-manifesting sex cannot be assessed directly, though some idea can be obtained from the manifesting sibs.

The type of maternal care a queen may lavish upon her kittens and the quality and quantity of her milk is determined in part by heredity.

A female which neglects her young or rears weakly offspring should always be examined for a possible ailment which may be undermining her health or stamina. However, if this examination is negative, the possibility that these undesirable traits are caused genetically should be considered. Other factors being equal she and her offspring should not be used for breeding. The point to be made is that it should not be imagined that these traits are inherited solely via the mother. A son from an excellent or poor mother is equally likely to pass on these desirable or undesirable qualities to his female offspring, as in a daughter from the same mother. A male cannot express any real forms of maternal instinct but, nevertheless, he will carry the genes for them.

Continuous Variation

The type of heredity described in previous sections is known as discrete or discontinuous because the characteristics involved are sharply defined. For instance, no one could confuse a tabby cat with a black nor, after a modicum of experience, a mackerel with a blotched striped tabby. Yet, not all variation is of this nature, many characteristics are known which vary continuously from one extreme to another. A good example, in the sense of being obvious to the eye, is the variation in intensity of yellow pigmentation, which can range all the way from light "ginger" to rich red. To be sure, a major step is required in the first instance to create the yellow cat but the variation of intensity is independent of this.

The question may be asked: is this continuous variation inherited and, if so, how? The answer to the first part of the question is, yes, very often a sizeable part of the variation is inherited, although the proportion may vary from character to character. In this respect, continuous variation differs from the discontinuous. With discrete heredity, the size of the step tends to swamp the incidental background variation, whether inherited or not. With continuous characters, on the other hand, the incidental background variation is included and it is not always wise to assume that all of the observed variation is inherited. It is also unwise to go to the other extreme and assume that none of the variation is inherited. The true situation lies in between, some of the variation is genetic and the remainder is not.

The answer to the second part of the question is that the heritable portion is due to many genes with similar effects, though the effect of any one gene is small relative to the total variation. Though the action of each is small, the total effect is cumulative, so that an individual which carries a number of these genes is phenotypically different from an individual which carries only a few. Because numerous genes with minor effects are involved, the inheritance of continuously varying characteristics is blending. The genes themselves do not blend, of course, but assort in the manner of genes with major effects. It is the phenotype which shows blending in the form of offspring which are generally intermediate to that of the parent, with the production of the odd individual which deviates from the average. Characters controlled by many genes are termed "polygenic" and the genes concerned are known collectively as "polygenes". The important point to remember is that many, rather than a few, polygenes are involved as a group and that the effect of each one is small compared with the cumulative effect of the group. Those genes with large effects (i.e. ordinary alleles) are "major genes" in this terminology.

It is convenient to speak of polygenes as possessing plus and minus effects with respect to the expression of a character. For example, take the variation of intensity of yellow. The ginger mongrel cat may be visualised as possessing minus polygenes, as opposed to the rich colouring of the exhibition Red Tabby which is brought into being by plus polygenes. Furthermore, these extreme forms breed relatively true; ginger cats rarely produce other than ginger young and red tabbies produce red tabbies. The colour may vary but, on the average, this is so. The reason is that they are at the extremes of the variation. Should the two forms be crossed, the offspring would be expected to be intermediate, richer in colour than the ginger but less so than the exhibition animal. Inbreeding these cross-breds would be expected to produce a generation consisting of very variable offspring. Most would be intermediate in colour but a number will approach either the ginger or the red of the grandparents. Should the intensity of yellow be divided into grades and the parentage of animals of each grade be tabulated for a large number of offspring, the result could be similar to Fig. 16.

The checkerboard of Fig. 8 may be used to convey a mental picture of the behaviour of polygenes. Suppose that three polygenes are involved and that the plus alleles can be represented by capitals

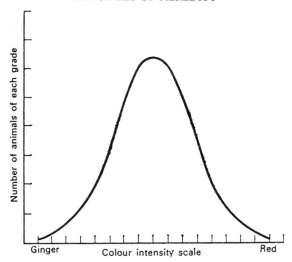

FIG. 16. Idealised curve to illustrate how the frequencies of animals, graded for intensity of yellow, might be distributed in the F_2 of a cross between a ginger and an exhibition red.

and the various minus alleles by small letters. Therefore, the ginger grade of yellow will have the genotype *aabbcc* and the red grade will be *AABBCC*. To keep the picture simple, assume there is no dominance and that the variation of intensity of yellow can be divided into seven grades (from 0 for ginger to 6 for the most intense red). The F_1 will be of an intermediate colour (grade 3) and have the genotype *AaBbCc*. When these are inter-bred, the polygenes will assort and combine at random to produce the totality of 64 genotypes as shown by Fig. 8 (by substituting the symbols *A*, *B*, *C*, etc. for *A*, *D*, *L*, etc. of the checkerboard). Let each plus polygene increase the intensity by one grade, so that the genotype *aabbcc* will be of grade 0 and the genotypes *Aabbcc*, *aaBbcc* and *aabbCc* will be of grade 1, and so forth. Proceeding in this manner over the whole range of genotypes, the 0 to 6 grades will be found to occur in the frequencies of 1, 6, 15, 20, 15, 6 and 1, respectively. Figure 16 shows the expectation in a rather idealized form. The curve on the figure is of the general type which occurs when numerous factors are operating to determine the expression of a character. Even with a hypothetical example of 64 individual, the shape of the curve can be seen in a plot of the expected frequencies.

If the F_1 are backcrossed to the red, the expectation is a range of grades from 3 to 7, with the majority of offspring being of the intermediate grades 4 and 5. Similarly, if the F_1 are backcrossed to the ginger, the range of variation will be from grades 0 to 3, with the majority of offspring being of the intermediate grades 1 and 2. The average in each case will be that of a grade of yellow which is half-way to that of the parents. This is a typical result of continuous or polygenic heredity. Note that it is the average of the offspring which is intermediate. The majority will in fact be intermediate but there will also be some individuals which will be either paler or darker. Any breeder who has had occasion to breed together yellow cats of various intensities will probably have noticed this behaviour.

The above remarks have deliberately simplified the mechanism of polygenic heredity for, apart from the obvious probability that many, rather than a few, polygenes will be involved, any of the attributes of genes with major effects could be shown by polygenes. These could include unequal effects for different polygenes, either alone or in company with certain others, dominance, masking of the effect of one gene by the presence of another and other odd behaviour. It is beyond the scope of this book to delve into this sort of complex behaviour. This is not to suggest that the topic is impossibly difficult but to cover the subject adequately would be to expand this chapter beyond reasonable bounds. The complexities of polygenic inheritance has been competently tackled and anyone wishing for further information should read either Mather (1977) or Falconer (1981).

Polygenic variation may be conveniently divided into two sorts: (1) the "pure" state, where no major genes are involved, and (2) where the variation is due in the first instance to the presence of a major mutant gene. The heredity of body size and conformity falls into the first category. No major genes are known to effect either of these features. On the assumption that the diet is adequate and the cat receives sufficient exercise for full development, the size and shape of the body is due to polygenes. "Size and shape" is an abstraction, of course, encompassing many individual features. Apart from bulk, *per se*—as measured by weight—a cat may be thick-set or long-bodied, heavy or lightly boned, short or long legged and so forth. These items do not vary independently but are correlated, and it is this fact which gives a meaning to the concept of "type" as visualized by the breeder seeking to perfect an ideal animal.

By far the commoner situation, however, is where a major gene is also concerned. The example of variation in intensity of yellow is most striking but may be justifiably held that the variation is brought into prominence in the first instance by the presence of the O gene. This is true and, what is more important, it has led to the idea of the polygenes being regarded as "modifying" genes. That is, the yellow colour is due to O but the expression of O is due to modifying polygenes or "modifiers" for short. The importance of this concept is considerable. In the first place, the concept is very general. For instance, long hair is primarily due to the mutant l but there is a great difference between the long haired mongrel and the exhibition animal. At present, there is no indication that the difference is due other than to polygenes modifying the length and texture of the long haired condition. Another example, which occupies the attention of breeders, is the variation of depth of colour of blue cats. The basic genotype is $aadd$ but the blue colour can vary quite appreciably. This variation is due to polygenes. Now, black cats also vary in depth of colour but to a less extent than do blues and, therefore it may be said that the polygenes involved are modifiers of the expression of the blue gene.

Some people have proposed that where the expression of a gene (particularly, a mutant) is dependent upon the presence of modifiers, these latter produce no effect on the alternative allele (particularly, the wild type). The variation in the shade of blue is a made-to-order example. Superficially, blacks are blacks and that's it! Yet, black cats do vary in intensity but certainly not to the same extent as blues and this fact provides a clue to the variation. The dilution modifiers probably modify the black phenotype but not so much as the blue. The action of the dilution polygenes are "damped down" where the former is concerned but "accentuated" for the latter. This aspect makes it rather difficult to assess the nature of any dilution polygenes carried by a black; whereas, it is fairly obvious that a light blue carries those polygenes lightening (minus alleles) the colour while a dark blue will carry those of opposite tendency (darkening or plus alleles).

In a similar manner, the coat length polygenes may have a greater effect in combination with l than with the type allele L. That is to say, their effects on hair fibre length is accentuated when the fibre has already been lengthened by the *l* gene. It is as if the normal stabilized development has been upset by the advent of *l*. Something of this nature is certainly conceivable. This would explain the relative minor effects of the polygenes on the wild type phenotype and yet the apparently greater effects on the mutant phenotype. The dilution polygenes in conjunction with *d* and the coat length polygenes in conjunction with *l*. On the other hand, the hair length modifiers may have some effect on the normal coat in view of the extraordinary full coat often shown by the F_1 between a normal coat animal and an exhibition type long hair. This result should be a warning not to generalize too readily with respect to the action of specific polygenes.

However, there is no reason why a definable group of polygenes should not be treated as a genetic entity in its own right. Especially where it can now be shown that the group is combining or interacting with more than one gene, since this would mean that the concept of the group as modifiers of a specific gene or phenotype will no longer hold in a rigid sense. Those polygenes responsible for the intensity of yellow pigmentation apparently behave in this manner. In addition to their effects on the yellow phenotype, the quality of the yellow pigment shown by the exhibition Brown Tabby and the Abyssinian, compared with the mongrel tabby, could be ascribed to the group. Also, the variation of the yellowish or tawny suffusion in the mongrel silver and the amount of yellow shown by the Red Siamese could be part of the variation. The thread running throughout these observations is variation in the intensity of yellow pigmentation, whether or not this be against a phenotype provided by the *O, C, I* or c^s genes. The *I* and c^s alleles reduce the amount of yellow in the coat but they do not eliminate it completely and the amount remaining is variable. In this connection, the exhibition silver displays no suffusion. This implies that selection has operated against yellow pigmentation, decreasing the amount to the point of total elimination.

The polygenes decreasing the amount of yellow may reveal themselves in a manner which is interesting enough to be mentioned. When an exhibition silver is crossed with a normal tabby, the offspring are often unusually pale in colour. It is as if the yellow coloration has been diluted (the black pigmentation is normal), such as might occur if *I* is incompletely dominant to *i*. Now, this is a possibility but, so far at least, it has not been proven. However, the interesting point is this. It is more likely that the polygenes carried by the silver are inherited in a typical blending manner. This means that although I is dominant to i, the intensity of yellow pigmentation will be diluted by the action of the polygenes. This sort of polygenic behaviour is not unusual whensoever the phenotype of one of the parents has been selected for extreme expression of a particular feature. The present case involves a colour trait but it may be noted that it parallels the situation described above for crosses with the exhibition long hair.

Apropos colour inheritance, it is necessary to recognize at least three or four groups of polygenes. The first is the group affecting the intensity of yellow and named (at least provisionally) rufus. The second are those modifying the depth of blue pigmentation (dilution group). A third group could be those modifying the depth of chocolate pigmentation, as found in the Chestnut Brown. The variation here is akin to that of the blue since it is possible to have light and dark chocolate coloured animals yet the corresponding blacks scarcely differ. If the dilution and chocolate groups are identical, the dark blue and rich chocolate animals would carry identical polygenes which darken the colour. It is by no means certain that the rufus polygenes are independent of the dilution group. Those polygenes which deepen the yellow to red could be the same as those which darken the other colours. For most purposes, the rufous and dilution groups can be treated as independent, but it is wise to be aware that this may not be so. The last group to be mentioned is that controlling the amount of agouti ticking in the tabby areas of the coat. This is variable and controlled to some extent by polygenes. As far as is known, the ticking polygenes produce no effect upon a non-agouti background.

Almost any feature of the cat which can be sensibly analysed will be found to vary, although not all of the variation will be genetic. The genetic proportion will vary from feature to feature and from strain to strain for the same feature. This explains in part why successful results can be obtained with some individuals and strains but not with others. The genetic variation, in general, will be of a polygenic nature. It may be, in fact, that the feature being studied was created in the first instance by the major gene and all the breeding animals are homozygous for it. This means that the major gene or genes becomes the basic genotype and subsequent modification of the phenotype will depend upon manipulation of the various groups of polygenes. How to attempt this manipulation will be discussed in a subsequent chapter.

Threshold Characters

Polygenic inheritance is usually associated with character which vary smoothly from one extreme of expression to the other. However, it is possible for polygenic variation to be involved with discontinuous variation which, at first sight, may be thought to be under the control of a major gene. The simplest explanation is the concept of a build-up of polygenes which enables a process to be carried past a "developmental threshold" so that a new mode of expression appears. This sort of character is called a "threshold character".

Alternatively, it is possible that a developmental process may fail to be carried through to completion because there are insufficient plus polygenes. Possibly this is a more comprehendable situation. Figure 8 may be pressed into service to exemplify the principle. Suppose that a vital physiological reaction requires the presence of a certain number of plus polygenes for fulfilment and that a population of cats may be represented by the figure. In this figure any individual may contain from one to six plus polygenes, together with a small number of deficient individuals (the 0 class). If the presence of at least one plus polygene is sufficient for full completion of the reaction, then only the zero class individuals will not come up to scratch; in other words, the failure rate will be about 2 per cent. However, suppose at least two plus polygenes are required, then both the 0 and 1 classes will be involved and the rate will rise to about 11 per cent. Therefore, generalizing, if many polygenic loci are involved and the essential polygenic complement varies from strain to strain, it is obvious that the incidence of a threshold character could vary within wide limits. Usually, the incidence is low because most individuals have a gene complement which leads to normal development.

Cases of threshold heredity occur in most domesticated animals and this is the main reason why the topic is mentioned. No definite instance is known for the cat although there is an air of general suspicion that certain gross anomalies could be generated in this manner. Any feature which differs rather sharply from the normal and occurs at a low frequency could be a threshold character. It could also be due, of course, to a mutant gene which is assorting at a low frequency in the cat population at large. This is particularly true if the gene is only partially penetrant, so that the occurrence is not only low but erratic. It is difficult to distinguish between these two situations unless it is possible to carry out precise breeding experiments. In most cases, the genetic diagnosis has to rely upon the known behaviour of similar traits in other animals and a "feeling" for the likely mode of inheritance. This is not scientific, it must be admitted but, if experiments are excluded and an explanation is still sought, this is the only line of approach.

It is perhaps just as well that cat breeders are not likely to be called upon to deal with threshold characters, for their manipulation can be tricky. However, for those who wish to delve deeper, Falconer (1981) has devoted a whole chapter to the topic and this excellent account should be consulted.

Genetic Fingerprints

An event of some interest to breeders is the discovery that minute but variable sections of the chromosomes can be portrayed as a series of dark bars on a photographic film. The significant findings of the discovery is that the bars are unique to the individual. This has led to the technique for revealing the bars being termed "genetic fingerprinting". The pattern of bars has a resemblance to the identifying computer codes to be found on many domestic items and for this reason these have come to be known as "genetic bar codes" which is, in some respects, an apt description.

The interesting aspect is that the individual bars are inherited from parent to offspring in a consistent manner. The uniqueness of the bar codes for the individual and the genetic descent implies that these have immediate practical applications. To give an example, they may be used to decide more decisively than hitherto cases of uncertain or disputed paternity. Instead of merely indicating that a certain stud could not have sired a specific kitten—as has been the case in the past—it is now possible to be more positive and state that only a certain stud could be the sire. This represents a considerable advance in paternity problems. Genetic fingerprinting is available as a service from a commercial laboratory by arrangement with a vet. The usual procedure is for small samples of blood to be taken from the cats under test for submission to the laboratory. The initial procedure is to consult a vet for his or her co-operation in procuring the blood samples (Jeffreys and Morton, 1987; Georges *et al.*, 1988).

4

Breeding Practice

IT IS entirely possible to breed cats without concerning oneself with quality nor complying with any particular system of mating. However, this sort of behaviour is not breeding in any worthwhile sense. It is scarcely removed from cat rearing since anyone can have a male and a few queens about the house and nature will do the rest. As cat breeders, it behoves us to do better than that. This means that certain animals are favoured to others and that no matings are allowed until careful consideration is given to the outcome. That is, the good and bad points of the individual cats are assessed and weighed against each other and the pairings arranged with the motive of improving the cats. With pedigree animals, the prime motives are usually two, improvement of the standard of the breed and success in the show pen against the best efforts of other breeders.

The skill of cat breeding resides in the choice of animals and how these may be mated with each other. Not everyone may regard these two acts as being separate but they should be so regarded, particularly if the subject is tackled analytically. True, they are complementary to each other and this is the correct way to view the situation. The choice of animal for breeding is embodied in the concept of "selection" and the mating of the selected animals as the "breeding system."

The main factors in the practice of animal breeding are shown by Fig. 17. The phenotype of the individual is made up of a large number of genetic characters of varying expression. The ideal animal is one in which the expression of each of these characters is just right in the eyes of the breeder. This means that an intermediate expression will be required for some but an extreme expression for others. The expression is controlled by selective breeding, of which there are several kinds. The simplest is choice of the individual but

73

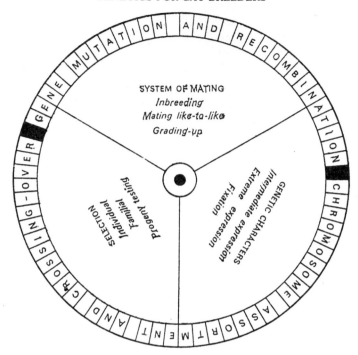

FIG. 17. The main factors of animal breeding portrayed as a wheel of chance. The breeder's art resides in the skilful manipulation of these to bring together genes which will engender the ideal individual.

selection can take in whole families and extend into progeny testing. Side by side with selection and reinforcing the process, there is the system of mating, which includes inbreeding of strong or moderate intensity, the matings of like to like and the grading up of poor quality animals. These are some of the tools which are at the disposal of the breeder should he so wish to use them. Just how they may be used and which ones are most suitable for particular problems is the substance of this chapter.

Selective breeding is by far the most potent factor, whether this be straightforward selection with no frills or one of the more sophisticated methods. The evidence for this is the existence of the various breeds of cats. Not so much that of coat colour (this can be easily juggled around) but that of body conformation which cannot be so easily manipulated though it is the real basis of breed differentiation. Among domesticated animals, the dog furnishes the finest examples of such differences. The differences between the larger hounds and the diminutive toy breeds is truly remarkable and testifies to the efficiency of selection. Yet selection alone is not enough. Breeds of animal breed relatively true otherwise they would not be worthy of the name. It might be thought that selection is responsible for this property. This is true to some extent but it is doubtful if it is the whole truth.

Selection by itself is not very efficient in eliminating heterozygous genotypes (the producers of deviating forms). Inbreeding is consistently more efficient in this respect. Not necessarily close inbreeding but the moderate form which results from mating of not too distantly related animals. It may come as a surprise but some inbreeding is essential during the formation of a breed in order that the conformation should stabilize around a definite type. Later, there can be some relaxation, but not too much, otherwise phenotypic divergence will occur. Those individuals which diverge too much are either not bred from or are mated to a typical animal of the breed. In general, a breed stabilizes itself and moves forward as an entity because the majority of animals tend to be descended from, or are bred to, a small group of elite animals commonly regarded as the most outstanding specimens (rosette winners and champions of various kinds). Quite often these are inter-related to a greater degree than the ordinary members of the breed. In short, the breeders who have worked to produce these outstanding specimens are exceedingly choosy in their mating and bitter experience has taught them the inadvisability of straying too far from the basic blood lines of the breed.

Selection and the Total Score

Selection of breeding stock can take a surprising number of forms. However, these all have one object in view, viz. the raising of the general quality of the stock. It is methods of selection which differ and this is where the skill of the animal breeder can be taxed in an endeavour to choose between the various methods and to fit these in with other factors which have to be considered. Most people have an idea of what is meant by selection but probably only a vague idea of the methods which can be brought to bear.

An important factor in selection is its intensity. It is not always easy to assess the strength of selection for all traits but a very convenient measure is that of calculating the proportion of kittens kept back for breeding. For example, a round of litters from one male and four queens could produce 16 kittens, out of which it might be decided to keep two queens as replacements for two of the mothers. This represents a selection intensity of two-sixteenths or 6 per cent. However, suppose, a second round of 16 kittens is produced by the same parents and two of the best kittens from the first are kept back for comparison with the second. Selection of the two best females would now represent a 3 per cent intensity. It is very desirable to have as many young as possible among which to pick and choose since, in many cases, the amount of progress by selection is closely related to the intensity. This is common sense, but is sometimes overlooked when other (extraneous!) factors have to be considered, such as cost of feeding and housing.

The simplest form of selection is that of individual merit, based almost entirely upon appearance. This is basic, regardless of whatever refinements may be employed. The first requirement is that the animal should be healthy, as shown by good growth, freedom from disease and lively behaviour. If a male, he should be morphologically normal, display keen interest in the oestrous female and be persistent in coitus. He should have a high rate of fertile matings. If a female, she should come into heat regularly, have easy parturitions, bring forth normal and healthy young in average numbers, and be able to rear these unaided. Some of the above items can only be seen after the animal has been bred which means that certain parts of the selective process have to be deferred. Reproductive performance is so important that it may be thought superfluous to mention the topic. Unfortunately, in the sorting out of the many traits which have to be selected, reproduction is not always given the priority it deserves. It is scarcely good policy to breed a superlative strain only to find that it is held in low esteem because of either poor health or reproduction.

The most spectacular results are obtained where it is possible to select for a single well-defined character. These are situations which produce the nice arcing curves of the results of selection to be found in genetic textbooks. In most cases, the practical breeder may find that he has to settle for something less. There are several reasons for this, of which three may be singled out. The first is lack of facilities in terms of space and time. Many breeders plead this but not always convincingly. It is largely a question of making do with the best that can be provided. If a breeder intends to breed cats, the job may as well be tackled properly and full use made of the available facilities. The second reason is to have a clearly defined objective in mind from the start. For most people, this will mean cats excelling in all of the fine qualities of the breed of their choice. Fair enough, then this means a close study of the standard of excellence for the breed and of those animals judged to be the best available. One's own stock should now be critically compared with these animals. This is the moment of truth and, the more objective the comparison, the more quickly can something be done to correct any failings which are evident.

Thirdly, the breeder is rarely in a position where he can concentrate entirely on one character. All sorts of characters have to be considered simultaneously if all-round excellence is to be achieved. There are three methods of setting about the problem. It might seem feasible to work on one feature at a time. Proceeding to the next only when the first have been raised to a sufficiently high standard. This is the so-called "tandem" method. The main objections to the method are the time required to produce worthwhile results for several characters and the real danger that the progress achieved with the early characters will be lost while the later ones are being dealt with.

A second procedure is to decide that any animal which falls below a given standard in any one character will be discarded. This is known as the method of "independent culling levels". The method is easy to apply and can be surprisingly effective, provided the breeder does not weaken in his resolve. As the culling levels rise with the improvement of the strain, so the selection becomes more stringent. Note, that the culling level need not be the same for each character. Some are not so important as others and some may need more drastic selection to realize the same results. All of these aspects should be considered. In fact, the more well thought-out the plan of action, the greater the overall improvement is likely to be.

An advantage of the method is that it necessitates a careful appraisal of the number of characters which can be dealt with and of their variation. The number of characters which can be effectively managed is limited and this implies that priorities have to be worked out. The manner in which the chosen characters vary individually has to be analysed in order to grade the animals as being above or below the culling level. The most serious objection to the method is that, on occasion, it may be too ruthless. It may be unwise to totally reject an animal possessing several admirable qualities just because it falls below a certain culling level in one character. To counter this argument, a third more flexible method has been devised.

The third method is that of the "total score" or "selection index" and it is the most efficient of the three. In company with the preceding method, it requires that the contribution of each character to the ideal cat be carefully assessed. The variation of each character should be graded by a convenient scale of points. The composition of the scale should be as accurate as possible without becoming unduly fussy. Even a simple grading of very poor (1), poor (2), average (3), good (4) and very good (5) gives a 5-point numerical scale. However, an endeavour should be made to do better than that and it is recommended that each animal should be scored against a 10-point judging scale, ranging from 1 for the lowest to 10 for the tip-top grade of expression of the character. The value of the scale will depend largely on the competence of the breeder in grading his charges. If in doubt, it may be wise to seek advice on this question from experienced judges.

Now, with the total score method, the problem of imposing a limit on the number of characters is not quite as important. In fact, it might be advisable to include as many as possible because it is difficult to foretell how a minor feature may turn out to be of first-rate importance. In this event, it is useful to be able to check on how the feature has been varying in past generations. In practice, a limit is set by the amount of time which can be devoted to the calculation of the index. The reason why a large number of characters can be considered is because the next step is to rank these by a system of "weights". These are numerical coefficients which reveal the relative importance of the various traits in the breeder's estimation. These are necessary because the points scoring of expression of each character cannot take this factor into account. This makes the total score two-tiered and this is a real advantage. The scale of points should be relatively unchanging, provided it is objectively drawn-up in the first instance, whereas, it may be necessary to change the coefficients from time to time in order to give greater emphasis to certain characters. For example, if a certain feature is showing no signs of improvement, the coefficient for it could be increased so that individuals with exceptionally good expression would score slightly higher. It must be warned, however, that the values of the coefficients should not be changed except for good cause.

The working of the method can probably be best explained by an illustration. There is no special virtue in the choice of characters considered nor in the values of the coefficients, since these must be chosen by the breeder for his particular cats and the task he has set himself. Suppose the following characters are graded: health (condition) (H), coat colour (CC), coat texture (CT), body build (BB), head shape (HS), feet (F) and tail (T). Now, the relative importance of these seven features might be assessed as follows:

Total score = 5 H + 4 CC + 3 CT + 3 BB + 2 HS + F + T.

That is to say, head shape is considered to be twice as important as either feet or tail and so forth. Health is ranked as the most important item and this is how it should be. All of the animals in the stud are doubtless healthy but giving it a high coefficient means that a weakly individual will be heavily penalized. To calculate the total score, each cat is appraised and graded on a 10-point scale for each character. The maximum total would be 190 but no animal would be expected to attain this exalted level.

Table 5 shows how eight cats might be evaluated according to the above formula. Cat A scores highly because it happens to be

TABLE 5. An Example of Calculating Total Scores as an Aid to Selective Breeding. (See text for meaning of the character abbreviations.)

Cat	Point grading for each character							Total score or Selection index
	H	CC	CT	BB	HS	F	T	
A	10	10	10	6	5	5	5	158
B	10	8	7	7	7	8	8	154
C	10	6	7	6	8	9	9	147
D	10	6	6	7	8	6	5	140
E	10	6	6	7	7	6	6	139
F	6	7	7	8	6	7	7	129
G	10	5	6	6	5	5	5	126
H	10	5	4	4	5	5	5	114

exceptionally good in the important character CC and CT although it is mediocre in other respects. Compare the score with that for cat C which graded highly for several unimportant traits but low on the important ones, thus producing a relatively low score. This shows how the coefficients will adjust the point rating in this respect. The best all-round cat is B, followed closely, perhaps by C. Individuals C, D and E tend to be similar, somewhat above average, animals, and, without the total score, it might be difficult to rank these in order of preference. This aspect reveals the discrimination possessed by the method. It should be noted that cat F is a fine animal except that it suffered an attack of undefinable sickness which makes its health suspect. This fact has reduced the total score rather sharply; had the cat been fully healthy, its score would have been as high as 149.

The table indicates the ranking of the eight cats for potential value to the breeding programme in terms of the total score. If three animals are required for the next generation, these would be A, B and C. Now, it might be interesting to compare this choice with that obtained by the use of the method of independent culling levels. Since only three individuals are required, the culling level will have to be rather high. If all animals which score grade 5 or less are eliminated, cats B, C, E and F remain or if all animals which grade 6 or less are eliminated, only cat B remains. Thus, the method does not possess the fine discrimination shown by the total score. In this example, cat F could be eliminated on the grounds of its suspected health and this leaves the three wanted animals. However, this is an arbitrary choice, taken after the selective processes had been completed which should have properly assessed the health factor in the first place.

It may be particularly noted that cat A is totally rejected since it grades poorly in several characters, in spite of its exceptional rating in the important traits CC and CT. Also, cat D is possibly unfairly discriminated against, though admittedly this is a debatable point. A refinement would be to vary the culling levels, being more stringent against the important traits and less so against the unimportant. To do this, however, is to move the practical application of the culling method closer to that of the total score but without quite gaining the flexibility of the latter. It might be worthwhile to employ the total score without more ado.

The total score is essentially an aid to selection and its value is no greater than (a) the ability of the breeder in defining the characters which are important for the task in hand, (b) his skill in grading and (c) the correct balance between the weighting coefficients. Instruction in the calculation is necessary for a person taking up the method for the first time but a "feeling" of a soundly constructed score only comes from experience. The example given above is probably crude in that it may be advisable to consider more characters, such as eye-colour and temperament. Also, it should be feasible to sub-divide those considered as one becomes more adept at grading. Coat colour (CC), for instance, could be further analysed in depth of colour (shade), tone quality and evenness of colour over the whole body.

Those readers who are familiar with the construction of selection indices may query the arbitrariness of the choice of weighting coefficients for the total score described above. It is possible to derive coefficients which are related to the innate qualities of the total variation and which should maximize the hoped-for improvement. Unfortunately, the derivation of these coefficients is beyond the level of this book. Details of the theory which underlies the derivation and their practical calculation may be found in Lush (1945), a book which has many interesting things to say on the whole topic of selection.

Family Selection and Progeny Testing

Selection is normally practised against the individual and this will always be the basis of selective breeding. However, selection may also be applied against a litter or a series of litters from the same parents. This is "familial" selection and, if it can be carried out, the effectiveness of the selection is enhanced. It can be applied regardless of the method employed, whether this be that of culling levels or the total score. The total score lends itself more easily to familial selection since it provides a numerical value from which to find an average.

Ordinary selection usually ignores familial relationships, the more superior animals being chosen from all litters. However, a critical appraisal would take into account the capability of certain pairings to produce better offspring on the average than others. The appraisal could take one or two forms, that of noting which pairings have the highest number of young above a certain level of excellence or that of deriving an average. Should the total score be in use, the latter can be calculated by summing the individual scores and dividing by the number of young. The parents with the highest average are clearly those producing the better offspring. These are the individuals upon which to concentrate. Further young should be obtained from these parents and preference should be given to their offspring. Indeed, to carry familial selection through to its logical conclusion, those parents which have produced the inferior litters should be discarded, together with their young. The effectiveness of familial selection stems from the fact that the selection is acting somewhat more drastically upon the genetic constitution than is possible by selection upon individual phenotype.

Quite often the same breeders are involved, the offspring being produced by different combinations of parents, some of which have resulted in better average offspring than others (a phenomenon known as "nicking"). In this case, those combinations which have produced the inferior offspring need not be repeated. This sort of difference can be deliberately exploited to reveal differences in breeding capability. Normally, queens cannot be examined in this manner because individually it is impossible to obtain enough young in a reasonable time. However, in theory at least, two or more stud males can be investigated. The procedure is to obtain a round of litters with several females from one male and a further round of litters with the same females from a second male. A comparison of the quality of each round of litters could be revealing as regards the breeding ability of the different males. This is "progeny testing" in one of its more direct forms, whereby the breeding worth of a male is determined by the average quality of his offspring.

Familial selection in conjunction with one of the systems of mating to be described in a subsequent section stand to give the maximum results. In particular, a comparison of the average total score for the offspring of two or more sib mating lines could indicate that one is consistently inferior. The breeder should consider abandoning this line and forming two separate lines from the superior. Two or more closed studs composed of a few animals could be similarly dealt with. This is "group selection". In both of the above cases, the procedure is to commence with more than one sib mating line or closed stud of a few individuals and, at an appropriate stage, make a comparison to ascertain if one line or group has made greater improvement than the other.

It is possible to combine familial selection with sib mating in the following way. A male can be mated with several sisters and the offspring for each litter be examined for the average score. The individuals for the next generation being chosen from the pair with the highest score. In any event, it is unwise to keep only two animals to continue a sib mating line since one may die and the line would come to a premature end. A male (or even two if so desired) and several sisters could be selected on merit for each generation and the availability of the extra animals put to good use. Be careful not to choose animals from different parents otherwise the mating would no longer be that of brother to sister.

The closed stud method of breeding is readily adaptable to progeny testing of the male when two or three are kept. This system requires a fairly constant number of females per generation and a point should be made of breeding a round of litters from each male in succession. Examination of the average score for each round of litters could indicate that one male is siring better (or worse) offspring than the others. It is also possible that certain combinations of male and female are producing exceptional litters, but this may not be easily established because of the small number of young per litter. A litter of exceptional young could be due to chance. It is probably better to rely upon the results from the whole series belonging to one male. Though litters may be procured from several males, it may be desirable to restrict the selection of animals for the next generation to those of one or two males. Obviously, the choice would be from the offspring of the male (or males) with the highest average score. In this manner, familial selection (by means of progeny testing) can be combined with some degree of inbreeding, with probably more fruitful results than if either is used alone.

The Stud Male and Grading-up

The stud male is the most important member of the cattery. Not because of his sex nor because characters are inherited more strongly via the male. The reason is statistical. A stud male can sire many more kittens than a queen can ever hope to produce. It follows, therefore, that a breeder should be particularly choosy in the choice of male. Fortunately, it is possible to be more selective of males because fewer are required. In general, this means insistence on at least as high a standard for the male as the best of the females or a higher standard whenever this can be managed.

For various practical reasons, not everyone can keep a male cat and the practice of placing exceptional animals at open stud has become common. This benefits the owner financially and the fancy as a whole by raising the overall quality of the breed. When circumstances warrant it, there should be no hesitation in taking advantage of the services of these males. The only problem which may doubtless arise is which male to use? The fact that the male is a well-known champion does not necessarily mean that he is the most suitable animal. For instance, he may have the same faults (despite his championship status) as the breeder is wishing to correct in his own stock. It is sound policy to visit shows and examine the various males on exhibition and to assess the good and bad features of each one. One or more should emerge as the appropriate mate for certain queens and arrangements can be made accordingly for a visit.

Queens may be sent to males at open stud for various reasons. Probably the more common is a desire for general improvement, especially if the queen is not outstanding in any way. Improvement in this manner is known as "grading-up", a term which may be used to denote most policies of mating mediocre stock to superior animals. The matings are usually repeated for more than one generation (i.e. backcrosses) in an attempt to firmly impress the superior qualities. This may not always succeed since this aspect is dependent upon the degree of purebreeding of the superior animal. This problem is discussed in more detail later since "pureness" of breeding is closely related to the amount of inbreeding which the superior stock has undergone. The backcrossing should be immediately halted should it become apparent that a general improvement is no longer occurring. However, leaving this aspect in abeyance, grading-up is the quickest method for the improvement of mediocre animals and one which can be recommended to the novice breeder. Superb exhibition stock is usually scarce and expensive, and the beginner often has to be content with lesser animals. These are not to be despised, especially if derived from a reputable strain and, correctly mated, could produce very good kittens.

Another important reason for sending queens to outside males is that of improvement of specific traits. If the breeder's animals have many good qualities already, extreme care has to be taken not to upset these while the new features are being incorporated. The whole situation has to be handled very adroitly, both the choice of mates and in the subsequent breeding. Unlike general grading-up these outcrosses are not necessarily repeated, since it is not a general improvement which is being sought. Much will depend upon whether the specific trait shows a desirable change and if this can be incorporated into the stock without either deterioration or less of the good points it now has. To do this, it may be better to inter-breed the offspring, rather than to outcross again.

It should be obvious that the next move does not lend itself to any worthwhile generalization. Only the breeder, with full knowledge of his cats, can decide. So much depends on the problem being tackled and the animal's response to the outcross. If the offspring show deterioration, this may be a sign that the outcross has not been successful and an outcross to another male might be the best policy.

Selection for Intermediate Versus Extreme Expression

Selection of characters falls into one of two categories; that of selecting for an intermediate degree of expression or selection for extreme expression. Now, since many different characteristics make up the ideal animal, this can mean that both sorts of selection may be operating at the same time. This is unfortunate, since the two forms of selection require different handling if each is to achieve maximum success. In the case of intermediate expression, the selection will be that of eliminating animals which deviate most from the optimum. More than anything else, it is a matter of fixing the character so that as many cats as possible will possess it. The quickest means of achieving this is by close inbreeding.

Selection for extreme expression, on the other hand, implies striving for something not yet obtained or found in only a few individuals. Extreme expression is displayed only by genotypes containing a large number of genes having either plus or minus effects with regard to the character (depending on which end of the scale is being considered). These genotypes are only formed by gathering together the appropriate plus or minus genes which are scattered throughout the general population. Something of this nature must be the situation otherwise the extreme expression would be common. This means searching for and breeding from any animal with a phenotype tending in the right direction in the hope that different polygenes are brought in and combined to bring into existence offspring of more extreme expression than that of the parents. This is the underlying mechanism, in principle at least. To achieve this, it is desirable to have individuals heterozygous for as many genes as possible, despite the fact that the selection will tend to pick out homozygotes. In other words, too early a decrease in the proportion of heterozygotes will hinder the free recombination of genes which is essential for the formation of the extreme phenotypes.

Here lies the conflict. For fixation of intermediate expression, the heterozygotes should be eliminated; for the realization of ever more extreme expression, the maximum number of heterozygous loci are required. A compromise must be found. This usually takes the form of a moderate amount of inbreeding—combined with intense selection—in the hope that there will be a steady fixation of intermediate characters but not too quickly so that there can be some progress towards extreme expression in other characters. The mediator is the breeding system which can be so arranged that the amount of inbreeding can be high, moderate or weak. How this can be managed is the main topic of succeeding sections.

Systems of Mating

As a prelude, it might be wise to consider what is meant by random mating, the antithesis of inbreeding. Most mongrel cats are representatives of random mating in the sense that there is an absence of control. With fancy cats, the situation is different. The matings are controlled and may in fact be carefully regulated in the choice of animal. Yet, as far as the array of genes is concerned and taking into account that the various breeders will be acting independently of one another, effectively, there will be random mating. Random mating in a strict sense implies the odd mating of brother to sister and other, less close, matings of related animals. Some of the closer matings may be studiously avoided by many people but perhaps not by everyone as an occasional event. Therefore, the assumption of random mating is not unreasonable.

Ordinarily speaking, inbreeding means the pairing together of closely related animals. This is so, though in practice the actual mating should be specified since this determines the relative intensity of inbreeding. Some forms of inbreeding can be regarded as close, others as less so, and still others as quite mild. The rate of inbreeding can be roughly assessed for most systems of mating and can be used as a measure of its strength. This is an advantage, since in some circumstances it might be desirable to inbreed closely and, in others, less closely.

Inbreeding may be the act of mating of individuals of various degrees of kinship but what does the process achieve? Briefly, if continued for generations, it will produce ever increasing homogeneity in the offspring. That is to say, genetically, the offspring will become more and more alike in appearance and general behaviour. This is because the common ancestry causes many of the same genes to be received by different individuals. The limitation in number of different ancestors and the absence of out-crossing are the key factors. Therefore, there is a tendency for the offspring to receive the same genes from each parent and to become progressively more homozygous.

The proportion of homozygotes in an inter-breeding group of animals is known as "homozygosis". Conversely, the proportion of heterozygotes is known as the "heterozygosis". These two terms are merely the opposite faces of the same coin but both are in use because some people like to speak of an increase in homozygosis while others of a decrease in heterozygosis. Crudely put, the proportion of homozygosis represents the "purity" of the group while the heterozygosis represents the "impurity". In this immediate context, group can mean either a strain or a breed.

One of the closest forms of inbreeding is that of mating of full brothers and sisters or sib mating for short. Since the inbreeding is intense, easily appreciated and can be quickly put into practice, the consequences of repeated sib mating have been carefully investigated. The breeding scheme is simple enough, the best individuals from the same parents (not necessarily belonging to the same litter, though it is an added convenience if they are) are paired together. The result is a decrease in the amount of heterozygosis as shown by Table 6. The interpretation of the table is as follows. After one generation of inbreeding, the proportion of heterozygosis is 75 per cent of what it was before inbreeding began, after two generations, the amount is 63

88 GENETICS FOR CAT BREEDERS

TABLE 6. THE STEADY DECREASE OF HETEROZYGOSIS FOR SUCCESSIVE GENERATIONS OF SIB MATING

Generation	Percentage	Generation	Percentage
1	75	7	22
2	63	8	17
3	50	9	14
4	41	10	11
5	33	11	9
6	27	12	7

per cent and so on. After 10 generations, the reduction has reached 11 per cent.

The figures given in the table are those expected, calculated for each generation starting from scratch. The successive values show that the decrease is a little unsteady for the first few generations but then the ratio of decrease becomes relatively constant. It is convenient to ignore the initial unsteadiness and to consider that the constant ratio of decrease will be characteristic of the type of inbreeding. The ratio could be regarded as an average over the generations and, for sib mating, the ratio is 81 per cent. This ratio somewhat overestimates the decrease for the early generations and this fact may be borne in mind. As will be seen later, the ability to describe the intensity of inbreeding by a simple ratio (an index, if you like) has certain advantages when the relative usefulness of close versus mild inbreeding and other problems are discussed.

There is one other system of pairing which is very similar to sib mating and its average effect on heterozygosis. This is where certain offspring are chosen to pair with the younger parent. That is, a given individual is mated twice, once to its younger parent and once to its offspring. For example, suppose the mother was the younger parent, then a suitable son would be selected as her next mate. From the offspring of this mating, a daughter would be chosen to continue the line and so on. The ratio of decrease of heterozygosis is 81 per cent per generation, as for sib mating. Although the two systems of mating have the same ratio, they should not be intermixed if the object of the inbreeding is to bring about the maximum amount of homozygosis in the shortest time. When the two systems are intermixed, the ratio is 84 per cent whenever a changeover is made from one system to the other.

Another regular system of mating is where a male may be mated to two half-sisters who are full sisters of each other. Three individuals are involved in each generation and two series of litters. The procedure is as follows. A male is paired with two females to produce two litters (or series of litters if a wider range of offspring are desired from which to choose the next generation, provided the same male and female are paired). From one litter, a male is selected while the other litter contributes the two females. The system is self-perpetuating, since it should not be difficult to find two females per generation, yet the rearing of two litters (or sires) allows a wider choice of offspring per generation than is possible with either sib mating or mating back to the younger parent (one litter or single series). The ratio of decline of heterozygosis is less than that for the latter systems but still respectable, with the value of 87 per cent.

The above methods of inbreeding are said to be regular, mainly because animals are paired according to set rules. A more flexible system may be held to be desirable in many cases. Many breeders will have at least one male and a variable number of females. Now, inbreeding may be practised with these, provided the stud is closed to outsiders. No new stock is brought in and no queens are sent out for mating. The animals for the next generation must be chosen from litters born within the stud. No rules need to be laid down that certain animals be mated to others. Indeed, these are purposefully waived to give the maximum freedom of pairing.

This is the "closed stud" method of breeding and is similar to that used by many people in their ordinary breeding. It differs from ordinary breeding, however, not only in the exclusion of outside influences but also in that there is no overlapping of generations. Each male and his retinue of queens are chosen afresh each generation. Any backcrossing of daughter to the father, for example, will result in a retardation of the trend towards homozygosis. In general, the matings will be between half brother and sister if the number of males are small.

The closed stud method will lead to a decline in heterozygosis because of the limited number of parents within each generation. In fact, the intensity of the inbreeding varies according to the number of parents as shown by Fig. 18. This gives values of the ratio of decline of heterozygosis for different numbers of males and females. It is worthwhile to study the values of the ratio since a decided tendency is

Number of females (rows) × Numbers of males (columns)

Females \ Males	1	2	3	4	5	6	8
1	0·81						
2	0·85	0·89					
3	0·86	0·91	0·92				
4	0·87	0·92	0·93	0·94			
5	0·87	0·92	0·94	0·95	0·96		
6	0·87	0·92	0·94	0·95	0·96	0·96	
7	0·88	0·93	0·94	0·95	0·96	0·96	0·97
8	0·88	0·93	0·95	0·96	0·96	0·96	0·97
9	0·88	0·93	0·95	0·96	0·96	0·97	0·97
10	0·88	0·93	0·95	0·96	0·96	0·97	0·97
12	0·88	0·93	0·95	0·96	0·97	0·97	0·97
15	0·88	0·93	0·95	0·96	0·97	0·97	0·98
Many	0·89	0·94	0·96	0·97	0·98	0·98	0·99

FIG. 18. The ratio of decrease of heterozygosis for various numbers of males and females for the closed stud breeding system.

apparent. The decline is only appreciable if the number of males and females are kept quite small. From a practical viewpoint, the number of males is the important item. With one male and one female, it is only possible to carry out sib mating, and the figure shows that this has the quickest decline of heterozygosis. With one male and successive additions of females, the decline can still be reasonable up to about six, and possibly not all that unreasonable for larger numbers. However, the situation changes rather abruptly even for the addition of one extra male. The value of the ratio rises until the decline is so small that very many generations are required to reduce the heterozygosis. In effect, the amount of inbreeding is so miniscule that it need scarcely be considered as such.

The decline of heterozygosis over the generations can be approximately calculated by successive multiplication of the appropriate ratio for any size of closed stud. In this way, a series of percentages can be derived which are comparable to that tabulated for sib mating. The use of the ratio probably over-estimates the decline for the first few generations but the decline is doubtless accurate enough to provide a comparison between studs of different sizes. For example, the decline for a typical stud of one male and five females will approximate the following pattern. After one generation, the amount of heterozygosis is reduced to 87 per cent of what it was formerly; after two generations, the proportion remaining is 76 per cent; and after five generations, it has fallen to 50 per cent. It is of interest to be able to judge the effectiveness of any size of stud and this can be gauged by finding the number of generations necessary to reduce the proportion of initial heterozygosis by 50 per cent. This is shown by Table 7 for sib mating and several studs composed of different

TABLE 7. THE NUMBER OF GENERATIONS REQUIRED TO HALVE THE PROPORTION OF HETEROZYGOSIS WITH VARIOUS BREEDING SYSTEMS

System	No. gens.	System	No. gens.
Sib mating	3	1 M and many F	6
1 M and 2 sisters	5	2 M and 6 F	8·8
1 M and 3 F	4·6	2 M and many F	11·4
1 M and 5 F	5	Group of 4 cousins	8·3
1 M and 8 F	5·5	Group of 8 cousins	18·9

Note: M = number of males, F = number of females.

numbers of males and females. The fewer generations required, the more effective the inbreeding. Sib mating is obviously the most efficient and the effectiveness of the other systems is inversely related to the number of animals involved.

The question whether or not to inbreed can be a difficult one to answer. However, one aspect is certain: if a breeder wishes to found his own strain with its own particular characteristics and uniformity of offspring, some measure of inbreeding is essential. The reason is that a high level of homozygosis cannot be attained in any other manner. Selection cannot do it. It can do so spuriously in the sense that the parents may be alike in appearance because a certain type are selected. But what of the offspring? These may be variable, with only the odd individual tending to resemble the parents. In breeders' jargon, inbreeding is necessary to "fix" the characteristics which are being selected. The appropriate genetic term is "fixation" of genes.

There is little doubt that inbreeding is valuable in stabilizing the results of selection. Does this imply that the inbreeding should be deferred until the selective breeding has proved successful or should it accompany and perhaps even aid the selection? There is something to be said for deferring inbreeding for a few generations, largely because the most significant results of selection are usually achieved during the early stages. Later, it is often a case of consolidating gains and seeking to make improvements which are less easily realized. This is where the inbreeding could commence. The merit of this policy is that it is simple and straightforward. The selection is not relaxed and the inbreeding is initiated whenever the breeder decides it is most opportune.

However, this is not the whole story. It might be pertinent to examine more closely what inbreeding can do. In practice, there are two systems to consider seriously. These are sib mating and the closed stud method (the latter usually centering on one or two specially chosen males per generation). Now, sib mating is the most intense form of inbreeding and engenders the most rapid increase of homozygosis. From the viewpoint of fixing a characteristic, it would produce the quickest results. However, this fixing of characteristics is double-edged. While it is desirable to have fixation of characters, once these are fixed, further progress is impossible. The characteristics of the strain are frozen in one mould, so to speak, and further selective breeding will have little effect. Should the animals of the strain be of a high order of excellence, the fixation may be deemed an advantage. Yet the cost must be considered. It may be that the fixation occurred before the full potentiality of the strain had been realized. No matter how excellent the strain may be, some faults are likely to be present and these are fixed as well.

What has happened is that the rapid increase in homozygosis has fixed both good and bad points with fine impartiality. On balance, the good points may predominate because the selective breeding has picked out the better individuals and these have left their impact. Now, suppose the increase has occurred less rapidly? In other words, if a less intense form of inbreeding had been adopted, it might have been possible to emphasize the good features of the strain still further and have eliminated more of the bad points before too much fixation had occurred. This is indeed so. A balance has to be struck between a rate of increase of homozygosis which will bring about fixation of desirable traits yet allow scope for the elimination of the undesirable. This is where the closed stud system has an advantage, for the intensity of inbreeding there is invariably less than that of sib mating.

In the majority of cases, the closed stud system of breeding will centre around one or perhaps two males. More than two males may be used but then the rate of loss of heterozygosity is very slow; possibly too slow except for very long-term projects. Should one male and a number of females constitute the stud, the inbreeding will be moderately high; the actual level being determined by the number of females. The king-pin being the common father which tends to hold the stud together. Within each generation, the actual individuals retained for breeding will be determined by the method of selection employed and the number of females required. A fair number of kittens should be obtained from each pairing in order that the intensity of selection can be reasonably high. In this manner, the two main factors in animal breeding will be operating simultaneously, one shaping the general appearance and quality of the strain and the other tending to fix these characteristics.

With the stud system, the temptation may be to backcross the daughters to the father, rather than to chose a male for the next generation. This temptation should be resisted unless the male is especially outstanding in some respect. The approach to homozygosis will be held up, particularly if the backcross is made during the early stages. This could mean a hold-up in the establishment of the strain by a generation or two. It is difficult to generalize in matters of this nature since the key-note of breeding is the ability to be flexible and to balance the results of one action against those of another.

Sometimes it may prove to be impossible to maintain a constant number of breeding animals per generation. One individual may regretfully die or two or more may be of such a high standard that it is decided to retain all of them for breeding. Could this have much of an effect on the progress towards homozygosis? If the numbers do not vary very much, the answer is no; as might be seen by the roughly similar values of the ratio given by adjacent entries in Fig. 18. On the other hand, should the numbers fluctuate rather widely, then a significant effect will emerge. Over a series of generations, the smaller numbers will have a more than proportionate influence over the larger. The simplest method of treating the problem would be to obtain the appropriate ratio for each generation and to multiply these together. This procedure will give the approximate percentage of remaining heterozygosity. For example, suppose that over a period of seven generations, a stud had consisted of a single male and the following number of females: 3, 4, 5, 6, 10, 12 and 15. The remaining proportion of heterozygosis would be estimated at 39 per cent. Now, the same reduction would be achieved by a stud of one male and a constant number of six females for each of the generations.

The difference between repeated sib mating and the closed stud is that the former leads to rapid fixation of all traits (sometimes so quickly as to block further progress by selective breeding) while the latter allows greater scope for selection to do its work but requires more generations for the stud to become true-breeding. On balance, the close inbreeding of sib mating might appear to be too drastic. Yet, there is another aspect of this form of inbreeding which has not been considered. Sib mating only requires two individuals per generation and this means that it may be possible to have more than one sib mating line in the cattery. Three of four such lines could be bred concurrently without too much trouble, whereas, the keeping of two or more separate studs could be difficult unless the number in each stud is restricted or the cattery is large.

The keeping of two or more sib mating lines has its advantages. The stud system carries the breeding group along as a whole, each individual tending towards the general average. The situation is otherwise for a series of sib mating lines. The rapid approach to complete homozygosis often induces a greater exposure of latent variation which can be seized upon by selective breeding. The outcome is phenotypic divergence between the inbred lines, some of which could be superior to the general average. Some may emerge as better than the results obtained by the study system. It is difficult to be certain of the latter, of course, but the point to be made is this: the full benefit of sib mating cannot be realized unless several lines are bred in parallel. Should one line fall behind the others in overall quality, it should be discarded and replaced by a splitting of the best line into two. In this manner, the number of lines are maintained and selection can operate at two levels, between individuals within each line and between lines. This may sound complicated but it is not; it is only making the fullest possible use of selection to raise the standard of one's cats.

Should the occasion arise that the ratio of decline of heterozygosity need be calculated more exactly than that given here or for numbers of males and females not given in the table, the following formula may be used:

$$\text{ratio} = 1\frac{1}{2} \{1 - 2A + \sqrt{(4A^2 + 1)}\}$$

where $A = (M + F)/8MF$ and M = number of males and F = number of females. If the number of generations to reduce the initial heterozygosis by half is required for this ratio, the following may be used:

$$\text{No. of generations} = \frac{0.301}{\log (\text{ratio})^{-1}}$$

The ratio of decline of heterozygosis which has been given for various systems of inbreeding should not be taken too literally for several reasons. The ratio is quite general in that it is independent of the initial proportion of heterozygosis and the total number of genes, for most practical purposes. It applies to autosomal genes but less accurately to sex-linked genes. However, for some systems, the ratio is similar for both sets of genes and, in others, the discrepancy is small. Since sex-linked genes are in a minority, the error is negligible unless the inbreeding is continued for a very long period which is an unlikely prospect. Another discrepancy could arise from selective breeding favouring the most vigorous and healthy animals and this may select out the more heterozygous individuals. As a result, the progress towards homozygosity may not be as quick as the ratio would indicate. However, only in exceptional circumstances, would a large difference emerge and, therefore, the ratio may be regarded as a useful index to the amount of inbreeding which will be taking place.

Grading-up and Prepotency

The extremely useful process of grading-up by the use of an outstanding male has two facets. One is that of gaining the genes which make the male so outstanding and the other is to raise the average quality of the stud. The likelihood of success of the latter is dependent upon the degree of homozygosis of the male. Repeated backcrossing of the females is a form of inbreeding since the successive matings are that of daughter, grand-daughter, great-grand-daughter etc., and this is contributing towards the grading-up. The repeated backcrossing alone, however, is not sufficient.

The decrease of heterozygosis is rapid but it does not lead to complete homozygosis unless the pivoted male is highly inbred. Initially, assume that the male is derived from an inbred strain and is largely homozygous. The decrease in the heterozygosis of the mediocre stock is 50 per cent for each generation. After only a few backcrosses, it would be expected that the offspring will come to take on some of the superior qualities of the male. Furthermore, should the male inadvertently die, another male (a son from the same strain, say) could be substituted and the backcrossing continued. The limit would be stock resembling the inbred strain in many respects. Since selection has been in progress at the same time, it is to be hoped the up-graded animals have gained most of the finer qualities of the strain but not the weaker. At some stage, before the characteristics of the male have become too fixed, it will seemingly be worthwhile to break off the backcross and to inter-breed, simultaneously maintaining or even intensifying the selection.

When the backcrossing is made to a male which is not derived from an inbred strain, the outcome is different. In appearance, the male may be a fine specimen of his breed but his heterozygous genotype will imply that he will not hand these qualities on to his offspring in a uniform manner. There is a decrease in heterozygosity as a result of inbreeding but the limit is 50 per cent of the proportion initially present and this is not attained for a very large number of generations. In the meantime, the male will have died of old age and there is no male of similar genotype to take his place. Hence, the backcrossing will come to an end. The value of an outstanding male of heterogeneous origin lies in the genes he may be able to pass on to a few offspring by chance assortment and it is usually worthwhile to endeavour to capture these genes by selective breeding. However, this is a far cry from a general grading-up in quality which one might expect from the use of a superior male. His heterozygosis would be a severe stumbling-block which will probably doom the attempt to failure at the onset.

It may be necessary to issue a warning against a breeding system which might trap the unwary into thinking that it represents grading-up. This is where a single backcross is made to a superior male and, from the offspring, the best son is chosen and used for breeding with the inferior stock. From his offspring another son is selected, and so on. Reflection should reveal that this is backcrossing in the wrong direction and any good points which might have been gained from the first cross will rapidly be lost.

"Prepotency" is a term employed to describe the situation when a male or a female possesses the remarkable property of producing offspring bearing a strong resemblance to his or her self. Males are usually referred to in this manner partly in error (incorrectly, it is often thought that the male has an innate propensity in this direction) and partly because they have greater opportunity to reveal the ability. Bad, as well as good features, may be transmitted, a point which is occasionally overlooked. Usually, the reason is that the individual has become homozygous for a gene or group of genes with dominant effects. This can happen by chance, especially if selection and inbreeding is being practised at the time. Should the characteristics be desirable there is every likelihood that these may be fixed in the stock since the animals bearing them will be retained.

The interesting aspect is that the more inbred an individual may be, the more homozygous he will be, and the greater the chance that he will display prepotency. This is where the male from an inbred strain will score over the male of heterozygous origin even should the latter be phenotypically superior. The prepotency may not be derived entirely from dominance in the case of an inbred male since he will be transmitting a uniform set of genes in every gamete whereas the queens will not. Hence, on average, the offspring will tend to resemble the male. The prepotency may be less striking but still evident.

Mating Like to Like and the Converse

The breeding together of animals of similar phenotype is often advocated and is known as mating "like to like". The usual reason for undertaking such matings is a belief that this will lead to fixation of characters. However, these matings are valuable for perpetuating a character but not, as a rule, for fixation. Inbreeding is the key to character fixation and this, coupled with mating like to like, is the surest means of stabilizing a desired degree of intermediate expression. In other words, mating of like to like is a form of selection and, as a general policy, has much to recommend it. The total score method produces a high proportion of such matings for the various characters which contribute towards the score. The converse of the above is the mating together of unlikes. This policy is often urged as a means of compensating for faults in one animal against those of another. It is implicit that the mating of animals with similar faults should be avoided at all costs, otherwise there is a danger of fixation. However, this may not necessarily occur, unless there is inbreeding, in which case it is true that there is a risk. The drawback of mating unlikes is that it tends to be a negative policy. It may be useful to combat the chance fixation of faults but it does so at the expense of encouraging heterozygosity. Even if the bad features disappeared or are mollified in the immediate generation, they could reappear in those following. This is especially true should there be over-compensation. That is, animals exceptionally good or bad in some points are appropriately matched with the intention of producing offspring with average all-round qualities.

Anyone who looks ahead to later generations should be able to appreciate the problems which matings of unlikes may entail. In general, this form of mating should not be viewed as a settled policy but only as an expedient in a rather difficult situation which cannot be resolved by other methods. The total score method undoubtedly will cause some matings of unlikes but these can be accepted unless they recur rather frequently, in which case a review of the composition of the score or the genetic behaviour of the constituent characters may be advisable. It may be that an inverse relationship (see later) has been exposed, in which improvement in one character can only be achieved at the expense of another.

Limits to Selection

It is impossible to eliminate all variation because a proportion is due to non-genetic causes. That is, to idiosyncrasies in the development of the individual cat and to the influence of the environment. Little can be done about the former but the effect of the latter can be minimized by providing as constant an environment as possible conducive to sturdy growth. However, even under optimum conditions, it is not always possible to remove all of the genetic variation nor to achieve a given objective at the first attempt. These two aspects may now be discussed.

The problem of fixing an intermediate expression of a character is the removal of genetic variation. The mating of like to like can make some contribution to this end but relatively slowly compared with inbreeding. Close inbreeding can induce the genetic proportion provided it is maintained for sufficient generations. On occasion, however, the progress is not so quick as might be expected or, in practical terms, the variation still seems to be as great as before the inbreeding began. There may be several possible reasons for this. The genetic proportion of the variation is not the same for all characters and it may be that the proportion is low for a particular character. Inbreeding will reduce this but the effect may be negligible because the genetic proportion was not making much of a contribution in the first place. Another possibility is that the more heterozygous animals are the more healthy and these may be preferably chosen for breeding. Hence, the genetic portion of the variation may persist. Choosing the less vigorous but more homozygous animals could lead to a reduction in variation but at the risk of the onset of inbreeding depression. This is not a necessary accompaniment of inbreeding, of course, but it is wise to be on the alert for it, more to the point, for factors which can bring it into being.

One of the peculiarities of selection for extreme expression is that the extreme phenotypes of some traits may remain tantalizingly out of reach. The odd individual may turn up but it is very difficult, if not impossible, to breed more of the same type. Again, there are several reasons which could be behind this. One is the same as that previously mentioned; namely, that the genetic proportion of the variation may be small. If this is the case, those few individuals which do turn up owe their appearance to non-genetic causes. Thus, it is not surprising that these cannot be produced by selective breeding; also, if the nature of the non-genetic factor is unknown, the appearance cannot be produced by manipulation of the environment. A rather similar situation is produced when the genetic proportion of the variation is small. Some progress may occur but this soon stops and further selection is unavailing.

Even when the variation is largely genetic, it may still be that the results fall short of expectation because the genes present in a particular stock are incapable of producing the extreme phenotype. The stock has not the genetic potential, despite the fact that another stock was able to reach the desired extreme. The solution in this case is to introduce genes from the successful stock by means of crosses. It is also possible for a stock to fail because, though it originally carried the necessary genes, some became homozygous and others were lost before they could become combined. Inbreeding could bring this situation into being. Once again, the solution is to outcross to a successful stud, either by the despatch of a queen to the stud male or by purchase of a suitable animal. It may be noticed that both of these solutions are forms of grading-up, by which advantage is taken of the availability of animals which apparently have the necessary genes to produce the coveted phenotype.

Another obstacle to selection for extreme expression is where an inverse relationship exists between the characters. This subtle phenomenon can occur, often unexpectedly, in a number of guises and it usually comes to notice because progress with selection in one character can hold back progress in another and vice versa. A fictitious example will illustrate the problem which could arise. Suppose a breeder of Longhairs is selecting simultaneously for very long hair fibres, especially in the underfur, and fur coat density. He may find over a period that those animals with good long coats appear to lack density and those with dense coats appear to be wanting in length. Try as he may, it does not seem possible to combine the two. Though such a situation may not exist, this example should convey the principle of inversity between two characters.

Whenever an inverse relationship is encountered, it usually means that a third character is mediating the other two. In the above example, the extra flexibility of the coat in the very long-haired cats may produce the illusion of lack of density. Or, the long hair fibres may only be produced at the expense of fibre thickness; again resulting in the illusion of lack of density. In both cases, the number of fibres per square inch of skin may be unaffected (the usual criterion of density). However, on the assumption that the lack of density is not an illusion, the increase in hair length may only occur at the expense of number of hairs for a given skin area. This could happen if the supply of hair substance (a keratin precursor, say) was limited, so that fibre length could only increase if there is a corresponding reduction in number. In these circumstances, an increase in hair length, with no reduction in number, could scarcely be managed by other than a greater supply of hair building substance. This may not be easily achieved (though perhaps not impossible) by selection based on either hair fibre length of density because changes in a trait (keratin substance) only subject to indirect selection (upon hair length and density simultaneously) are usually more intractable than if selection can be applied directly. It may be remarked that the example is fictitious, as far as known, though it could have a modicum of truth.

Finally, limited progress may be made because the selective breeding is being sloppily or inconsistently applied. Half-hearted attempts at selection may produce results of a sort but it is more probable that they will not. Or, the achievement in one generation may be frittered away in the next. Illogical changes in the emphasis upon the selection of different characters could undo years of careful selection. If the total score method is used, it may be that it is badly constructed, either for the characters considered, their grading or weighting. These items should be checked.

Inbreeding Depression and Hybrid Vigour

The fear is often expressed that inbreeding will bring about a decline in vigour or general weakness. This is "inbreeding depression", as it is usually termed. The loss of vigour is due to the homozygosity of an increasing number of genes with deleterious effects. These are polygenes in as much that the effect of any one in isolation is small. However, the cumulative effect can mount up and become noticeable. in the ordinary random bred population, most of these genes will be present as heterozygotes and their existence may be unsuspected until exposed by the inbreeding. This is not to suggest that all cats carry these genes or that inbreeding must inevitably produce weakly stock. On the contrary, the inbreeding of innately healthy stock is usually quite safe.

On the other hand, some animals do carry deleterious genes and these may make their presence felt on inbreeding. For this reason, the nature of inbreeding depression should be known. Almost any feature of the normal cat may be affected. There may be a decline in birth weight, as shown by small, thin or lethargic kittens, poor growth in later life and below standard adult individuals. There may be a fall in average litter size, an increase in the number of still-born or abnormal kittens. It is not uncommon for the reproductive performance to fall off. This may be shown by a reluctance of the male to copulate, the female to come into heat or partial sterility in either sex. There may be a greater proneness to illness. Perhaps one of these features may be rather strongly evident or several may show a small yet detectable deterioration. It is impossible to foretell the form the depression may take. It usually comes on gradually, affecting some individuals and not others. This means it can be countered by breeding only from the most healthy animals. This is a general maxim, of course, but it particularly holds when inbreeding is practised.

Should inbreeding depression become established in spite of efforts to counteract its effects, there is little recourse but to outcross to unrelated stock. If the outcross is made wisely, it ought to be possible to preserve many of the better qualities of the strain or, at least, not to lose too many. However, this is a matter of selection and skill of the breeder. It may be desirable to inter-cross two inbred strains which are displaying signs of depression. This could occur when several inbred lines are being bred in parallel. Should this be done, the first-cross offspring may turn out to be exceptionally healthy and fertile. This phenomenon is known as hybrid vigour or "heterosis". It does not always occur, of course, but it occurs often enough that most breeders have heard of the phenomenon. Random bred animals rarely show heterosis because much of their taken-for-granted vigour is in fact heterosis of a less obvious kind.

Some strains of pedigree cats show mild signs of inbreeding depression (i.e. they are more "delicate" or "temperamental") as a consequence of generations of selection and their somewhat inbred ancestry. This is tolerated, provided it is not too severe, because to outcross would destroy their proved characteristics and possibly their pedigree status. The depression is very insidious and it is not unknown for it to pervade many individuals of a breed, particularly if a majority of animals are related in one way or another. Weak inbreeding is then difficult to avoid and every endeavour should be made to breed only from the most healthy stock in order to counter a possible worsening of the situation.

Maximum Avoidance of Inbreeding

The occasion may arise where it is necessary to maintain a small group of animals with the minimum loss of heterozygosis. Such a case could be where a stud has attained a high level of perfection but signs of inbreeding depression have become evident. An outcross would be the obvious remedy but this is judged undesirable. For practical or sentimental reasons, the owner may not wish to break-up the blood line or it may be that no outside stock is available of comparable quality. In this event, the decision whether to outcross or not may not be easy. One solution would be to increase the size of the stud so that larger numbers are available from which to select the most vigorous animals. However, if the selection is intense, as it should be in the circumstances, the number of parents will be reduced and the stud will be exposed to inbreeding which may lead to further deterioration. The position is aggravated if it is only possible to keep a small number of animals.

A possible alternative would be to adopt a system of breeding in which the loss of heterozygosis is minimized. These take the form of groups of animals equally divided into males and females and are forms of cousin matings. Two of the simplest will be described, requiring only four and eight individuals per generation as shown by Figs. 19 and 20, respectively. In the first, two males and two females are so paired that the resulting two litters (or two series of litters) provide either both the males or females for the next generation. It is important that the sexes be chosen from litters with different parents otherwise the system reverts to sib mating which it is expressly designed to avoid. The ratio of decrease of heterozygosity is 92 per cent, a value which cannot be bettered by any other breeding system consisting of so few parents in each generation.

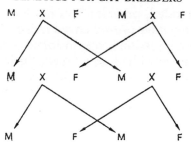

FIG. 19. Diagram of pairings for a group of four cousins. Two different males (M) and two different females (F) form the group in each succeeding generation. These must be paired as shown by the lines of descent. The pairings repeat for each generation.

The second system requires four males and four females. The arrangement of pairing is more complicated and is best understood by reference to the figure. Each of the four litters must provide two offspring for the next generation, a male and female. In the diagram, the letter M represents a male and the letter F a female, the lines of descent showing how the eight offspring must be paired for the next round of litters. Whence, the whole process is repeated. In practice, both for the previous system and the present one, it is advisable to

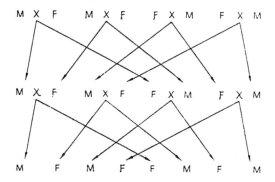

FIG. 20. Diagram of pairings for a group of eight cousins. Four different males (M) and four different females (F) form the group in each succeeding generation. These must be paired as shown by the lines of descent. The pairings repeat for each generation. Note the reversal of arrangement of the males and females in the two halves of the diagram; this is for clearer presentation of the lines of descent.

make out a sketch-plan showing the lines of descent but filling in the names of the animals in the cattery instead of the M and F symbols. The sketch-plan should be completed for two generations so that the pairing of the kittens is definitely fixed. Later, it will only be necessary to add a row of names for the next generation. This can avoid the sort of mistakes which can occur, by trying to operate the system in the mind. The ratio for the second system is 97 per cent which is again larger than other systems for a similar number of parents per generation. The last two entries in Table 7 reveal how the two cousin groups preserve the amount of heterozygosis compared with other systems.

It is possible to propose a somewhat more flexible system of pairing than that outlined above for people who find it difficult to follow a set pattern. However, there are rules attached even to this system. The main one is that each pairing must contribute two offspring to the new generation. This is the same as before, of course, except that now there is no insistence that the pairs of offspring must be consistently of the same or unlike sex. Nor is there any need for the number of animals to be invariably 4 or 8. The numbers kept for breeding in each generation must necessarily be in multiples of two but this means that it is possible to have, for example, 6 or 10. However, there are certain rules which must be observed if the system is truly to be one of minimized inbreeding. Though the choice of sex is left open as regards individual pairings, the total number of cats per generation must be equally divided into males and females. Thus, strictly speaking, complete freedom of choice only exists for the initial animals. Later selection of animals must take into account that the sexes should balance.

The advantages of the present system is the greater freedom of choice for at least half of the animals and that the pairing between the selected individuals need not follow a defined pattern. This is true, provided there is no inadvertent brother-to-sister pairing for too many consecutive generations. In fact, for the system to function as minimized inbreeding, it may be necessary to arrange that some brother-to-sister pairings are deliberately interspersed among more distant pairings. This policy implies that pairing within the system is not entirely at random but ought to be planned to some extent. At least, the pairings in successive generations will have to be watched so as to avoid prolonged inbreeding, inadvertent as this may be.

Similarly, care must be taken that a group of eight breeding animals, for instance, are truly interbreeding and are not by mischance actually divided into two lines of four. The two cousin systems described above, on the other hand, obviate these worries because all of the pairings are fixed beforehand.

Once inbreeding depression has set it, sooner or later it is difficult to avoid making an outcross if the strain is to be saved. It is possible that one of the present breeding systems may defer the event and it is just possible that ruthless selection within the system might counter the depression. It is a hope, if the avoidance of outcrossing is that important. The usefulness of the two systems is that of a holding operation until suitable animals become available to which an outcross may be made.

Inbreeding and the Appearance of Anomalies

Some hesitancy may be expressed because it is felt that inbreeding can cause anomalies. This is not an unjustified feeling but possibly over-emphasized and sometimes misplaced. In the first instance, inbreeding itself cannot induce anomalies, although it can bring to light genetic defects which may be latent in the stock. Random mating tends to keep defects hidden or prevents their recurrence except for the odd animal here and there. It is possible for a recessive anomaly to be brought into the stock, persist for a few generations, and be bred out without anyone being aware. Those heterozygotes which may carry the defect are likely to be fully healthy, hence there is no reason why anyone should be suspicious.

The chances of discovery of such a recessive defect will vary with the amount of inbreeding. The chances are small for weak and not very great for moderate inbreeding. However, the chances increase rather sharply for close inbreeding and this is the reason why inbreeding and the appearance of anomalies are believed to be associated. Only a minority of studs possibly carry a recessive anomaly and in most cases inbreeding will not produce anything abnormal. No one would be exactly pleased to discover an inherited anomaly yet should one be present in the stock it is wise to be aware of the fact and to take active steps to eliminate it. Fortunately, recessive defects can be removed and several methods are described in a later chapter. In some respects, inbreeding can be regarded as a cleansing operation, for it has a propensity to bring recessive defects to light, it also leads to their eradication far more quickly than random mating. The chance occurrence of anomalies is not the same as inbreeding depression discussed earlier. This is a more vexsome and difficult problem to control.

The Meaning of Strain

Many people at some time of their life may feel that they would like to have a strain of their own. This is very natural and leads to the question "What is a strain?" In the cat fancy, all breeders may register a stud name and all kittens which are bred to previously registered parents. This introduces a small degree of control and ensures that a stud will become widely known when the animals from it are regular winners. Almost certainly, there will be demand for kittens—and queens will be sent to the stud males. A certain amount of inbreeding may occur and it may be legitimate to speak of a blood line. Eventually, the word "strain" may be mentioned, perhaps in a general sense, but more specifically to those animals bred within the stud or from purchased animals not too many generations removed.

The terms "blood line" and "strain" are often used rather loosely in animal breeding, most commonly to indicate relationship rather than anything else. This is particularly true for blood line which in its most precise use means a line of ancestry tracing back to an exceptional animal or lineage of animals. Collateral descent is an important aspect of blood lines when it is desired to show that certain animals are related via a remote but common ancestor. Blood lines are held in high regard in the cat fancy, particularly when outstanding animals feature in the pedigree. Unfortunately, this must not be equated to genetic worth because animals of championship status may produce mediocre or downright inferior kittens. The appearance of the cat should always have first consideration and the pedigree examined with a critical eye. This is especially true when the names of champions are absent from one side of the pedigree or do not occur in the more recent generations. This could indicate that some grading-up has been taking place for the first case and that the stud has not been faring very well recently on the show bench for the second case.

In animal breeding, the term "strain" should not be lightly applied. Ideally, it should be used to denote a stock of animals of distinctive, if not exceptional merit. It should represent a stud of relatively true breeding animals possessing unique features which tend to make them stand out. This sort of reputation is not achieved overnight and is the culmination of years of unremitting selective breeding. On a lower level, a group of closely related animals which have been inbred for several generations (e.g. beyond 5 or 6) would qualify as a stain, even if these are not of particular note in other respects.

The founding of a strain of elite cats should be the goal of all breeders. Not everyone may have the opportunity nor will everyone who attempts the task be able to succeed. Nonetheless, the attempt should be made just for the pleasure which animal breeding and tending can bring to people of all ages. Especially those who have to live in urban areas yet yearn for the company of animals.

Synopsis

Despite a risk of repetition, it seems desirable to summarize the main tenets of the foregoing sections. This may be expeditiously achieved by contrasting the effects of selection and inbreeding as follows:

Selection	Inbreeding
1. Small decline of heterozygosis	1. Steady decline of heterozygosis
2. Perpetuation of certain genes	2. Steady fixation of all genes
3. Increasing phenotypic similarity	3. Increasing genotypic similarity

A first reading of the tendencies induced by either selection of inbreeding might cause one to consider that the two processes are complementary and all one has to do is select the right animals and inbreed them. In very favourable circumstances, this might be feasible. The outcome would be (1) a low level of heterozygosis, (2) perpetuation of the desired phenotype and (3) both phenotypic and genotypic fixation. Unfortunately, in practice, it is usually impossible to obtain animals correct in all of the characters which should be considered and too much inbreeding could bring about fixation of bad points before these can be eliminated.

A compromise has to be found and, generally, th is will have the form of selective breeding (using any method which seems best for the problem in hand) in conjunction with moderate inbreeding. The rationale is that this programme should bring together desirable combinations of genes and hold them until the inbreeding has led to the appropriate fixation. It must be emphasized that this is a general compromise. In special circumstances selection with the barest inbreeding may be the correct policy or selection with intense inbreeding may be more fitting. In essence, the degree of inbreeding is the factor which cannot be decided without knowledge of the problems to be overcome or the ultimate goal of the breeder.

The concepts of animal breeding are firmly rooted in genetic principles and the two topics cannot be separated. In fact, most books on genetics touch upon animal breeding practice and may devote a chapter or two to it. However, the topic is worthy of serious study in its own right and a number of books are available which do just that. The previous sections present an introductory grounding which should assist breeders broaching the subject for the first time. Those who wish to extend their reading should consult Bogart (1959) and Hutt (1964) for elementary expositions. One of the best books ever written on animal improvement is that of Lush (1945).

5

Colour and Coat Inheritance

IN ALMOST all species which are subjected to scientific study, it is desirable to have a standard to which all deviating forms can be compared. In genetics, it is convenient to choose the type present in the wild and, in cats, this is the short coated mackerel striped tabby as found in the European wild cat (*Felis silvestris*). Specimens of this type of tabby may be seen in almost all mongrel cat populations of the world. Doubtless this has been handed down from primordial wild ancestors, countless generations ago, persisting more or less unchanged to the present day.

Tabby Striping

The tabby pattern consists of dark melanotic striping apparently superposed upon a yellowish-grey ground colour. This ground colour is present in most animals and is known as agouti (so-called after a rodent of this colour). In particular, the hair fibres are not solid black from base to tip but are banded and/or tipped with yellow. It is the manner of the overlay of the fibres which produces the characteristic agouti coat. The colour is probably most well known for the wild mouse or rabbit. The cat, however, possesses a second system of pigmentation which these species lack, and this is responsible for the tabby striping. This striping is due to a marked reduction in the quality of the yellow band, leading to its elimination, with the result that a dark pattern is produced. The effect is to create the impression of one pattern imposed upon another; a coexistence of concealing colours which is seemingly basic to most members of the cat family.

The mackerel tabby may be observed in almost any mongrel

COLOUR AND COAT INHERITANCE

population. It is characterized by the presence of vertical gently curving stripes on the sides of the body. These may be continuous or be broken into bars and spots, particularly low down on the flanks and on the stomach. A second type of tabby is also found in most mongrel populations. This is the blotched tabby. The head markings of this form are similar to those of the mackerel but the body pattern is very different. The even vertical striping is replaced by broader bands which form whorls and spiral arrangements. The legs and tail are relatively heavily barred. The actual blotched pattern is variable with respect to the width of the bands and the amount of fusion they may display. Where the coalescence is extensive, a very dark tabby is produced.

A third type of tabby is that found in the Abyssinian breed. This is an interesting form since the tabby striping is extremely evanescent (or should it perhaps be nascent?). In any event, little or no evidence of striping is normally present on the body, though some may be observed on the face, legs and tail. Usually, the barring is finer than that shown by the mackerel type, though this is not always so. In the Abyssinian breed, the legs and tail may be devoid of barring or, at least, can only be seen after careful scrutiny. The interest created by the Abyssinian type centres around the relative absence of the tabby striping. On the body, the colour is that of typical agouti. The depth of colour may vary from yellowish-grey to a ruddy-brown but this variation is independent of the Abyssinian gene. Thus, while the striping is usually regarded as an integral part of the tabby pattern (certainly in the popular mind and perhaps beyond), it is possible to find a genetic form which is largely devoid of it.

The three forms of tabby pattern are inherited as an allelic series. The Abyssinian type is semidominant to both mackerel and to blotched, while mackerel is dominant to blotched. The symbols for the three genes are Abyssinian T^a, mackerel T and blotched t^b. Breeders will probably recognise blotched as the classic tabby. The incomplete dominance of the Abyssinian allele manifests as weak striping on the legs and rings on the tail for the heterozygote T^aT or T^at^b, and the absence or reduction of these markings for the homozygote T^aT^a. There is variation in the expression of the markings and it is not impossible for some homozygotes to have faint markings. However, the two forms usually can be distinguished (Lomax and Robinson, 1988).

A fourth type of tabby deserves to be mentioned. This is the spotted tabby. There seems to be two forms of this type. The first appears to be a modification of the mackerel in which the vertical stripes are discontinuous so that these appear as short bars or spots. As such, of course, the form may not be a new genetic type but the mackerel under a new guise. The break-up of the stripes is almost certainly polygenic. The second form has more distinctive and rounded spots. The case for a new genetic type is much stronger for this form.

At one time, it was thought that the spotted tabby could be yet another allele of the tabby series. It could be, of course, but the evidence—although meagre—seems to be against the idea. The alternative concept is the existence of an independent gene which modifies or "interrupts" the continuous pattern of the mackerel and blotched patterns to produce the spotted tabby. In particular, the combination of the gene with blotched tabby is seemingly responsible for the attractive round spotted "Ocicat" type. However, despite the amount of supported breeding data being so meagre, these are suggestive for a modifying gene (provisionally symbolised as Sp) for the creation of the spotted tabby.

Non-agouti

The gene responsible for the agouti-grey of the tabby has produced a mutant allele known as non-agouti. The resultant phenotype is the black cat. Though the animal is uniformly black in appearance, it will carry one of the tabby alleles. The presence of these can usually be seen in the coat of young kittens and sometimes in the adult under certain circumstances. The trick is to manipulate the animal so that the pattern can be seen by reflected light. Either the mackerel or blotched pattern should be discernible. If no pattern is observed, this could mean that the Abyssinian type is present but not necessarily so, of course. The non-agouti gene is inherited as a recessive and is represented by the symbol a.

Brown Alleles

The two mutant brown alleles change the normal black pigmentation to different intensities of chocolate or brown. The colour change is most obvious when combined with non-agouti to produce the dark chocolate of the Havana (*aabb*) or the lighter (milk) chocolate form (*aab¹b¹*). In almost all combinations with other genes, the *b* and *b¹* alleles engender a generally similar coloration but in two phases, a dark and a light. Gene *B* is dominant to *b* and *b¹*, and *b* to *b¹*.

By analogy with microscopic studies on brown mutant forms in other mammals, the colour change is due to modifications of the pigment granules in the hairs to successively paler shades. To the eye, this manifests as two levels of chocolate or brown. By a quirk of pigment chemistry, the brown alleles do not modify yellow pigment or, if they do, it is in the direction of producing a "brighter" colour. It seems probable that *b¹* has a greater effect than *b*. The effect could be purely optical, of course.

Albino Alleles

The albino series are particularly noteworthy because, between them, the various alleles are responsible for several of the cat fancier's most popular breeds. In order of dominance, the members of the series are full colour (*C*), Burmese (*c^b*), Siamese (*c^s*), blue-eyed albino (*c^a*) and pink-eyed albino (*c*). All four of the mutant alleles are recessive to full colour but not necessarily to each other (Table 3). It has actually been demonstrated that *c^b* is incompletely dominant to *c^s*. It is too soon for precise information to be available for the interrelationships of *c^b* to *c^a* or *c* but incomplete dominance is almost certain according to preliminary observations.

The effect of each allele upon the coat colour has a certain consistency. The normal gene *C* produces black and orange pigment at full strength (hence the designation "full colour"). Biochemically, the various alleles cause a progressive degrading of pigment quality. With *c^b*, the black pigment is changed to a dark sepia or seal brown, while the orange becomes yellow. The points (nose, ears, feet and tail) are usually darker than the body, a feature which is obvious for kittens but less so for adults. The eyes are probably less deeply pigmented than normal because these tend to be yellowish-grey, rarely rich yellow (Thompson *et al.*, 1943). With *c^s*, the dark sepia is restricted to the points, the body fur being off-white or pale sepia, varying in colour. The eyes are partially deficient in pigment as evinced by their blue colour. With c^a, no pigment develops in the coat, not even on the points, but the eyes are a pale blue. Finally, with c, pigment is totally absent. The fur is white and the eyes are pink due to the blood being illuminated by light rays passing through the translucent tissue of the eye structures.

The so-called albino reported from the USA and continental Europe does not appear to be true albinism. The coat is white but the eyes are a ruby red and the irises are a pale milky-blue instead of being pink. This coloration could indicate either the presence of a small amount of pigment (less than in the eyes of the Siamese) or that the iris of the cat is bluish because of its structure. The former appears to be the more likely explanation. The few genetic studies which have been completed indicate that the blue-eyed albino is inherited as a recessive to full colour and to Siamese (Turner, Robinson and Dye, 1981). Tentatively, it is assumed that a mutation has occurred to an allele (c^a) just short of true albinism and positioned between Siamese and pink-eyed albino.

The existence of the complete pink-eyed albino has been described by Bamber and Herdman (1931) but without reporting any breeding experiments. However, the complete form has been discovered in the USA in more recent years (Leventhal et al., 1985). The albino allele is inherited as a recessive to full colour (C) and by implication to all the other albino alleles.

The difference in depth of pigmentation of the extremities and body for the Burmese and Siamese is due to temperature gradients over the surface of the body. The effect is most marked for the Siamese, when the phenomenon has been experimentally verified (Iljin and Iljin, 1930). The important factor is probably amount of heat loss from the skin. In one experiment, where the cat was left in a cold environment during a period of moult, the body became covered with light sepia fur and new sites of intense pigmentation appeared on the shoulders and hips where the skin was stretched across the underlying bones. In another case, a bandage applied to a small area of shaven skin caused the growing hair to be white.

The eye of the Siamese is deficient in pigment, especially the choroid tissues, but sufficient remains in the iris to produce the characteristic blue colour. A tapetum is present, a finding which contrasts with the blue eye of dominant white (see later) which regularly lacks a tapetum (Thibos et al., 1980).

Blue Dilution

In the blue diluted cat the coat is modified to a lighter colour, namely, black to blue, chocolate to lilac, cinnamon to fawn and red to cream. The change may be most clearly appreciated for the self or non-agouti colours. The reason resides in the distribution of pigment granules in the hair. Instead of being laid down evenly throughout the hair shaft, as in black and other dense colours, in the dilute colours the pigment granules are deposited in clumps which sometimes can be quite large. Segments of the hair may be sparsely pigmented or even lack pigment. (Prieur and Collier, 1981b). To the human eye, this impairment causes the coat to appear "diluted". It is of interest that the clumping of the granules does not occur in the tissue of the eye (Prieur and Collier, 1984). Consequently, the eye colour is not paler than usual, as might be expected. The dilute gene is inherited as a recessive and is symbolized by d.

Dilute Modifier

Dilute modifier is a dominant gene Dm which—as the designation implies—lightens the coat colour of dilute (dd) cats. The gene is a modifier because it has no effect on dense coloured animals. Blue now takes on a brownish cast but not as light in tone as the lilac and is known as caramel. With dilute brown or lilac, the combination becomes a little paler and is known as taupe. The cream is also paler than usual and has been called apricot (Patricia Turner, personal communication).

The situation may be made clearer by tabulating the colours and genotypes as follows:

Black	*aaBBDD* (*Md* or *dm*)
Brown	*aabbDD* (*Dm* or *dm*)
Blue	*aaBBdddmdm*
Lilac	*aabbdddmdm*
Caramel	*aaBBddDm–*
Taupe	*aabbddDm–*
Red	*DDOO* (*Dm* or *dm*)
Cream	*ddOOdmdm*
Apricot	*ddOODm–*

Inhibitor of Melanin

The dominant inhibitor gene *I* suppresses the development of pigment in the hair of the coat. It does this presumably by limiting the amount of pigment fed into the growing hair, because the typical expression is that of white hairs with coloured tips. By the same principle, the gene has greater effect upon the more lightly pigmented agouti areas between the tabby striping. A feature of the gene is the wide variation of expression which ranges from a barely perceptible lightening of the undercolour to an almost white animal with the pigment restricted to the hair tips. The silver (*A—I—*) shows the typical expression of the gene while the chinchilla is a fine example of the extreme phenotype. The smoke is the non-agouti form (*aaI—*). The white undercolour is evident but the coat contains appreciably more pigment due to the presence of non-agouti (Turner and Robinson, 1973). The restriction of the pigment granules to the upper portion of the hairs has been confirmed by microscopic examination by Prieur and Collier (1981a).

Pink-eyed Dilution

In addition to blue dilution, a second type of dilution occurs commonly in mammals. This is pink-eyed dilution, so-called because it imparts a characteristic pinkish or ruby glimmer to the eye. The coat colour is often a bluish-fawn. The genes responsible for this colour are usually inherited as recessives. A female cat of this general description is reported by Todd (1961). The eye is said to be pink and the coat a light tan in colour. Mated with a chocolate pointed Siamese, this unique animal gave birth to three kittens, born 10 days prematurely and none survived. However, it was possible to see that all three were typical tabbies. Therefore, the implication is that the colour is inherited as a recessive trait and is independent of the albino alleles. This would be expected if the colour is due to pink-eyed dilution. Examination of the pigment granules of the hairs revealed that these were smaller and yellowish brown in colour, when compared with the normal brown-black granules. The change is responsible for the unique coat colour (Prieur and Collier, 1981b).

Wide Band

There is some intriguing evidence for a gene which is responsible for changing the ordinary tabby into the more brightly coloured golden tabby. The assumed effect of the gene is to widen the agouti band on the hairs. In addition, the gene tends to make the tabby pattern less distinct or blurred. The overall effect is a tabby of a rich golden hue. The golden tabby has long hair and this is a factor in the production of the colour. Long-haired cats expose more of the agouti band and do not have such an obvious tabby pattern as do short-haired cats. Examination of the hair revealed that it is nearly all yellow with a black tip and a suggestion of pale blue at the base, just as would be expected for a wide band phenotype. The golden tabby was developed from the chinchilla breed and is instructive in suggesting the nature of the difference between the silver and chinchilla phenotypes. This aspect is discussed anon. The breeding data to substantiate the existence of the wide band gene are slim but the gene is apparently dominant (either complete or incomplete) and has been provisionally symbolized by Wb (Robinson, unpublished observations).

Dominant Black

The existence of a gene for dominant black is something of an enigma. Tjebbes in 1924 published a report on crosses between a Siamese and a tabby which indicated that the Siamese transmitted a gene which obscured the tabby pattern. The F_1 offspring were black but the tabby re-appeared in the F_2. Attentive reading of the report revealed that the black F_1 were probably the offspring of a single female Siamese. Only two Siamese cats are described and only the female was used in the cross-breeding. The two Siamese were stated to be descendants of a pair of Siamese originally imported from Bangkok by a Dutch breeder about ten years previously. The Siamese strain has always been kept pure and has bred true to type. In view of the apparent absence of the dominant black gene from the general population, the gene is not considered in the subsequent chapter on breed genotypes. There is no point in discussing combinations which may not be in existence. Should the gene be rediscovered, of course, the situation can be reassessed.

Orange

Until recently, the gene responsible for the ginger or marmalade cat was known as yellow but the standard designation is now orange. It is unique because it is sex-linked, a statement which means that the gene is carried by one of the sex chromosomes. The chromosome is the X and a depiction of the principles of the heredity is shown by Figs. 14 and 15. A complete list of possible matings and expectations is provided by Table 4. The recognized symbol for the gene is O.

The action of the O gene is to eliminate all melanic pigment (black and brown) from the hair fibres. This is accomplished by a biochemical diversion of those substances destined to become dark melanism into the cognate compound phaenomelanin. The result is a lighter pigment granule, with different optical properties. The O gene removes the melanic pigment impartially from both agouti and non-agouti animals, so that the genotypes $A-OO$ and $aaOO$ are identically orange. That this is so is demonstrated by the existence of the two tortoiseshell forms: tabby tortoiseshell, with contiguous tabby and yellow fur and black tortoiseshell, with contiguous black and yellow fur. In the tabby tortoiseshell, it should be noted that the deeper tabby striping is carried through from the tabby areas into the yellow, where the barring is transformed into rich orange. Incidentally, the emergence of the tabby striping in the yellow areas of the black tortoiseshell is additional evidence that the a gene does indeed mask the presence of striping. All three tabby patterns are to be found combined with yellow. The mackerel and blotched forms can be readily identified but the Abyssinian is subtly changed. The contrast between the yellow and black ticking of the predominantly agouti coat is now lost and the yellow Abyssinian may seem surprisingly uniform at first sight.

An interesting aspect of the genetics of orange is that the heterozygous (Oo) female is the tortoiseshell cat. The mosaic of orange and black is most striking and has led to considerable speculation upon its origin. The most convincing explanation is that only one of the two X chromosomes is functional in the cells of females. This occurs at an early stage of development and all cells in the same lineage have the same functioning X. Ordinarily, this behaviour of the X would not be noticed, but the tortoiseshell has an O gene on one chromosome and o on the other. All cells with the O bearing functioning X will be producing orange pigment while those cells with the o bearing functioning X will be producing black pigment. The outcome, as the embryonic cat develops, is a female with a mosaic coat of orange and black.

The belief voiced by some breeders that tortoiseshell and white cats have a clearer segregation of orange and black than ordinary tortoiseshells has been upheld by the studies of Norby and Thuline (1965). It was observed that all non-spotted animals tend to be brindled, having an intimate mixture of small areas of yellow and black. As the amount of white increased, so the size of the patchwork areas increased, until in cats with much white, the coloured spots are usually of one colour. It is probably significant that the coloured areas in mostly white cats are contoured, with little of the breaks or runs leading to extensive intermingling of colour and white, as found with white spotting in certain other mammals. This phenomenon is intriguing and probably provides an explanation of how white spotting is produced in the cat.

It is not uncommon for yellow pigmented mammals to vary very considerably in depth of colour. The cat is no different in this respect. The yellow cat may vary in colour from a sandy yellow to a rich red and all graduations of colour may be found between these extremes. This variation is almost certainly due to polygenes which enrich the colour independently of the O gene. This deepening of the colour has been termed rufism, meaning to redden. The variation is most noticeable in all-yellow phenotypes but is definitely not limited to these. The auburn coloration of the exhibition Brown Tabby and ruddiness of the Abyssinian, and the variable tawny suffusion shown by many silvers are manifestations of the rufus polygenes.

The present section would be incomplete without a word on the tortoiseshell Tom cat. Theoretically, it would be held that these curious animals should not occur but they do, though at a low frequency, and an explanation must be sought. The fact that they occur only rarely is an indication that they must arise from a rather exceptional event.

Three possibilities for the occurrence of the tortoiseshell male will be outlined. The first is that of somatic mutation. Yellow animals occasionally have small spots of tabby or black hair on their bodies. Now, few people would presume to call these animals tortoiseshells, whether they be male or female. However, rarely, it is possible for the black markings to be more extensive and to simulate a tortoiseshell which is predominantly yellow. Little notice would probably be taken if the animal is a female but it could attract attention if it was a male. Such animals would be fertile and would breed as an ordinary yellow male. The reason for this is that a mutation has occurred in the body cells (from O to o) of a yellow cat, with the result that these now produce black pigment and not yellow. The size of the area would depend upon the development stage at which the presumed mutation occurred. The earlier in development, the larger the anomalous area would be expected to be. Somatic mutations may be likened to mistakes in development, for the germ-cells are usually not involved.

The third explanation revolves around the proposition that only one of the X chromosomes is functional in the body cells. The discovery that most tortoiseshell males have extra X chromosomes in their cells immediately prompts the hypothesis that this is the reason for their occurrence. The simplest situation is where the male has one extra X, giving the chromosome constitution XXY. Only one X chromosome is functional, hence the effective constitution is XY, the same as a normal male, and the animal accordingly develops into a male. In reality, the cat will have tissues of two XY constitutions, depending upon which of the two Xs is functioning. If one X carries O and the other carries o, one tissue (O) will be producing orange pigment and the other (o) will be producing black. That the animal is a male is incidental in this connection. The XXY constitution has one effect, however, for it usually confers sterility.

Microscopic studies have revealed that the tortoiseshell male may result from quite a variety of unusual chromosome constitutions. Their tissues may be comprised of mixtures of XX and XY cells, XX and XXY cells or XY and XXY cells, among others, or even of three different sorts of cells. The above examples certainly do not exhaust the range of possibilities. The principle is that the male must carry at least two X chromosomes and the tortoiseshell mosaicism is derived from the presence of an O gene on one X chromosome. The fertility of the extremely rare tortoiseshell male may be explained in a general manner by the presence of XY cells in the germ-cell tissue. Whereas, the XXY are outright abnormal and the XX abnormal for testis tissue, the XY are quite at home and these may be capable of producing functional sperms. The male may be fully or only partly fertile, depending how much of the testes are capable of producing viable germ-cells, among other factors. Now that chimaeric animals are known to exist, it has been conjectured that a tortoiseshell male of XY and XY cells could arise. The difference between the two cells is that the X in one could carry O while the X in the other could carry o. Paradoxically, the animals would appear to be uniformly XY under the microscope and be fully fertile.

Complementary to the rare occurrence of tortoiseshell males are the occurrence of a number of exceptional black females. These are exceptional because they arise from matings in which the colour is not expected (Table 8). These animals do not excite attention because they do not represent such a unique phenotype as the tortoiseshell male but, nevertheless, they are of genetic interest. Many of them could be tortoiseshells which have failed to manifest any orange or yellow hairs. However, there is reason to believe that some could have the chromosome constitution XO. A count of the number of chromosomes would probably decide if a suspected black female is in fact XO. If the female is fertile, it is possible to check the constitution by a breeding test. The exceptional female should be mated to a yellow male. Should a yellow female occur among the kittens, it is likely that she is XO.

TABLE 8. REPORTED OBSERVATIONS ON THE INHERITANCE OF YELLOW AND TORTOISESHELL; AND THE OCCURRENCE OF EXCEPTIONAL TORTOISESHELL MALES AND BLACK FEMALES

Mating		Offspring					
		Males			Females		
Dam	Sire	Yellow	Tort	Black	Yellow	Tort	Black
Black	Yellow	—	1*	58	—	53	13*
Tortoiseshell	Yellow	63	1*	44	58	46	6*
Tortoiseshell	Black	45	1*	43	—	29	24
Yellow	Black	23	—	—	—	19	—

Note: In the above table, black is used as a euphemism for non-yellow (black, tabby, blue, etc.) and yellow covers orange and cream. Exceptional or unexpected colours are marked with an asterisk.

The breeding data of Table 8 present an interesting picture of the inheritance of yellow and tortoiseshell and of the occurrence of the exceptional colours. The frequency of tortoiseshell males would appear to be about 0.6 per cent, while the black females would be about 3.6 per cent. These figures should be accepted with caution. It is probable that the frequency of tortoiseshell males is less than this, while the frequency of black females may be much overestimated. Some of the black females could be tortoiseshell females in which the yellow areas have not been detected. Two other features may be noted. The number of exceptional black females is six times as great as that of tortoiseshell males whereas the two forms might be expected to occur with equal frequency. This is suggestive that the black females could be misclassified tortoiseshells. Also, no exceptional yellow females are recorded; though these would conceivably be expected to occur as frequently as the exceptional blacks.

Piebald Spotting

Piebald or white spotted cats are exceedingly common. The spotting may occur in company with any colour and, therefore, is an independent entity *per se*. The manifestation of the spotting varies from small tufts of white hair on the breast and on the belly to extensive white areas, with the pigment areas confined to the tail and to small spots on the head or body. The increase in amount of white is variable but is not without a certain regularity. With progressive increases, the belly becomes largely white, with the neck and chin becoming involved, together with the front paws. Later, the white extends up the sides and appears on the head and hind paws. From this point onwards, white is spreading all over the animal, breaking up the remaining coloured areas on the back into spots of decreasing size. Figure 21 is an attempt to portray the progression of white.

The genetics of white spotting are not exactly known. However, it seems to be inherited as a dominant in the sense that the breeding of nonspotted animals does not usually produce spotted offspring (unfortunately, there can be exceptions). Conversely, white marked kittens are usually produced whenever one or both parents are spotted (again, there can be exceptions). These results could imply that at least one dominant gene for white spotting is in existence. This seems to be generally accepted and the gene is symbolized by S.

In one series of observations by Kühn and Kröning (1928) the

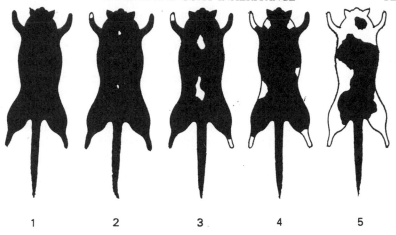

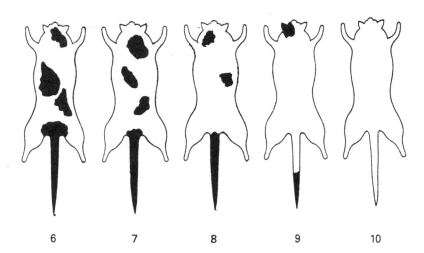

FIG. 21. Variation of expression of piebald white spotting. Grades 2 and 3 show the typical location on the stomach while grades 4 to 9 show the progressive increase in the amount of white and the break-up of the coloured areas. Grade 10 represents the all-white cat. (Courtesy of the editors and publishers of *Bibliographia Genetica*.)

heredity of the spotting was that of an incompletely dominant gene. On the average, the spotting varied from grades 4 to 6 of the figure for Ss and from 5 to 8 for SS. Clearly, there is overlapping of expression for the two genotypes. Equally clearly, the variation could be different for other observations based on animals with different genetic backgrounds even if the same S gene is present. However, the same principle will doubtless apply. The main differences are likely to be that the Ss could range down into the low grades of 2 and 3 or the expression of Ss could be close to SS to give a more fully dominant mode of heredity.

If there is one thing which is certain about piebald spotting, that is its variability. Some of this variation will be non-genetic, being due to random eccentricities of individual development. On the other hand, some will be due to polygenes, although just how much is uncertain. This means by selective breeding it may be possible to stabilize (in so far as such an erratic character can be stabilized!) the spotting about certain grades. For example, the almost all-white cat of genotype $aaSS$, with a black tail and one or two spots of black fur on the head and body, is quite an attractive animal and one which some people consider should be recognized as a breed.

It may be that the postulation of a single gene for piebald spotting is a genetic oversimplification. There is in fact grounds for thinking that a second gene, which produces a very low grade of spotting (just a small spot on the breast or pubes) may exist (Kühn and Kröning, 1928). The inheritance of this suspected second gene is not fully understood but it seems to be that of a semi-dominant with variable expression in some crosses or possibly as a recessive in others. It also seems possible that some cats which should show the weak spotting, by virtue of their genotype, fail to do so; a fact which complicates the issue. The presence of this second gene, interacting with S could be partly responsible for wide variation of the spotting.

Comparatively recently, observations on the progeny of matings between the Birman breed with self and Colourpoint cats by K.J. Clark (personal communication) are suggestive that the white gloves of the former are inherited as a recessive. As a recessive in most mating, that is, because, while the majority of the progeny did not show white, one or two showed a little white. Clark has proposed that the relevant gene be designated as gloving and symbolized by g. At this time, acceptance of this should be provisional since it is unknown if the gene is an allele of piebald spotting S or is an independent entity.

There would appear to be three basic mechanisms by which white spotting occurs in mammals. The pigment producing cells in the skin originate from a limited number of sites (probably of the order of 34) in the developing embryo. Presumably, the number of sites are sufficient to allow the cells to spread to all parts of the body in the time allotted to the process. White spotting represents areas of skin in which the pigment producing cells are absent. This absence could be due to (1) a reduction in the number of sites, (2) a slowing down of the rate of spread of the cells or (3) failure of the cells to function in certain areas. Tortoiseshell cats without white have an intermingled mosaic of orange (O) and black (o), mostly brindled with a few patches of solid colour. This indicates that the spread of both O and o cells do so at an equal speed and probably competitively. The presence of white causes the orange and black to form patches, the greater the amount of white the larger the patches, as a rule. This phenomenon could not occur under mechanisms two and three. It could under mechanism one because O is carried by an X chromosome. Only one X chromosome is functional so that about half of the original sites will be generating cells capable of producing either orange (O) or black (o) pigment. The consequence of this is the ordinary tortoiseshell. Reduction of the number of original sites would produce some white areas and decreased competition between spreading pigment-producing cells. Hence, a given area would have cells derived from few or even a single site and the greater the chance of a black or orange patch. The greater the amount of white, assumably, the fewer the number of original sites, and the greater the chance of the remaining coloured spots being either orange or black. This deduction is borne out by observation (Norby and Thuline, 1965).

Dominant White

The completely white cat, either with yellow, blue or odd eyes, is depicted in this book as due to a dominant gene symbolized by W. Since the coat colour is pure white it is impossible to ascertain by inspection which other genes are carried. In other words, W is epistatic to all other colour mutants. The only possible exceptions are those which have an effect on eye colour and there may be uncertainty even for these.

The results of crosses with dominant white, as reported in the literature, is indicative that the form is inherited as a simple entity (Robinson, 1959). This is important since it has been proposed that the all-white cat is simply an instance of the accumulative presence of several piebald genes. This is a plausible proposal but one which seems to be untrue. It has also been suggested that the dominant white gene is not independent of the main piebald gene but is an allele of it (Whiting, 1919). It may not be an easy task to experimentally examine the likelihood of this suggestion although it is a project which deserves attention. For the moment, however, it is assumed—purely on the useful premise that it is wise to adopt only the simplest assumptions that the data demand—that the S and W genes are inherited independently.

The W has manifold effects on coat and eye colour, and is associated with deafness. The production of a white coat is the most regular expression of the gene. A proportion of kittens may possess a spot or smudge of coloured fur on the head but this rarely persists into the adult coat. The eye colour is changed to blue in a large proportion of cats, either bilaterally or unilaterally (the odd-eyed white). The deafness is more likely to occur with blue-eyed animals but the association is not complete. In a recent survey of 185 white cats, 25 per cent had yellow eyes and normal hearing, 31 per cent had blue eyes and normal hearing, 7 per cent had yellow eyes but deaf, while 37 per cent had blue eyes but deaf (Bergsma and Brown, 1971). The deafness is due to degenerative changes in the succule and cochlea (Bosher and Hallpike, 1965). As with eye colour, the deafness may be either bilateral or unilateral.

Cats with white coats are significantly more liable to skin cancer due to absorption of solar ultraviolet rays (Dorn *et al.*, 1971). The study focused on white cats which included very white piebald as well as dominant white individuals. Breeders who reside in semi-tropical or tropical countries should ensure that their cats have the opportunity to rest in areas shaded from strong sunlight.

Rufism

This is a term given to denote the relative wide variation of yellow pigmentation, especially the deepening of the colour to engender the red found in the exhibition cat. This is the opposite to the "ginger" of the mongrel animals although this, of course, represents the "wild type" degree of colouring. The variation appears to be continuous from the lightest to the darkest colour and the heredity is almost certainly polygenic.

The range of variation is quite noteworthy. It is most obvious in the contrast between the ginger alley cat and the rich red of the exhibition Red Tabby. However, the same polygenes are doubtless involved in producing the warm ruddy-brown colour of the Abyssinian. Without these, the Abyssinian would be a drab and nondescript animal. The variation of amount of yellow pigment found in mongrel silver animals probably owes its origin to the same group of polygenes. The implication is that variable quantities of rufous polygenes may be present in various exhibition breeds of cats.

The exhibition silver and the Chinchilla, on the other hand, represent breeds in which selective breeding has operated to eliminate the polygenes. The outcome is a phenotype exceptionally devoid of yellow pigment. It should never be overlooked that any polygenic complex has plus and minus polygenes (in a formal manner of writing) and that diligent breeding will result in accumulations of either one or the other type in specific breeds in an effort to approximate an ideal.

Eye Colour

The cat shows rather conspicuous variation of eye colour. The iris colour may vary from grey-green to yellow and from yellow to orange, the former occurring mostly in mongrels and the latter among exhibition animals. Despite claims to the contrary, there appears to be no reliable evidence for monogenic control of eye colour. The variation from yellow to orange is particularly distinctive and every graduation seems to occur. It may be assumed that the inheritance of this feature is polygenic.

A few of the colour genes have an influence on eye colour and, to this extent, it is possible to speak of monogenic variation. The most obvious effect is the blue or bluish eye colour produced by the genes for dominant white, Siamese and blue-eyed albino. It seems feasible that the brown and dilution genes could have some effect on eye colour, especially in conjunction with Siamese, yet, if so, the effect appears to be swamped by the general variation. The cat appears to be remarkable among mammals in having such variation of iris colour.

Coat Composition

Before proceeding to discuss the distinctive features of the various coat texture genes, it seems opportune to give a general description of the hair fibres which make up the normal coat. Three main types may be recognized: These are (1) guard hairs, (2) bristle or awn hairs, and (3) down or wool hairs. The guard and awn hairs are sometimes called collectively, the top-coat, and the down hairs, the underfur. All of the hair types are important to the animal, mainly as an insulating barrier against excessive heat loss for the down hairs and, in the case of the guard and awn hairs, as a protective covering to the soft underfur and for sensory purposes. The vibrissae or facial whiskers are extra stout hairs devoted primarily to a tactile function.

The three hair types are distinctive and their differences may be easily seen with the aid of a good lens. The guard hairs are normally straight and taper evenly to a very fine point. The awn hairs are thinner than the guard hairs and have a characteristic thickening in diameter (sub-apical swelling) near the tip of the hair before tapering to a fine point. The down hairs are the thinnest of the three types. They are of similar diameter throughout their length and are more or less evenly undulated or "crimped" as it is termed. The awn hairs tend to be variable. Some may approach the guard hairs in thickness and form; while others may approach the down hairs in thinness, even to the extent of becoming crimped and showing a barely perceptible sub-apical swelling. The latter have been called awn-down hairs. If necessary, it is possible to distinguish three categories of awn hairs but it must be emphasized that all three grade into one another. The guard hairs are slightly longer than the other two types and the awn hairs are longer than the down. The difference may result, in part, from the crimping.

All three types of hair display a rather abrupt constriction in diameter at the point of entry into the skin but thickening again to form a slightly elongated club. This constriction probably enables the skin follicle which surrounds the hair to grip and hold the hair. The hair seemingly will lie in a sheath of flexible and probably contractile tissue which is of smaller diameter than that of the club. The club could function, therefore, as an anchor, apart from the likelihood that there is cell adhesion at the base of the thickened region.

The adult cat has a diffuse moult in that new hairs are being produced throughout the year and old hairs are being shed. However, this is combined with a seasonal moult in that replacement of new hairs reaches a peak in late summer and slows to a minimum in mid-winter. The cycle of moult is similar for each sex, but the male is about two months in advance of the female. Neutering of the male appeared to have no effect on the amount of moulting nor on the cycle. The hairs of the winter coat are slightly longer than those of the summer, possibly as a result of an extended growth period.

The coat of the long-haired cat contains all three types of hair fibre. Their form appears to be unaltered except for length. The remarkable difference in length between the mongrel and exhibition long hair is due to modifying genes. The long hair fibres may arise from one of two causes (or both in combination if one wants to consider all possibilities). Firstly, the hairs may grow more quickly and attain a longer length before the growth phase is ended or, secondly, the rate of growth is unchanged but the period of growth is extended. Little serious effort seems to have been put in hand to distinguish between these alternatives but, if observations on other animals can be thought to be a guide, a longer growth period is the more likely cause. In contrast, if observations on other animals can be applied to the cat, the ultra short coat of the rex is due to a slower rate of growth. The period of growth being the same or similar in both the normal and rex animal.

It is a common fallacy that the rex genes completely eliminate guard and awn hairs. The typical soft rex coat being produced by abundant down hairs which are more or less normal. This is a very over-simplified picture of the changes which take place. More typically, the rex coat is produced because, while all of the various hair fibres are reduced in length and thickness, the guard and awn hairs are affected to a greater extent than the down. In some individuals, the guard hairs may indeed be largely suppressed but, in most, the guard hairs persist but so closely resemble the down hairs that a microscopic examination is necessary to distinguish the differences. However, in some animals, the guard hairs may be seen to be persisting above the underfur as mere shadows of their former selves.

The length of the rex coat is variable and this probably parallels to a great extent the variation to be found in the normal coat. The nature and degree of wave or curliness varies between different animals and is related to the length of the hair fibres, the presence of an exaggerated curvature to the rex hair and a tendency for the individual fibres to "lay" in a similar direction. This can cause a streaming effect and bring about a marcelled type of wave in contrast to a more randomized pattern of tight curls. Rex cats with these two extremes of curliness appear very different and different again from the rex with a smooth coat having a minimum of wave or curl.

Four of the various rex coats have been examined in detail. In three rexes (Cornish, German and Oregon) the guard hairs appear to be lacking or, if not lacking, reduced to the appearance of awn hairs. Their numbers vary from cat to cat and many display the sub-apical swelling which is characteristic of the hair type. The relative thickening, however, does not seem to be as great as that shown by the normal awn hair. In fact, it is not unusual for the distal swelling to be absent or barely perceptible. In this event, the hairs appear as extra thick down hairs. It is not uncommon for a graduation in thickness to occur between the down hairs and the presumptive awn type hairs. This aspect may not have special significance because the awn hairs are variable in the normal coat and the present variation could arise from this.

The German rex coat contains awn hairs. More persistently, in as much as no individual has yet been found to be devoid of them, and more obviously. The difference in thickness between the down fibres and the awn hairs is more marked and the sub-apical swelling is a little more pronounced than that found in the awn hairs of the Cornish rex. The awn hairs in the German rex would seem to reach a higher level of development than the Cornish. This is revealed in another connection. Not only are the awn hairs more well formed but they seem to be more abundantly distributed in comparison with those present in the Cornish rex coat. It is of interest that, while the awn hairs vary in thickness, there is no real evidence for the presence of a third type which could be depicted as a guard hair. Since the Cornish and German rexes have shown to be identical, the variation in number of awn hairs probably reflects a difference of genetic background between the West of England and East German cat populations. The German population containing polygenes encouraging the formation of numerous awn hairs.

If the awn hairs are just that slightly more well formed in the German rex, compared with those of the Cornish, the awn hairs of the Oregon rex are somewhat more well formed and thicker than those of the German. In the Oregon rex, awn hairs are abundant in all fur samples examined, and showed unmistakable sub-apical swelling. The awn hairs also seemed to project a little more above the general coat level provided by the down hairs. This is supported by the impression that the Oregon awn hairs are noticeably less bent and curved over than those of the Cornish and German rexes. Once again, though the Oregon awn hairs show variation, there is no indication that a guard hair type is present.

The coat of the Devon rex, on the other hand, appears to have three types of hair. Both guard and awn hairs seem to be represented by stouter hairs of two grades of thickness. These hairs, however, are more grossly abnormal than the awn hairs of the other rexes. Instead of being of even or smoothly changing diameter, they are strikingly uneven and given to excessive constructions in places. They also terminate abruptly in most cases, as if growth never commenced as a fine point or as if distal portions have been broken off. This latter possibility is supported by the observation of broken, but unparted, hairs on several occasions, something which has not been observed in hair samples of any of the other rexes. The Devon rex guard or awn hair could be more brittle than the ordinary hair or the irregularities of diameter noted earlier could produce weak points along its length. The constant grooming by the rough tongue of the cat could be responsible for the breakage. The Devon rex rarely has a full complement of whiskers, not even as young kittens. As older kittens or as adults, it is quite common for the whiskers to be absent or merely represented by a few bent stubs. This fact and the rapid loss of hair prior to the growth of a new coat distinguishes the Devon from the other rexes.

The question which now arises is how much of the observed differences is due to the action of the rex genes themselves and how much is due to the genetic background? Only extensive inter-crossing of the various rexes could provide a positive answer to this question. Alas, from a genetic viewpoint, such inter-crossing is not likely to occur. On the other hand, a little speculation may be in order. As will be discussed later, simple crosses between the Cornish, Devon and Oregon rexes have revealed that each one is due to a distinct mutation. Now, it is improbable that each gene will produce exactly the same effect and this implies that differences due to the type of rex gene may well occur. In general, however, the various rexes look grossly alike. Only the Devon differs rather sharply from the others in the often lack of whiskers and the premature moulting. Quite often, too, the coarse hairs present in the Devon rex can be felt by a sensitive hand.

Long Hair

The long haired cat owes its unusually long coat to a recessive gene with the symbol *l*. The length of coat is variable enough in the normal cat and these differences are more noticeable for the long hairs. The mongrel long hair has a shorter and coarser coat than that of the exhibition animal. In the latter, the coat is not merely longer but feels more silky. This could result solely from the increase in length, but it seems possible that there has been a greater proportional increase in the length of the down hairs. The effect of this would be to produce a "fuller" coat of exquisite texture. These differences of length and texture are due to polygenes and are the consequence of decades of patient selective breeding.

Cornish Rex

The first of the mutants to become popularly known was discovered in 1950 and is the Cornish rex (or rex—1, as it was formerly known). The rex coat is very different from the normal coated cat and, once seen, can never be forgotten. The coat is soft to the touch, mole-like, with an apparent absence of projecting guard and awn hairs. There is a definite tendency towards waviness in many individuals, either to produce a marcelled-effect or that of waves of tight curls. The whiskers are shorter than normal, more curved and often bent. This latter feature provides a ready means of identification of rex mutants from an early age. The coat density varies from a thin, limp covering to one in which the hairs form a thick even pelage. The Cornish rex is inherited as a recessive and has the symbol *r*.

The long-haired Cornish rex has been produced and the resulting animal is clearly rex as evinced by its bent whiskers. The coat fibres are longer than normal but shorter and seemingly thinner than those

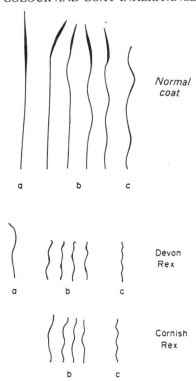

FIG. 22. Hairs of the normal and rex coats; (a) guard hair, (b) awn hairs and (c) down hair. Note the bristle tip to the awn hairs and their variation. The Devon rex has all three types of hair but these are abnormally short, constricted and bent. The Cornish lacks guard hairs while the awn and down hairs are short but a little less abnormal than the Devon.

of the ordinary long-hair. The coat, therefore, has features of both hair types. This shows that the action of each gene is independent of each other and can function harmoniously in combination.

Devon Rex

A second rex mutant was found in Devonshire in 1960 and crosses between it and the Cornish rex soon revealed that the two are unrelated. The new form was known as rex–2 for a period but this ungainly designation has been discarded in favour of the more appropriate title of Devon rex. In appearance, the Devon rex is very similar to the Cornish. The coat is short and even in length, with a spurious lack of guard hairs by ordinary inspection. Again, there is a tendency towards waviness. There is a greater propensity for the Devon rex to lose its coat and to have bare areas, especially on the belly, which persist until the next moult. The amount of hair loss varies between different individuals and is seemingly due to genes inherited independently of the rex. The Devon rex gene behaves as a recessive and has been symbolized by *re*.

A notable and probably a distinctive feature of the Devon rex is that the whiskers of the majority of animals are lost at an early age and that many animals never seem able to retain more than a few stubs for any length of time. The existence of these stubs is suggestive that the whiskers are lost by breakage, rather than by a falling out of the hairs. Even at the best of times, the Devon rex cat never, or rarely, has such a full complement of whiskers as carried by other rex mutants. The effect is enhanced by the relatively greater crookiness of those which do remain.

It is not entirely certain if the homozygous "double rex" of genotypes *rrrere* has been produced but, if it has, it will be a rex cat possessing the main features of each mutant. The coat would be expected to be softer in texture than the coat produced by either mutant by itself. The coat would lack guard hairs (due to the effect of *r*) and have hairs with constrictions along their length (due to *re*). The whiskers would be sparse or mere stubs, due again to *re*. There may be bare areas. One such rex has been identified by microscopic examination but not confirmed by breeding tests.

German Rex

A third rex has appeared in East Germany; in East Berlin to be precise, in 1951. There is circumstantial evidence that the animal, a female, was born several years previously and could be the first of the recognized rex cats, chronologically speaking. The coat is typical, being smooth and soft, with a tendency to wave. There is an apparent absence of guard hairs and the whiskers are bent. Experiments soon disclosed that the German rex was inherited as a recessive. The most interesting finding was destined not to be made until many years later. A few animals had been exported to the United States whence crosses between Cornish and German rexes produced rex kittens. This revealed that the two rexes are genetically identical.

Oregon Rex

One of the most interesting of the various American rex mutants is that known as "Oregon rex" after its place of origin. This rex was found in 1959 and is being bred by a band of enthusiasts. It is inherited as a recessive to the normal coat as in the case of all of the other forms. What is interesting is that crosses between the Oregon rex and both the Cornish and Devon rexes have produced kittens with normal coats. Thus, it would appear that three independent rex mutants are known for the cat. In fact, it is tempting to add the words "at least" to the last sentence. The symbol ro is proposed for the gene.

Selkirk Rex

Within recent years, a new type of rex has made an appearance in Wyoming, USA, in about 1986 or 1987. As kittens, the coat is soft and wavy, giving way in the adult cat to a dense, still exceptionally soft and wavy coat. Microscopic examination of the coat revealed that the hairs are shorter and thinner than normal. The coat on the body lacks both guard and awn hairs, a finding which would account for the softness. However, long thin guard or awn hairs could be seen on the tail. The whiskers and brow hairs are short and crooked. The Selkirk rex is inherited as a dominant to normal coat and may be symbolized by Se. The combination of Selkirk rex with long hair results in a longer coat which is soft to the touch although the waviness is less evident.

Other Rexoid Mutants

It is of interest to record that yet other instances of rex mutants have been observed. One occurred in Italy about 1951. Little is known of the Italian rex except that three rex kittens were bred from a normal mother. Without placing undue emphasis on this evidence, it could be surmised that the form is due to a recessive gene.

The Oregon rex of the United States has already been described but it is worth mentioning that other cases have been reported from this country. By all accounts, these have occurred at widely separated points. A form from Ohio was observed as early as 1952 but was treated very casually and was allowed to die out. Several rex animals were bred from the same normal coated parents and this would suggest that a single recessive gene has been observed.

Another instance occurred in California in 1960. On this occasion, apparently combined with long hair. Inter-breeding with normal coated animals indicated that the rex type was inherited as a recessive. Hearsay evidence has it that crosses between the Californian rex and the Cornish rex produced normal kittens.

TABLE 9. CHECK LIST OF COLOUR AND COAT MUTANT GENES AND SYMBOLS

Symbol	Name	Symbol	Name	
a	Non-agouti	O	Orange	
b	Brown	r	Cornish rex	
b^l	Light brown	re	Devon rex	
c^b	Burmese	ro	Oregon rex	
c^s	Siamese	Se	Selkirk rex	
c^a	Blue-eyed albino	S	White spotting	
c	Pink-eyed albino	T^a	Abyssinian	
d	Blue dilution	t^b	Blotched tabby	
I	Melanin inhibitor	W	Dominant white	
l	Long hair	Wh	Wire hair	

The following mutant genes are probable but can only be listed as provisional at present: Dm, dilute modifier; g, gloving; Sp, spotted tabby modifier; Wb, wide band. See text for details of each gene.

All of the early occurrences of rexoid mutants have been, or are surmised to be, inherited as recessive to normal coat. This is not obligatory, of course, and, more recently, two cases of rex type coats have found to be inherited as dominant to normal coat. The first occurred in Holland and there was some indication that the gene was not fully dominant, the homozygote appearing to have a more sparse coat than the heterozygote. The second case is the Selkirk rex which was discovered in the United States and described above.

Wire-hair

This curious coat type occurred in the United States. In appearance, the coat is rough and unruly in contrast to the smooth even coat of the normal animal. The new form has been termed wire-hair. All three hair types are present but are abnormal. The guard hairs appear thinner than normal and are curved rather than straight. The awn hairs seem to be characteristically abnormal. These are thin but have the typical sub-apical swelling. Most of them show exaggerated undulation and a "shepherd's crook" type of configuration in the region of the sub-apical swelling. The down hairs also display exaggerated and irregular curvature; unlike the more regular undulation of the normal hair. The overall effect is a sparse, wiry coat, coarse to the touch.

The breeding data on the wire-haired condition are meagre at present. However, it seems to be inherited as a simple monogenic trait and, subject to confirmation, as a dominant to normal coat. The symbol *Wh* is proposed for it.

6

Genetics of Colour Variation and Breeds

THE RAW material of the creation of breeds of cats is gene mutation. In the main, these are mutants affecting colour and fur characters. A note-worthy exception, of course, is the Manx. If a mutant gene or a combination of genes furnishes the raw material, the process certainly does not end there. Numerous finer points contribute towards the superb exhibition animal, which may differ quite considerably from a mongrel cat of equivalent basic genotype. An attempt will be made to indicate a number of the more important differences; although it must be appreciated that to define all differences is well-nigh impossible. Indeed, this may not even be necessary, for anyone who is keenly interested and is closely associated with breeds of cats soon learns to detect—by an almost proverbial sixth sense—the subtle qualities possessed by each one.

This chapter constitutes a detailed discussion of colour variation; both, generally, as the genes combine to engender an ever-increasing range of colour varieties and, specifically, where a particular genotype has come to be a recognized breed. The chapter is largely self-contained, but not entirely so, and it should be read in conjunction with Chapters III and V. It attempts to clothe the bare bones of heredity as set out in these former chapters. The beginner should not hesitate to constantly refer from one chapter to the other, armed if necessary with pencil and paper, to convince him or herself of the principles involved. This is a friendly hint to the wise.

The genetics of coat colour in breeds of cat has proved to be a fascinating subject. Though the basic groundwork has been laid for decades, only comparatively recently has it been possible to unravel many of the finer details. Despite this, however, the serious inquirer will undoubtedly encounter many vexing unsolved problems. In a

138

manner of speaking, this should be viewed as a challenge, not as a set-back, and an endeavour should be made to find a solution.

Conformation and Type

An established breed may be considered to have three components: general conformation (as shown by body structure and stance, head shape and ear carriage), coat type and coat colour. The first attribute is by far the most important and determines the status of a breed in most cases. Changes in coat type or colour are usually trivial. This is not wholly true, of course, since the Long Hair and Rex breeds have their origin in simple coat mutants but, even so, body conformation must still be regarded as important. Although coat colour cannot be entirely disregarded, its relegation to a subordinate role is seen by the recognition of several colours, within the same breed; the Burmese and Siamese are outstanding examples. Thus, a "breed" must signify something more substantial than a difference in colour. This is usually a characteristic body type, recognizable regardless of coat colour. Colour differences within a breed are properly termed "varieties".

Little is known on the heredity of body conformation in cats. Two rather distinctive conformations tend to stand out. One is a compact, powerfully built frame, with a round head and the other is a sinuous more lightly built frame, with a "wedge-shaped" head. These tend to characterize the "British" versus the "foreign" or "oriental" breeds. There are, of course, differences within these two broad categories. It is not easy to define the exact differences, nor possibly wholly advisable, since differences of opinion exist on their nature. It is of interest that cats of intermediate conformation can be seen, implying that the two types represent the extremes of a range of variation. Body build is usually under polygenic control which interacts with diet and general care. On the assumption that the last two items are adequate, conformation is determined in the last resort by selective breeding. The polygenes concerned will be determining size and shape of the individual bones of the skeleton and the size and shape of the musculative. These are the determinants of conformation and are the features which breeders will be manipulating in their efforts to improve and maintain "type" as it is termed.

The view is held by some breeders that an insistence upon

distinctive body conformation for all breeds may not be wholly in the best interest of the cat fancier. It is certainly satisfying for a breed to have an impressive appearance. However, it must be recognized that the attribute can be two-edged. The disadvantage is that matings have to be made within the breed if the ideal conformation is not to be lost or suffer deterioration. This is fine if the breed is popular and the number of stud males is reasonably large. Should the breed not be too numerous, and the stud males few in number, inbreeding will occur with possible bad effects in the long-term. Any attempt to counteract the inbreeding by outcrossing will run up against the problem of finding another breed which will not destroy the carefully nurtured distinctive body type. As a compromise, it may be advisable to build up certain broad categories of body type which will deter but not inhibit absolutely the occasional judicious outcross.

In the domestic dog, selective breeding of body conformation has been carried to fantastic, if not bizarre, lengths. It is doubtful whether the cat should be manipulated in this manner or even, if it is possible to do so. That is, the species may not have the latent genetic variation to produce, for instance, either miniature or excessively massive breeds. However, the existence of several breeds with distinctive body types indicates that bone structures, such as skull shape, length and thickness of the leg bones, spine and rib cage, as well as tail thickness and length, can be influenced by the processes of selection.

The Selfs

The self or one-coloured breeds will be discussed firstly with the express object of introducing early the idea of the four basic colours, viz. black, blue, chocolate and lilac. To do this, it seems advisable to discuss these in their most obvious form, as the uncomplicated non-agouti or self phenotype. All self coloured cats are non-agouti *aa* in genetic constitution. White is excluded because this is not a "colour" in the sense defined here.

The black cat is produced by the genes *a* (non-agouti), *B* (black pigment) and *D* (dense coloration), giving the genotype *aaB–D–*. Two conventions will be observed as far as possible in writing the genotypes throughout this chapter. The order of genes will be alphabetical. This is usual practice but has no special significance. A dash will indicate the possible presence of a recessive gene. Thus, *B*– should be taken to represent either *BB*, *Bb* or *Bb^1*. Although one could write *aaBBDD*, this assumes that black is true breeding (as it may be) but it seemed wiser to have a reminder that this is not necessarily the case.

The beauty of the black resides in a solid jet black colour, as absolute as possible, with no sign of rustiness. Any animal which has a persistently brownish tinge should not be used for breeding unless it is positively outstanding in other respects. It must not be overlooked, of course, that sunlight is the biggest enemy of a rich black coat. Continuous exposure will ruin the best of colours. All of the self colours, in fact, can be adversely affected by sunlight, some to a greater degree than others. This aspect should be remembered at all times, provided it is not used to overlook a poor-coloured cat due to genetic causes.

The blue is produced by the dilution gene, gene *d* in the formula *aaB*–*dd*. It is black but with the colour diluted. The depth of colour is somewhat variable and can be manipulated to some extent by selective breeding. Cats approaching most closely to the ideal breed colour should always have preference for breeding, provided other important features are considered. Three breeds have the basic *aaB*–*dd* genotype. These are the British blue, Russian blue and Korat. The continental breed of Chartreuse may be regarded as approximately equal to the British blue. The more subtle differences between the breeds lies in the shade of blue and in their body type, neither of which can be symbolized at the present level of knowledge.

The Havana (sometime Chestnut Brown) is the self chocolate cat of genotype *aabbD*–. It is a dense-coloured animal but with chocolate pigment replacing black. The ideal colour will only be maintained by careful selective breeding of those individuals which approach most closely to it. The same remarks apply just as cogently to body type and other characteristics of the breed. The fourth self colour is the lilac of genotype *aabbdd*. As indicated by the genetic constitution, the lilac is dilute brown; bearing the same relationship to brown as does blue to black. The lilac colour is most attractive, being a "softer" shade of blue.

The above colours have been known in the cat for fifty to a hundred years, possibly much longer for the black. However, a comparative newcomer is the cinnamon. The colour is pleasing medium brown as opposed to the dark chocolate of the Havana. The colour is produced by a recessive allele of B and b, and is denoted by b^1. The genotype is aab^1b^1D-.

The fawn is the dilute version of the cinnamon, being of genotype aab^1b^1dd, in a similar manner to lilac being the dilute of chocolate. The colour has a resemblance to lilac but is a lighter shade. It may be noted that because both lilac and fawn contain three recessive genes, the colours are more true breeding than the others.

The Tabbies

Three forms of tabby will be discussed in this section; a fourth, the Abyssinian, differs so much from the traditional tabby to deserve a separate section. Nearly everyone must know of the tabby cat. They abound in mongrel populations of both town and countryside. The tabby is grey in colour with characteristic darker patterns which differ from cat to cat but are consistent enough to fall into three generally recognizable forms. These are the mackerel striped, the blotched or classic and the spotted tabby.

The mackerel tabby is the wild type, as defined earlier, and has the genotype $A-B-D-T-$. As a recognizable variety, it differs (or should differ, shall it be said) from the mongrel mackerel tabby in several respects. The vertical striping should be well defined, evenly spaced and as unbroken as possible. The ground colour is agouti, not drab or "cold" in tone but more auburn or "warm" due to enrichment by rufus modifiers.

The exhibition Brown Tabby is the blotched tabby of genetics. The genotype is $A-B-D-t^bt^b$, differing from the mackerel in the possession of the t^b allele. The tabby pattern can be very variable but Brown Tabby breeders have managed to bring about some degree of stabilization. The tabby markings must be well defined, as black as possible and nicely balanced. The agouti ground colour should be a rich warm colour, not dull and lifeless. There is a tendency for the tabby pattern to be invaded by agouti ticking and a continuous watch must be kept on this, otherwise the pattern will become ill-defined and lose its solid appearance. This aspect should command the attention for other breeds where a good solid tabby pattern is desired.

The last form of tabby is the spotted. The genetics of this tabby

PLATE 1. A fine illustration of a silver mackerel striped tabby. In the silver, the yellow pigment is eliminated but the black tabby markings remain. On this individual, the mackerel striping is not continuous but tending to "break-up" into short bars or spots. The genotype is $A-I-T-$.

PLATE 2. An ordinary blotched tabby. Note the irregular pattern on the side compared with the regular striping of the mackerel form. This is the so-called "classic" type of tabby cat pattern. The genotype is $A\text{--}t^bt^b$.

PLATE 3. A superb Abyssinian tabby. Observe particularly the complete absence of
tabby markings on the body and fore-legs, and the virtual absence of markings on
the tail. Cross-bred Abyssinians often show vestigial tabby markings on the forelegs
and tails. The genotype is $A–T^a–$.

PLATE 4. A charming scene of four kittens enjoying a meal. The kitten at top left is a nicely marked mackerel tabby, with almost unbroken and evenly spaced vertical stripes; while the tabby at bottom right is the blotched form, with thicker and irregular markings. The kitten at bottom left is non-agouti black. The kitten at top right is a black tortoiseshell. Three of the kittens show small amounts of piebald

PLATE 5. A typical tabby pointed Siamese. The tabby markings are clearly evident on the tail and nose but not on the legs. The genotype is $A{-}c^sc^s$.

PLATE 6. A young long-haired cat, illustrating the soft fluffy coat of these breeds. The colour is red and the genotype, therefore, is either *llOY* or *llOO*.

PLATE 7. A delightful study of a normal coated queen, heterozygous for Cornish rex, and her two rex kittens. In addition to rex, these kittens carry the dominant white gene which produces a white coat and yellow or orange eyes. The genotype of the mother is $RrW-$ and that of the kittens $rrW-$.

PLATE 8. A Manx cat with several interesting features. The complete absence of tail can be clearly seen. The whorl of black pattern on the flank is characteristic of many blotched tabbies. The white markings are a typical expression of low-grade piebald, occurring on the nose and forehead in the shape of an inverted V and on the lower part of the legs (grade 4). The genotype is *A–MmSs*.

is unknown in the sense that it could be due to a distinct mutation or it may merely be a variant of the mackerel. The striping of the mackerel has a decided tendency to break up into short bars or spots. It is fairly easy to take advantage of the tendency and to develop a spotted tabby. Some really remarkable and beautiful spotted cats have been produced. The fact that these cats can be bred is consistent with either of the above explanations. However, the latter one is adopted because it is not politic to assume the existence of mutant genes unless these have been well founded. The almost continuous variation from mackerel to clearly spotted is indicative that the difference between the two is polygenic. Breeders would be wise to breed only from those spotted cats which come closest to their ideal animal. The spotted tabby can occur as a variety of British Short Hair or be the main component in the constitution of the Egyptian Mau. These latter cats are discussed in a later section.

To avoid unnecessary repetition in the following discussion of the various coloured tabbies, these will be assumed to be blotched ($t^b t^b$). This is the pattern most commonly found. In general, all of the remarks apply equally to all tabbies. However, there is one difference to be remembered. The mackerel tabby is less heavily pigmented than the blotched and the contrast between the tabby pattern and the agouti background is less. This difference can make the recognition of certain phenotypes easier for one sort of tabby than the other.

Blue tabby result from the substitution of d for D in the genotype, namely $A-B-ddt^b t^b$. The tabby markings are a slate blue and the agouti areas are cream or fawn. The chocolate tabby has the genotype $A-bbD-t^b t^b$. Here, the tabby markings are rich chocolate in colour, interspersed with yellowish agouti. The cinnamon tabby ($A-b^1 b^1 D-t^b t^b$) is brighter in colour. It may be noted that the genetically brown tabby is not the same as the breed of this name. The breed Brown Tabby is a black tabby genetically because it has the B gene for black pigmentation. To avoid confusion, the genetically brown tabbies could be called either chocolate or cinnamon tabby, as the case may be. The lilac tabby ($A-bbddt^b t^b$) and the fawn tabby ($A-b^1 b^1 ddt^b t^b$) complete the sextet of basic tabby varieties. The last two colours possess a lilac-fawn coat, the lilac being darker than the fawn on average but there may be too much overlapping of the actual colour for reliable separation.

It is probably worthwhile making the point once again that all tabby cats are agouti, i.e. have the agouti gene A. The reason is that the uniformly dark coat of non-agouti is epistatic to the expression of tabby pattern. It is difficult for a dark pattern to be observed in a coat which is already dark. This is not wholly true, of course, a "ghost" tabby pattern can frequently be seen in kittens, disappearing after growth of the more deeply pigmented later coats. This fact confirms the epistatic nature of non-agouti to the tabby alleles. It also shows that all cats must have at least one tabby allele in the genetic make-up.

A point of genetic terminology may be commented upon at this stage. It will be noted then in discussing the various non-agouti cats, the tabby alleles were omitted from the genotypes. It is true that a tabby allele must be present but, since the a gene effectively "covers them up", there is no point in including them. Another practical aspect is that the actual tabby allele present may be unknown. This means that the tabby allele cannot be symbolized, even if one so desired.

There is an important exception to the rule that all tabbies are agouti. This is the orange or red tabby. These need not necessarily be agouti. The reason for this is that a different sort of epistasis is involved in their case. The nature of this will be taken up in the next section.

TABLE 10. GENOTYPES OF THE BASIC COLOURS OF CATS

Tabby	Genotype	Self	Genotype
Brown		Black	aa
Chocolate	bb	Chocolate	$aabb$
Blue	dd	Blue	$aadd$
Lilac	$bbdd$	Lilac	$aabbdd$
Cinnamon	b^1b^1	Cinnamon	aab^1b^1
Fawn	b^1b^1dd	Fawn	aab^1b^1dd
Red	OO	Tortoiseshell	Oo
Cream	$ddOO$	Blue tortie	$ddOo$

For clarity of exposition, in the above and subsequent tables, only mutant genes are listed, all other genes are taken to be normal; i.e., non-mutant as found in the normal cat genotype. The brown tabby has no mutant genes; its genotype written in full would be $AABBDD$. Genetically, the brown tabby would be described as "normal". To list normal genes for every genotype would distract from the essential genes for the genotypes. No account has been taken of the pattern shown by the tabby. The blue tortie is otherwise known as the blue-cream.

Red Tabby and Tortoiseshell

All of the ginger, marmalade and red tabbies are controlled by the sex-linked orange gene O. The gene is carried by the X chromosome and this means that the inheritance of the gene is a little more complicated than ordinarily. The sex of the parent introducing the O gene into any cross has to be taken into consideration (Table 4). Males have only one X chromosome while the females have two (XX). Therefore, the orange male can only have one O gene while the female may have either one (Oo) or two (OO). If merely one, it is the tortoiseshell, if two, it is orange. Tortoiseshell cats are invariably heterozygous, as implied by their brindled or patchwork phenotype, and are always female.

The action of the O gene is to convert all black pigment to orange, changing the tabby or black to a yellow cat with a rich red tabby pattern at a stroke, so to speak. The implications of this pigment conversion deserves careful consideration. The agouti and black genes operate upon the black pigment, the former causing the hairs to be banded yellow while the latter allows the hairs to be unbanded. Since all black pigment has been removed, this means that the effect of agouti cannot be seen. The orange, therefore, can be either of the genotypes $A-O$ or aaO (male) or $A-OO$ or $aaOO$ (female). Visually, it is impossible to distinguish between an agouti or non-agouti orange.

A second pair of genes are affected in a similar manner. These are B for black pigment and b for chocolate. If no black pigment is present in the coat, one cannot discern if it is solid black or has been changed to chocolate by the action of b. Therefore, once again, the orange may have either of the genotypes $B-O$ or bbO (male), or $B-OO$ or $bbOO$ (female). Gene O effectively can mask the possible presence of a or b to give four possible genotypes: $A-B-O$, $aaB-O$, $A-bbO$ or $aabbO$ (males), or $A-B-oo$, $aaB-oo$, $A-bbOO$ or $aabbOO$ (females). This may seem confusing at first but the principle is that any gene which acts only on black pigment cannot be detected in orange animals. Similarly, there is little reason for thinking that b^1 can be distinguished in orange cats.

The presence of tabby pattern in orange cats is a clear indication that the disposition of pigment in these areas is greater than in the agouti areas (the paler regions between the deeper orange). It might be wondered if the non-agouti orange (aaO) could be a more self orange colour than the orange agouti A–O. However, it is not, presumably because the amount of extra pigment required to change agouti into black is too small to produce any change of phenotype between A–O versus aaO. The type of tabby pattern is independent of O, so orange cats of constitution OT^a–, OT– and Ot^bt^b are yellow with orange or red tabby pattern of Abyssinian, mackerel or blotched markings.

The magnificent exhibition Red Tabby differs from the alley ginger cat in many features. Body conformation is one, of course, but the most obvious is that of colour. The intensely rich red of the tabby pattern of the breed is due to the selection of rufous type polygenes. The intensity is enhanced by the presence of blotched tabby in the genotype (Ot^bt^b) as opposed to mackerel (OT–) since the tabby markings are more pronounced.

There are three kinds of self red; cats with the minimum of tabby markings. There are the orange Abyssinian (OT^a–), orange mackerel (OT–), where selection has minimized and diffused the tabby markings (exemplified by the red Burmese) and the so-called red self (Ot^bt^b), where the tabby markings on the body have spread and coalesced into large patches of solid red. These latter creatures are gorgeous cats. These are discussed in a later section on the long hairs since the red self as a breed falls into this category.

The tortoiseshell is a remarkable cat in a number of respects. Tortoiseshells are mosaic of orange and non-orange areas. The orange areas are orange regardless of the type of tortoiseshell, whereas the non-orange areas show the effects of genes A, a, B, b, or b^1. This fact substantiates the statement that O masks the effects of these genes. Thus, the tabby tortoiseshell (A-Oot^bt^b) is orange and tabby while the black tortoiseshell ($aaOot^bt^b$) is orange and tabby. The equivalency of tabby striping in the tabby and orange is shown by the behaviour of the pattern in the tabby tortoiseshell. The pattern carries through from the tabby to the orange areas without a break except for a change of colour. The existence of tabby pattern in the orange areas but none in the black areas (in black tortoiseshells) confirms that gene a masks tabby pattern, a point made in a previous section.

Since all tortoiseshells are obligate heterozygotes, the colour cannot be true breeding. Being females, they have to be mated to either orange or non-orange males to give the results shown by Table 4.

There is no reason to prefer one sort of mating to the other. The actual tortoiseshell pattern is due largely to non-genetic (i.e. embryonic development) causes and beyond the control of the breeder. The wide variation of expression of tortoiseshell can sometimes produce unexpected results. These arise from situations where the tortoiseshell appears non-tortoiseshell (due to an absence or apparent absence of orange areas) or orange (due to an absence or apparent absence of non-orange areas). These rare cats will breed as tortoiseshell although they are not tortoiseshell in appearance.

The tortoiseshell and white has the genotype $aaOoS-t^bt^b$, the white areas being produced by the S gene. In most respects, and in breeding behaviour, the tortie and white is identical to the ordinary tortoiseshell. There is a tendency for the variety to be less brindled, with clearer and larger patches of orange and non-orange. Often, the greater the amount of white, the larger are the patches of single colour. However, there is tremendous variation and even the best tortie and white will show some brindling. The tortie and white is the calico of USA breeders.

The cream and blue-cream are dilute editions of the red tabby and tortoiseshell, respectively. The colour change follows from the incorporation of d into the genotype: cream male ddO, cream female $ddOO$ and blue-cream $aaddOo$. Inasmuch as any sign of tabby pattern is held to be undesirable, it is advantageous for the various genotypes to have T rather than t^b. A pale, rather than a rich, cream is preferable for exhibition and these are the animals to be favoured for breeding purposes. In Britain, the colours of the blue-cream should be softly intermingled whereas, in the USA preference is given to those cats with segregated patches of blue and cream. It may be mentioned in parenthesis that US breeders recognizing a Cream Tabby, where, in contrast to the cream, a definite tabby pattern of darker cream is desired. The genetic difference between the two phenotypes derives from the nature of the modifying polygenes governing the expression of tabby pattern; whether this be ill-defined and diffuse or well-defined and intense, respectively. The mackerel tabby pattern can be more easily manipulated in this manner than the blotched.

The chocolate ($aabbOo$) and cinnamon (aab^1b^1Oo) are rather fascinating tortoiseshells, despite the relative lack of contrast between the orange and non-orange areas. The lilac ($aabbddOo$) and fawn

(aab^1b^1ddOo), with cream coloration in place of orange, complete the range of self-coloured varieties.

A comparable range of tabby tortoiseshells can be bred. Their genotypes are identical to those discussed above, with the substitution of the agouti gene A for a. These cats are becoming known as Torbies. Finally, the addition of the inhibitor gene I will extend the spectrum of colours into the silver and shaded silver varieties. Each of these will be found in the usual standard colours. It should be apparent how the number of varieties can multiply for each addition of a mutant gene to the genotype. Increases of this nature will occur for other breeds, as will be evident from subsequent sections.

Spotted Tabby

The spotted tabby is something of an enigma at this time. It was noted in an earlier chapter that two forms of spotted tabby are conceivable. The first is the mackerel tabby in which the stripes are broken up into short bars or spots. The mackerel pattern has a natural tendency in this direction which could be exploited by selective breeding. The second form is more exciting since the spots are more prominent and rounded. The form seems to have reached the peak of perfection in the Ocicat, a superbly spotted cat. The spots are so well formed that it is possible to speculate on the existence of a definite gene Sp for spotting, seemingly to convert the blotched tabby to a distinctive round spotted tabby.

It should be particularly noted that the better spotted tabbies are not the ordinary brown tabby but silver tabbies. This is probably not a coincidence since the inhibitor gene I eliminates pigment from the less intensely pigmented areas, such as the undercolour and the agouti areas between the tabby pattern. Now, if the pattern had been broken up into lighter and darker segments, the I gene would accentuate the process by removing pigment preferentially from the lighter segments. A distinctively spotted tabby could be the result.

Some superbly rounded chocolate spotted tabbies have been produced and the same principle could apply to them. If the tabby pattern had been broken up into darker and lighter segments, the darker segments would stand out more than the lighter because the sparse chocolate coloured hairs of the latter would blend into the reddish/yellowish background.

Abyssinian

The Abyssinian is an interesting cat genetically. Fundamentally, the breed owes its appearance to a unique mutant of the usual tabby pattern of the cat. The Abyssinian gene produces a restricted form of tabby, the pattern occurring on the head, limbs and tail but only faintly on some parts of the body. Breeders of exhibition Abyssinians have further restricted the pattern but the ancestral form often reappears with crossbred animals. The body fur is agouti as shown by the evenly ticked appearance. The early Abyssinians were in fact affectionately known as "bunny cats" because of the resemblance to the agouti rabbit.

The usual (black) is produced by homozygosity of the T^a allele of the agouti series. The full genotype may be written as $A-B-D-T^aT^a$, exactly the same as the genotypes of the tabbies discussed earlier, except that T^a replaces either T or t^b. This Abyssinian is a handsome cat and first-class specimens show minimal traces of tabby pattern. The body colour has been intensified to a warm ruddy brown. This increase in depth of colour is on par with the change from ginger cat

TABLE 11. GENOTYPES OF ABYSSINIAN COLOURS

Colour	Genotype	Colour	Genotype
Usual		Tortie	Oo
Chocolate	bb	Choc. tortie	$bbOo$
Blue	dd	Blue tortie	$ddOo$
Lilac	$bbdd$	Lilac tortie	$bbddOo$
Sorrel	b^1b^1	Sorrel tortie	b^1b^1Oo
Fawn	b^1b^1dd	Fawn tortie	b^1b^1ddoo
Silver	II	Silver tortie	$IIOo$
Choc. silver	$bbII$	Choc. sil. tortie	$bbIIOo$
Blue silver	$ddII$	Blue sil. tortie	$ddIIOo$
Lilac silver	$bbddII$	Lilac sil. tortie	$bbddIIOo$
Sorrel silver	b^1b^1II	Sorrel sil. tortie	b^1b^1IIOo
Fawn silver	b^1b^1ddII	Fawn sil. tortie	$b^1b^1ddIIOo$
Red	OO	Red silver	$IIOO$
Cream	$ddOO$	Cream silver	$ddIIOO$

All Abyssinian colours are T^aT^a and this must be added to the above genotypes. The colour described as usual is the normal or black and has no mutant colour genes. The Somali colours have identical genotypes to the above with the addition of llT^aT^a, that is, the breed is a long-haired Abyssinian.

to the richly coloured red tabby. It is probably, if not certain, that the same polygenes are concerned.

The sorrel Abyssinian was known as the red before its true genetic nature was discovered and the colour was renamed. The genotype is $A\text{-}b^1b^1D\text{-}t^aT^a$, differing from the usual by the substitution of the b^1 allele for B. The colour is a distinctive and attractive reddish brown, fully justifying its popularity.

The chocolate Abyssinian ($A\text{-}bbD\text{-}T^aT^a$) is a somewhat darker coloured version of the sorrel Abyssinian, resulting from the replacement of the b^1 allele by b. The two forms are usually distinctive in general appearance but, if difficulty is experienced, the solid coloured tail tip is a ready means of differentiation. The colour of the tip is light brown for the sorrel but chocolate for the chocolate.

The blue Abyssinian has the genotype $A\text{-}B\text{-}ddT^aT^a$, with bluish ticking over a cream ground colour. The lilac has the genotype $A\text{-}bbddT^aT^a$, with lilac ticking over the cream ground colour. It is fairly easy to distinguish the two dilute forms, with experience. In any event, the colour of the solid tail tip should decide matters. The fawn Abyssinian is the dilute of the sorrel, with the genotype $A\text{-}b^1b^1ddT^aT^a$. The ticking is lighter than that shown by the lilac and the coat is more cream in appearance. Unfortunately, taking into account the colour variation of the lilac and fawn, it is often difficult to separate the two varieties.

The red Abyssinian is engendered by the orange O gene to give the genotypes $A\text{-}B\text{-}D\text{-}OT^aT^a$ for the male and $A\text{-}B\text{-}D\text{-}OOT^aT^a$ for the female. The coat colour is bright orange and the tip of the tail is red. The substitution of the b or b^1 allele for B in the above genotypes will make little change in the phenotype. As a consequence, the red may have several different genotypes and this will be reflected in the breeding behaviour when mated to other varieties. The cream Abyssinian is the dilute form of the red. The genotypes for the colour will be identical to those of the red except that the d allele replaces D. The colour is a clear cream.

The tortoiseshell Abyssinian is a mixture of red and non-red areas, with the basic genotype $A\text{-}OoT^aT^a$. The non-red areas will be the colour of the particular tortoiseshell variety—usual, sorrel, chocolate, etc.—with the appropriate genotype to match. A problem with the tortoiseshell Abyssinian, unlike the other tabby pattern tortoiseshells, is that they are not always easy to identify, especially if the red areas are dispersed throughout the coat. This problem can be acute for some coloured varieties.

Introducing the inhibitor gene I into the breed has created the silver series of varieties. Effectively, a white undercolour is produced, the red or cream ground colour, as the case may be, disappearing completely. The coloured tipping to the hairs will be one of the varieties described previously. The six basic colours, usual to fawn, red and cream, and the six tortoiseshells can all be bred as silver varieties. Their respective genotypes will contain the I gene in addition to the usual complement. For instance, the genotype of the fawn silver tortoiseshell is $A-b^1b^1ddI-OoT^aT^a$, to cite the variety with the maximum number of mutant genes. In toto, there can be 28 varieties of Abyssinian.

Somali

The Somali is a long-haired version of the Abyssinian. The name is fanciful, of course, since the breed was developed in the USA by careful selection of long-haired kittens produced by the Abyssinian. The basic genotype is llT^aT^a. The Somali can be bred in all the colour varieties found in the Abyssinian. Their genotypes are identical but with the addition of the long-haired gene l. The Somali variant is a short-haired Somali with long-haired ancestry, such as may arise from a cross with the Abyssinian to maintain good body type. These variants may be mated to Somalis but not to Abyssinians because of the probability of inadvertently introducing the long gene into the Abyssinian breed.

Singapura

The Singapura is a sleek cat of unusual colouring. The breed results from a combination of the Abyssinian and Burmese alleles, as in the genotype $c^bc^bT^aT^a$. The Abyssinian pattern is clearly evident, while the colour is a pleasing tone of dark sepia brown, shading over the body, upon a cream background. It is possible that colour varieties may make an appearance in the future.

Siamese

The Siamese is an elegant animal and represents, in many people's eyes, the quintessence of cat breeding. The breed may be taken as archetypal of the foreign or oriental body type. The phenotype is a form of "Himalayan albinism", to be found in many animals (rabbit, mouse) but showing more pigment than is typical. This means that the eyes are blue (instead of pink) and the body is sepia shaded (instead of white). Apart from this, the Siamese is typical in that the kitten is born devoid of pigment but commences to form pigment on the nose and ears within a few days. This behaviour is characteristic of this class of mutant.

Formation of pigment in the hair of the Siamese is temperature dependent and is responsible for the contrast between the colour of the body and the points. Pigment forms on the points because their temperature is sufficiently low but the temperature of the body is just a wee bit too high for much pigment to be produced. As a result, the coat varies from pale to medium sepia, according to a number of factors. Groups of Siamese will not all colour to the same degree even if kept in the same room temperature, and some cats will respond to changes of temperature whereas others will not. In general, the cooler the surrounding temperature, the darker the colour; the higher the temperature, the paler the colour.

The seal Siamese is a non-agouti black with the addition of the Siamese gene c^s, i.e. $aaB-c^sc^sD-$. Note that the colour of the points is not black but a dark seal brown. This degrading of the colour intensity is characteristic of c^s and this fact should be remembered for all varieties of Siamese. The colour of the points will differ slightly from the corresponding normal colour. The blue Siamese has the genotype $aaB-c^sc^s-dd$, the chocolate $aabbc^sc^sD-$ and the lilac $aabbc^sc^s dd$ (frost point in the United States).

The tabby point or Lynx Siamese has the genotype $A-B-c^sc^sD-$, displaying tabby markings on the head, feet and tail. Only the seal or black tabby point is recognized at present but it is obvious that the four basic colours could be developed easily and at any time. The genotypes of the other three colours are: blue tabby point $A-B-c^sc^sdd$, chocolate tabby point $A-bb-c^sc^sD-$ and lilac tabby point $A-bbc^sc^sdd$. Note that the type of tabby is not included in these formulae because so little of the tabby is expressed that this item is relatively unimportant. However, in most cases, the allele present seems to be mackerel (*T*). If it is desirable that no tabby markings are apparent on the body, the *T* allele is preferable to *t^b*, and selection should aim at minimizing and diffusing the expression of the striping.

The red and tortie point Siamese involves the sex-linked orange gene. The formula for the red is c^sc^sO in the case of the male and c^sc^sOO for the female. The *O* gene is carried by the *X* chromosome and the inheritance of the gene is exactly similar to that for an ordinary yellow (Table 4). Since the *O* masks both *A* and *b*, these two genes cannot be detected in the red point. Consequently, these are omitted from the genotype. The presence or absence of either of these genes can only be found from knowledge of the parents or by breeding behaviour. The cream point has the genotype c^sc^sddO (male) or c^sc^sddOO (female); the colour being produced by the *d* gene acting upon the red pigment.

The tortie point Siamese can exist in a large number of different colours. The seal point is $aaB-c^sc^sD-Oo$, with seal and reddish tortoiseshell markings. It should be clear that the various tortie points are simply the combination of Siamese and tortoiseshell, the expression of the latter being almost exclusively confined to the points. The blue tortie point is $aaB-c^sc^sddOo$, the chocolate $aabbc^sc^sD-Oo$, and the lilac $aabbc^sc^sddOo$. A similar series of four colours will occur for

TABLE 12. GENOTYPES OF SIAMESE COLOURS

Colour	Genotype	Colour	Genotype
Seal	*aa*	Seal tortie	*aaOo*
Choc.	*aabb*	Choc. tortie	*aabbOo*
Blue	*aadd*	Blue tortie	*aaddOo*
Lilac	*aabbdd*	Lilac tortie	*aabbddOo*
Seal tabby		Seal tab. tortie	*Oo*
Choc. tabby	*bb*	Choc. tab. tortie	*bbOo*
Blue tabby	*dd*	Blue tab. tortie	*ddOo*
Lilac tabby	*bbdd*	Lilac tab. tortie	*bbddOo*
Red	*aaOO*	Red tabby	*OO*
Cream	*aaddOO*	Cream tabby	*ddOO*

All Siamese are *c^sc^s* and this must be added to the above genotypes. Red and red tabby (as well as cream and cream tabby) look alike but have different genotypes. The Balinese colours have identical genotypes to the above but with addition of *c^sc^sll*, that is, the breed is a long-haired Siamese.

the tabby tortie points, with the substitution of the A gene for a. For instance, the seal tabby tortie is $A-B-c^sc^sD-Oo$ and so on.

It should be particularly noticed that a red point and a red tabby point Siamese are recognised. The former denotes the non-agouti red of genotype aac^sc^sOO while the latter denotes the agouti red of genotype $A-c^sc^sOO$. The reason for the distinction is to avoid the situation of mating a red point to a seal point and breeding tabby point kittens instead of the desired seal points. This is possible because the two red Siamese cannot be distinguished visually. The breeding policy is to assume that all red Siamese are agouti until proven otherwise. This may be done by mating a red to one of the self colours (seal, blue, chocolate or lilac) or self tortie (same colours) and noting that all of the non-red progeny are self coloured. Red point bred from proven red point Siamese parents would be acceptable. However, be on guard not to mate a proven red point to an unknown red Siamese. This would undo all previous careful breeding. The above comments apply with equal relevance to the differences between the cream point and the cream tabby point Siamese.

Balinese

These cats are a long-haired relation of the Siamese. The name is as fanciful as that of Somali, since the breed was developed in the USA by selective breeding of long-haired segregants from the Siamese. The basic genotype is c^sc^sll. Other genes are added to create particular colour varieties, for example $aac^s\,c^s\,ll$ for the seal point Balinese or aac^sc^sddll for the blue point Balinese. All of the colours recognized for the Siamese may be bred in the Balinese. The Balinese variant is a short-haired Balinese with long-haired ancestry, such as may arise from a cross with the Siamese to improve good body type. These variants may be mated to Balinese but not to Siamese to avoid the probability of inadvertently introducing the long gene into the Siamese breed.

Burmese

The gene responsible for the Burmese is a member of the albino series, a step up from Siamese in terms of amount of pigment produced in the coat but failing to attain the full production of the normal coloured cat. The result is that the black is changed to a dark sepia brown (seal) and the orange to a golden red. The points are darker than the body colour, the difference being most perceptible in kittens but becoming less obvious in the adult. This effect suggests that the formation of pigment may be thermo-sensitive as in the Siamese. The fact that pigment in the Burmese is close to, but of slightly less intensity, than that of full strength, means that while the four basic colours are recognizable, these are subtly paler in tone.

All of the Burmese bred at the moment are non-agouti. The brown has the genotype $aaB-c^bc^bD-$, being a dark seal brown. The blue is $aaB-c^bc^bdd$, being bluish grey, the chocolate $aabbc^bc^bD-$, being a medium chocolate brown, while the lilac is $aabbc^bc^bdd$, being a delectable dove grey. In the USA, the chocolate and lilac are known as "champagne" and "platignum", respectively. Generally, the fur colour is lighter in the kitten but darker in the adult coat. Also, traces of tabby striping may be evident in the kitten but this fades upon adulthood. It is of interest that most, if not all, Burmese have the Abyssinian T^a allele in the genotype, not the more usual mackerel T or blotched t^b alleles. This may be of significance since the T^a allele would minimise the expression of tabby pattern in the coat.

The red Burmese has the formula c^bc^bD-O (male) and c^bc^bD-OO (female) and is golden red in colour. This colour results from a reduction of intensity due to c^b, on the one hand, and a policy of breeding for minimal tabby marking. The latter would result in a dissipation of the deeper pigment which is produced by the tabby pattern in red cats. The cream is a lighter-coloured edition of the red, but otherwise identical, and has the genotype c^bc^bddO and c^bc^bddOO, according to sex. The tortie and blue-cream varieties are simply Burmese analogues of the usual tortie and blue-cream, with genotypes $aaB-c^dc^dD-Oo$ and $aaB-c^dc^dddOo$, respectively. It only requires the breeding of the chocolate tortie ($aabbc^dc^dD-Oo$, and lilac tortie ($aabbc^bc^bddOo$) to complete the series of varieties of Burmese. Parenthetically, the red and cream varieties are non-agouti (aa) because of the method by which the Burmese are bred at this time.

Tonkinese

Since the Burmese c^b allele is incompletely dominant to the Siamese c^s allele, it is possible to have a light phase Burmese, and this has become known as the Tonkinese. The fundamental genotype is aac^bc^s. Other genes are added to produce the colour varieties. The above genotype is that of the black (known as seal); when written in full this is $aaB-c^bc^sD-$, while the chocolate is $aabbc^bc^sD-$, and so on for all of the recognised colour varieties. The difference between the two phases is most obvious for kittens. The body colour of the light phase is distinctly lighter and the contrast between the depth of pigment of the points and that of the body is emphasized. There is some variation, the lightest appear as extremely dark Siamese while the darkest approach the dark phase in colour. As adults, the difference between the phases is less noticeable.

TABLE 13. GENOTYPES OF BURMESE COLOURS

Colour	Genotype	Colour	Genotype
Brown	aa	Brown tortie	$aaOo$
Chocolate	$aabb$	Choc. tortie	$aabbOo$
Blue	$aadd$	Blue tortie	$aaddOo$
Lilac	$aabbdd$	Lilac tortie	$aabbddOo$
Red	$aaOO$	Cream	$aaddOO$

All Burmese colours are c^bc^b and this must be added to the genotypes.

Burmilla

The Burmilla originated from a mating between a lilac Burmese and a Chinchilla. The first cross cats were so striking in appearance and type that these were developed by assiduous selection into a breed. The coat is short, with white undercolour, profusely shaded with tipping of various colours. In effect, all of the colours found in the Burmese are permitted. The fundamental genotype is c^bc^bII, with addition of the pertinent other genes to engender each of the coloured varieties. The Burmilla is an agouti, and when non-agouti is added to the genotype the Burmoire is produced. These have light or white undercolour but are more heavily shaded. The basic genotype is aac^bc^bII, together with the pertinent genes for the colour varieties. All of the above have the I gene to produce the white undercolour. Those colours which lack the I gene will also occur within the breed. The agoutis (as represented by tabbies) are known as Asians and the non-agouti as the Bombay—at least, as regards the self black.

Tiffany

The Tiffany is a long-haired development of the brown Burmese with the genotype aac^bc^bll. The long coat induces a greater contrast between the sepia-brown tones over the body and the darker points.

Albino

The complete albino with pink eyes and white coat is almost unknown in the cat. Not totally unknown because there have been two reports of albinism in the past, one from North America and one from France. In the most authenticated case, the pupil is described as blood red and the iris a translucent white. It is a little surprising that the albino has not been established in cats because the mutant is extremely common among mammals and has been accepted by most fanciers as a respectable breed.

The "Albino Siamese" bred in the USA is a Siamese-type cat with a completely white coat (no points) and eye colour of a pale bluish-pink. The limited amount of information which has become available on the variety indicates that it inherited as a recessive to both normal coloured and Siamese. The pale blue eye is suggestive that the variety is not true albino.

More recently an Albino variety is being bred in Belgium under the name of "European albino". The coat is fully white while the eyes are ruby-red, with pale translucent blue irises. The body type is that of the European short hair. The colour is inherited as a recessive. Apart from body conformation, which is immaterial, the similar phenotype and heredity would imply that the two mutants are similar if not actually identical. Both forms are ascribed to a mutant allele c^a which is assumed to be just short of true albinism.

It is unfortunate that the blue-eyed albino is sometimes confused with the blue-eyed white due to W. The two are similar but only superficially, for close examination will reveal the eye colour is different. The fear has been voiced that the albino may suffer from eye defects or deafness but this does not seem to be so. There is some photophobia but this is also shown by the Siamese to some extent. Deafness is not a property of albinism and has not been observed. It must be emphasized that W and c^a have nothing in common genetically.

Silver

The silver tabby owes its name to an absence of yellow pigment from the agouti areas of the coat. Consequently, the black tabby pattern stands out against a white background. The exhibition cat of championship status is a handsome beast. The silver looks its best when devoid of any suggestion of a tawny or yellow suffusion. This often appears in cross-bred silvers, indicating how successful breeders have been in eliminating the blemish by careful selective breeding.

An investigation into the inheritance of silver showed that the colour is produced by a dominant gene I (Turner and Robinson, 1973). The disappearance of yellow pigment from the coat is fortuitous. Gene I suppresses the development of pigment from the coat and produces its greatest effect on those areas which are the least heavily pigmented. These are the agouti areas between the intensely coloured tabby pattern. Presumably, the first silver showed some yellow in the coat, but breeders have selected against this and eventually the silver became devoid of yellow.

The exhibition silver has the genotype $A-B-I-t^b t^b$. It is possible to have a mackerel-striped silver of genotype $A-B-I-T-$. Other colours do exist and may occasionally be seen. The blue silver of genotype $A-B-ddI-t^b t^b$ is not an unattractive colour for those people who like the softer colours. It has a bluish tabby pattern against an off-white background. The chocolate silver ($A-bb-I-t^b t^b$) could be bred if anyone is sufficiently interested. Also the lilac silver ($A-bbI-t^b t^b$) to complete the quartet. All of these are shown with the blotch tabby gene because this form probably would be the most acceptable. However, if mackerel tabby is desired, T could be substituted for t^b in the above formulae.

Egyptian Mau

The Egyptian Mau is a spotted tabby of graceful foreign type. The interesting aspect of the breed is the adoption of a spotted tabby as the "hallmark". It is unknown if the spotted form is a distinct genetic entity or if it is a modified mackerel tabby of basic genotype $A-T-$. There is some variation in sharpness of definition, size and roundness of the spots but this can be overcome by selective breeding. In fact, it will probably be found that careful and diligent selection is essential to maintain the ideal spotted pattern.

The ordinary Egyptian Mau is a black tabby (A–B–D–T–) while the Bronze Mau is the chocolate tabby (A-$bb$$D$–$T$–). These latter are most attractive cats, with rich chocolate spots against a yellowish background. The cinnamon Mau (A–$b^lb^l$$D$–$T$–) is also an attractive cat, differing from the Bronze in having lighter brown spots. Introducing the dilution gene produces the blue Mau (A–B–$dd$$T$–) and the lilac Mau, the latter appearing in two shades, a dark (A–$bb$$dd$$T$–) and a light ($A$–$b^lb^l$$dd$$T$–). The light form is described as having a rosy-pink aura to the pastel blend of the lilac and fawn. One further variety which certainly merits comment is the silver Mau (A–B–D–I–T–), with its contrasting pattern of black spots on a white ground.

Bicolour

White-marked cats are very common among mongrel or alley cats but few breeds have white spotting as an essential part of their make-up. A notable exception is the bicoloured, short or long haired. Formerly known as the Magpie, the white areas are not extensive, which implies either the heterozygous expression of the piebald gene S or the homozygous expression where the amount of white has been reduced. For many years, the Bicolour was bred only as black and white (aaB–D–Ss) or as blue and white (aaB–$ddSs$). However, in more recent times, any or most of the standard colours have been acceptable.

Chinese Harlequin

An attempt was made some years ago to popularize a nearly all-white cat under the name of "Chinese Harlequin", based upon an alleged, probably mythical, ancient Chinese cat. The variety is mainly white except for small patches of black on the head, sometimes on the body, and a black tail. The genotype is aaB–SS. Only black were produced but presumably the blue (aaB–$ddSS$) would be excellent foil for the black. The phenotype is undoubtedly "pretty", more perhaps to the casual cat keeper than to the serious breeder.

Smoke

Smoke is formed by the combination of the inhibitor gene with non-agouti (*aaI*–). The action of *I* in producing white undercolour is clearly seen in this breed. "Ghost" tabby marking of dark and light pigmentation may be observed in most kittens, if not all, if one searches carefully enough. The extent of the white undercolour is very variable. The majority of smokes have white undercolour although these may be spoken of as dark, medium or light, depending upon the amount of top colour. The white undercolour itself is not (or only rarely) white in the smoke. It should more properly be termed light. The colour may vary from off-white to bluish, barely distinguishable from the blue undercolour of ordinary black. Very dark smoke can be confused with black, producing the apparently paradoxical situation of smoke kitten, being bred from black parents. It is likely that one of the parents is actually a smoke in genotype but not in appearance. The great variation in undercolour is comparable to that which differs silver from chinchilla and is presumably due to the same modifying genes.

The exhibition smoke may be short or long haired (*aaB–D–I–*) but it is the latter which are so well known. It will be appreciated that the combination of *I* with other mutant genes will produce smokes of various colours. For instance, the blue smoke (*aaB–ddI–ll*), chocolate (*aabbD–I–ll*) and the lilac (*aabbddI–ll*). Some people may be apprehensive regarding the breeding of these colours but their possibility (in a few cases, their existence) cannot be ignored. The light undercolour is not only more apparent with long coat but its beauty is enhanced. The corresponding short-haired smokes have their points but cannot compare with the sheer magnificence of the long haired.

Chinchilla

Basically, the genotype of the chinchilla (*A–I–llT–* or *A–I–llt^{b}t^b*) is similar to that of the silver. In fact, for a time, until the hairs grow long enough to show the pronounced white undercolour, the chinchilla looks like a silver, even to the extent of exhibiting a tabby pattern. It seems that the majority are blotched or classic tabby. Later, as the hair becomes longer, the pattern disappears. The reason, as may be confirmed by observation, is that only the extreme tips of some hairs are pigmented. During the phase when merely the points of the hairs are protruding through the skin, the tabby pattern is apparent because it is hairs from these regions which are tipped with pigment.

Two factors enter into the production of the superb chinchilla: highly successful selection for an extreme phenotype and the long hair. The absence of pigment has been achieved by increasing the white undercolour to the utmost. The long hair has been conducive to the overall effect by exposing the undercolour and preventing the pigment hair tips from forming any sort of pattern.

It appears, however, that this is not the end of the story. Tabby patterned cats bred from heterozygous Chinchilla Ii are not of the usual colour, as would be expected, but are much brighter, as indicated by the name of golden tabby. What could be the nature of the difference? These have the appearance of being agouti with the yellow band being greatly widened. Examination of hairs of the golden is in keeping with the suggestion, since these are nearly all yellow with a dark tip and slight blue undercolour at the base. It may be proposed that the Chinchilla owes its unique phenotype to the presence of a wide band gene—provisionally denoted by Wb. Since the wide band tabby is less heavily pigmented than the ordinary tabby, in combination with the I gene this would facilitate the action of the latter in removing pigment from most of the hair, to produce the Chinchilla as opposed to the typical silver tabby. Modifying polygenes could be involved to put the finishing touches to the Chinchilla phenotype.

The standard chinchilla has black-tipped hairs and will have the genotype $A-B-D-I-ll$. However, chinchillas with blue-tipped hairs are not unknown, with the genotype $A-B-ddI-ll$, presumably arising from an out-cross to a long-haired blue several generations previously. These cats are not easy to detect as adults but are obviously blue as baby kittens. The theoretically possible chocolate chinchilla ($A-bbD-I-ll$) would appear ticked with dusky brown or off-coloured black as adults although more readily detectable as baby kittens.

Cameo

The bringing together of the genes I and O results in the Cameo or red smoke. These cats are very delightful creatures. In appearance, they are a blend of orange-yellow tipping or veiling over a whitish background. The genotype is $I–llO$ or $I–llOO$ for the male or female, respectively. The particolour or tortoiseshell cameo has the genotype $aaI–llOo$, if the non-cameo areas of the coat are smoke or $A–I–llOo$, if these areas are shaded-silver or chinchilla. The tabby genes are relatively unimportant in the cameo. The t^b allele could be involved in producing the darker-shaded forms while the T allele is probably involved with the lighter. However, this must not be regarded as a hard and fast rule.

A property of the cameo is the considerable variation in the amount of orange veiling. This is recognized by the general acceptance of three grades. The most heavily shaded is the smoke cameo, with rather dense veiling, followed by the shaded cameo, with noticeably less intense veiling, and the shell cameo, the lightest of all. In very light animals, only the tips of the hairs are orange. The major difference between the shaded silver and chinchilla versus the cameo is the conversion of black pigment to orange by the O gene. The fundamental gene in the creation of these two series of varieties is the inhibitor gene I.

Unlike the chinchilla breeders who are breeding for extreme expression of the I gene to produce their ideal cat, cameo breeders have a wider choice. Their policy is to cultivate a variety of intensities of veiling in their breeding operations. If anything, this will call for a greater degree of skilful breeding. It may not make the task easier but it certainly adds interest.

The various cream cameos have genotypes identical with the corresponding red cameo with the addition of the d gene. The two fundamental constitutions, therefore, are $I–ddllO$ (male) and $I–ddllOO$ (female). These will occur in three intensities of veiling as discussed previously. The dilute particolour may be either $aaddI–llOo$ if the non-cream cameo areas of the coat are blue smoke or $A–ddI–llOo$, if the areas are blue-shaded silver or chinchilla.

Colourpoint

A development of the Long Hairs has produced the splendour of the Colourpoint. These lovely cats are not simply long-haired Siamese, for the body type is completely different. The Colourpoints tend to have clearer body colour than the Siamese and this emphasizes the contrast between the body and the points.

Colourpoints may be bred in all of the colours known for Siamese. The constitutions are the same, with the addition of the long-hair gene: seal ($aaB–c^sc^sD–ll$), blue ($aaB–c^sc^sddll$), chocolate ($aabbc^sc^sD–ll$), lilac ($aabbc^sc^sddll$), red ($c^sc^sD–llOO$), cream ($c^sc^sddllOO$), tortoiseshell ($c^sc^sD–llOo$) and blue-cream ($c^sc^sddllOo$). In the United States those with self points are known as Himalayan while those with points other than self are known as Kashmir.

TABLE 14. GENOTYPES OF COLOURPOINT COLOURS

Colour	Genotype	Colour	Genotype
Seal	*aa*	Seal Tortie	*aaOo*
Chocolate	*aabb*	Choc. tortie	*aabbOo*
Blue	*aadd*	Blue tortie	*aaddOo*
Lilac	*aabbdd*	Lilac tortie	*aabbddOo*
Seal tabby		Seal tab. tortie	*Oo*
Choc. tabby	*bb*	Choc. tab. tortie	*bbOo*
Blue tabby	*dd*	Blue tab. tortie	*ddOo*
Lilac tabby	*bbdd*	lilac tab. tortie	*bbddOo*
Red	*aaOO*	Cream	*aaddOO*
Red tabby	*OO*	Cream tabby	*ddOO*

All Colourpoints are *c^sc^sll* and this should be added to the genotypes. Red and red tabby (as well as cream and cream tabby) look alike but have different genotypes. The blue and lilac torties are also known as blue-cream and lilac-cream, respectively. The Birman colours have identical genotypes to the above but with the addition of *c^sc^sggll*; that is, the breed is a Colourpoint with white on the extremeties.

Birman

This breed is an unusual cat. It is not, as one might think, simply a variation of the Colourpoint. True, there is a close resemblance in that the two breeds are long coated and have a Siamese type pattern. For example, while the seal variety of each breed has the genotype *aac^sc^sll*, the Birman has white "gloves" on the feet whereas the Colourpoint does not. The white should not be too extensive so as to appear as a "stocking". It may be surmised that the white spotting is due to restricted expression of the piebald gene S but the observations of K.J. Clark do not support this. It seems that a gene for minor white spotting is involved, provisionally denoted by the symbol g. The genotype of the seal variety may, therefore, be written as *aac^sc^sggll*. All the colours of the Colourpoint may occur in the Birman.

Ragdoll

The breed has elements of the Colourpoint in the background, together with piebald spotting which, it may be said, can result in a cat of pleasing appearance. All Ragdolls are colourpointed and long-haired, as shown by the genotype aac^sc^sll for the seal. Other colours are chocolate $aabbc^sc^sll$, blue aac^sc^sddll and lilac $aabbc^sc^sddll$. Each of the above can be combined with piebald S to produce two grades of white pattern: a limited amount of white on the face and feet, when the Ragdoll is said to be mitted; or more extensive where the white also occurs on the body, when the Ragdoll is said to be bicolour. The former could be the heterozygous Ss expression of piebald, while the latter is the homozygous SS. It has been commented that the Ragdoll is extraordinarily placid, becoming limp when cuddled, but it is doubtful if it is more so than any trusting cat.

Turkish

The Turkish (or Van) has extensive white spotting combined with orange and long hair. The basic genotype is $llOSS$. The coloured areas are confined mostly to the head, elsewhere only on occasion, with a coloured tail. These are orange, indicating the presence of O. An interesting variation is the cream Turkish of genotype $ddllOOSS$. Black and blue varieties, of genotype $aallSS$ and $aaddllSS$, respectively, are being contemplated.

Foreign White

Among the many varieties of foreign short-haired cats, the Foreign White deserves special mention. Apart from the fact that it is a beautiful cat, the breed was created by the application of genetic principles. The object was to produce a true-breeding blue-eyed white cat. This was accomplished by combining the Siamese allele c^s with the dominant white gene W. The coat is completely white due to the W gene and eyes are always blue due to the c^s allele. The eye colour may vary in intensity and the correct shade must be maintained by selective breeding. The genotype of the breed is c^sc^sWW. The other colours of foreign, as well as of oriental, are short-haired types produced by the usual combination of genes.

Snowshoe

These are rather pretty short-coated cats of Siamese pattern with white "gloves" to the feet. It might be thought that the gloves are produced by a minor white spotting but apparently this is not the case (Patricia Turner, personal communication). The gloves are produced by the heterozygous expression of the piebald gene S. The heterozygote Ss typically induces white toes but also small streaks of white on the face and stomach.

White

The completely white animal with orange, blue or odd eyes (one eye orange, the other blue), is due to the dominant gene W. The short-haired breed is $L–W$ and the long-haired is $llW–$. The gene is fully dominant, hence the presence of one gene is sufficient to create a solid white animal. The majority of whites are in fact heterozygotes (Ww), mainly it seems because of a propensity of breeders to cross the white to a black or blue, either to improve eye colour (in the case of the orange-eyed variety), coat quality or body type. There is no disadvantage in this; indeed in skilled hands, the results can be beneficial. The deep orange eye, so desired for the orange-eyed variety, will only be achieved or maintained by breeding from the better animals in this respect.

The blue- or odd-eyed white is engendered by one of the expressions of the W gene. In addition to producing the white coat, the gene also produces blue eyes. It does not do this in all animals (otherwise the orange-eyed variety would not exist) but in a fair proportion of cats. The completely blue-eyed form appears more frequently than the odd-eyed, as a rule. If a breeder prefers the blue-eyed variety, only matings between blue-eyed animals should be made. This is the only method by which the chances of breeding blue-eyed kittens can be maximized. However, the occurrence of either orange- or blue-eyed kittens is such a chancy business that the breeder has little control over the breeding at will of any particular eye colour. The mating of orange-eyed animals together can produce blue-eyed kittens and vice versa. The occurrence of the odd-eyed cat is even more a chance event and there is little prospect of these ever being bred to order.

The deafness associated with the blue-eyed variety is an expression of the W gene. Not all blue-eyed white cats are deaf nor do all orange-eyed white animals have normal hearing. The proportion of deaf animals is fairly low, but too high for any complacency in the opinion of many people. In a protected environment, deafness is not a major hazard although deaf queens can be indifferent mothers because they cannot respond to the piping of kittens. Most people object to the presence of deafness on ethical or aesthetic grounds because it distracts from the wholesomeness of the cat. The only practical method of counteracting the deafness is not to breed from detectable deaf individuals. The deafness will probably never be totally eradicated but attempts can be made to keep the incidence at a low level.

It is possible to create a true breeding strain of blue-eyed white cats by combining the c^s and W genes. The genotype $c^s c^s WW$ will be blue eyed due to c^s and white due to W. This animal has indeed been produced in the lithely built Foreign White. It is unfortunate that deafness may be a recurring problem. Much will depend in this connection upon the effectiveness of keeping the incidence at a low level.

The completely white coat should not be taken at its face value of an apparent absence of all other coat colour genes. This false idea occasionally finds expression in the belief that the mating of a white cat with a coloured will produce offspring of the same colour as that of the coloured parent. A few matings will soon show that the belief is untrue. In general, white cats may carry a variety of genes masked by the whiteness and unexpected results will occur. Sometimes close study of the parentage of a white cat can give a good idea of the genes which may be carried by the animal and the results which may be expected from various matings.

Long Hairs

It has been truly said that the Long-Haired cat is one of Nature's most beautiful creations. There is little doubt that the breed has been brought to a high level of perfection. The coat is due mainly to homozygosity of the long-hair gene. In the exhibition animal, the coat is long, full bodied and exquisitely soft, quite different from that of the mongrel long-haired cat. In these, the coat is usually not so long, less dense and coarse to the touch. These differences are due to modifying polygenes which are inherited independently of the l gene. This fact explains why the coat may differ in length or texture between breeds whose only kinship is that they have the l gene in common. The coat, of course, is the most important feature of the Long Hair and particular attention should be given to it in planning matings. The Long Hairs were formerly known as Persians and still are in the United States.

Any of the colours found in short-haired cats may be found in the Long Hair. There are subtle differences and these arise from the extra hair length. The tabby pattern, for example, is less well defined and less easily recognizable. This is not an important aspect for the experienced but could confuse the novice. The main factor to remember in long-haired cats is that the hairs overlap each other to a greater extent and not always regularly. A much greater length of the hair shaft is exposed and, since this is less intensely pigmented than the tip, this often produces a spurious reduction of colour. Breeders have countered this effect to some extent by selection for deep undercolour. This is most desirable for the black.

The black and the blue have the genotypes $aaB–D–ll$ and $aaB–ddll$, respectively. In the breeding of these, quality of coat, evenness and depth of colour and richness of eye colour are of prime importance. These characters are not necessarily of equal importance, as may be imagined, since this aspect will depend partly on the particular stock. The self brown or chocolate will have the genotype $aabbD–ll$ and the self lilac, $aabbddll$. Similar remarks to the above will apply to those colours. The Brown Tabby has the genotype $A–B–D–llt^b t^b$, or occasionally, $A–B–D–llT–$.

The Red Tabby ($D–llOt^b t^b$, male; $D–llOOt^b t^b$, female) should possess all of the qualities of the short-haired breed plus long coat. Similarly, for the tortoiseshell ($aaD–llOosst^b t^b$) and the tortoiseshell and white ($aaD–llOoS–t^b t^b$). The red self is of the same basic genotype as the Red Tabby except that the tabby pattern has been encouraged to spread into large patches of deep red. The long hair tends to blur the pattern but, in developing the variety, reliance should not be placed upon this. Nor should one rely upon the chance occurrence of heavily patterned individuals deriving from ordinary red tabbies. There should be deliberate selection for cats with extended blotched pattern where the whorls and spirals have joined to form patches of intense pigmentation. These animals are distinct from the ordinary blotched tabby and probably would be regarded as too heavily patterned but these should be eagerly sought after for self red breeding.

The Maine Coon and the Norwegian Forest cats are long-haired breeds with firm coats, lacking the fullness associated with the British long hairs. These are study cats of different conformation from the traditional long hair and, can occur in all of the usual colours. These cats developed in geographical isolation and are unrelated to each other.

Rex

The two established rex breeds are the Cornish and Devon rexes. These differ in body conformation and in the nature of the rex coat. The Cornish rex lacks the primary guard hairs but, in general, has the denser and more complete coat. The Devon rex coat possesses guard hairs but tends to have a thinner coat and is more prone to have bare areas, especially on the chest and stomach. This question of density of coat and the ability to retain the coat from one moult to the next are items which breeders would be wise to pay particular attention. A cat with a coat so thin that the skin is evident and/or with the bare areas is not a pretty sight, however affectionate or lively the animal may be. There is little doubt that these aspects are under polygenic control and every effort should be made to rectify matters. It is regrettable that the rex should have this propensity but there is hope in that not every cat is severely affected and selective breeding should be able to bring about an improvement.

Any of the colours known to occur in the normal furred cat may be found, or can be produced, in either of the rex breeds. It only requires patience and familiarity in manipulating the relevant genes. For example, the black or blue Cornish would have the genotypes $aaB-D-rr$ and $aaB-ddrr$, respectively. Again, the seal Devon Si-rex (Siamese rex) would have the constitution $aaB-c^sc^sD-rere$ or the white Devon rex, $rereW-$. These examples could be almost endlessly extended.

It has been decreed by the rex breed societies that the two rexes be kept separated and never be crossed. This is advisable policy since this avoids the confusion of normal coated kittens turning up when least expected. During the early days of the rex, a presumptive double rex (*rrere*) was bred, combining features of both rexes and having a soft, thin coat. Unfortunately, this finding requires confirmation.

Also during the initial development of the Cornish rex, the long haired rex (*llrr*) was produced. The coat was longer than normal, but not so long as the usual long haired, and very fine in texture. The whiskers were bent and curled, a sure sign of the presence of a rex gene. The phenotype is not particularly attractive and was not pursued.

Sphinx

The Sphinx is described as a hairless cat but this is not strictly true. The Sphinx kitten has a soft covering of hair which is subsequently lost. The adult animal may have a transitional covering of fine hair but this is also lost until the cat is permanently hairless except for a few thin hairs on various parts of the body. The whiskers are short and bent, rather similar to those of the rex. In fact, the similarity of Sphinx to the Devon rex induced breeders to intermate the two breeds, behaviour which led to the finding that the Sphinx loss of hair is dominant to the rex coat. Sphinx and Devon rex are now commonly bred together, each maintaining its own identity, at least for the Devon rex, since even Sphinx to Sphinx matings can produce rex coated kittens if they are heterozygotes.

American Curl

The American Curl is due to a dominant gene *Cu* which causes the external ear (pinna) to curve gently backwards. The pinnae are of normal appearance for the first 12 to 16 weeks of kittenhood but then begin to develop the curve, which is permanent. This gives the cat a rather alert appearance. There is variation in the degree of curvature and selection must be practised to arrive at the desired curve. The American Curl can be bred in any colour, together with long hair or rex coats. Large numbers of heterozygous curl *Cucu* have been produced, with no reported anomalies. At least one homozygous *CuCu* Curl has been examined, again with no obvious anomaly. However, although there is no reason to suspect that the homozygote will be defective in any way, it is wise to be cautious at this early stage in the development of the breed.

Scottish fold

This breed takes its name from the country in which it was found and from the fact that the apex of the ear pinna is bent forward. The ear fold is not present for the first four weeks or so of life but then the peak tilts forwards to become a permanent feature at about 12 weeks. The fold is produced by a dominant gene *Fd*. The only effect of the gene for the majority of heterozygotes *Fdfd* is the ear fold; otherwise they are healthy enough. Unfortunately for the popularity of the breed, the homozygote not only has the ear fold but also a crippling overgrowth of the cartilage of the bones. The bones of the tail become thickened, which might just be tolerable, but the bones of the legs become thickened, especially around the feet. Eventually, the cat cannot walk properly and suffers considerable discomfort.

To avoid the breeding of the homozygote, Scottish Fold should only be mated to normal-eared partners which have been bred from Scottish Fold. In this manner, the integrity of the breed is maintained but no anomalous homozygotes will be produced. It is disturbing, however, that a small proportion of heterozygotes do eventually develop the same crippling anomaly. The Fold may be found in any colour, pattern or coat type.

Manx

The Manx is one of the most well-known breeds, even by people who do not keep cats. It is bred in a number of colours, mostly the more common, as may be expected. However, it is patent that any of the known colours could be combined with the Manx gene *M*, if one is so willed.

The homozygote *MM* is a prenatal lethal and all Manx cats are necessarily heterozygotes *Mm*. This is no disadvantage provided one accepts that it is impossible to produce pure-breeding lines. It is unfortunate that the Manx is associated with various anomalies of the lower vertebrae and anal region. Even the stilted or stiff-legged gait is the result of pelvic defects. The various anomalies arise from the action of the *M* gene in causing the taillessness and are inescapable in Manx breeding. It is urged that only the most robust and healthy cats should be allowed to breed. Any obvious crippled kitten should be painlessly put to sleep. In other cases, do consult a veterinarian.

The long-haired Manx (*llMm*) has been produced in the USA under the name of "Cymric". Despite the appellation, the variety has no connection with Wales. Several different colours are known. The synthesis of either the Cornish rex (*Mmrr*) or Devon rex (*Mmrere*) Manx, in a variety of colours, should not present any special problems, should this ever be considered a worthwhile undertaking.

Japanese Bob-tail

There is a form of short tail occurring in Far Eastern cats which is different from Manx. The tail is shorter, rather than absent, and there are no overt signs of abnormality. A breed is being popularized in the USA under the name of "Japanese Bob-tail" which possesses the short tail as its primary characteristic. The tail length is variable but usually of about 3 to 5 inches long. It is often curved and rigid, not flexible. The fur on the tail is often bushier than that of the covering of a normal tail. There is an effort to restrict the known colours to non-agouti (*a*), orange (*O*) and spotting (*S*). Tricolour cats of high-grade spotting (*aaOoSS*) are particularly highly prized. These are individuals, mostly white, with patches of orange and black, either occurring as separate islands of colour or as islands composed of patches of colour with the minimum of brindling. It is believed that the short tail is inherited as an incompletely dominant trait.

7

Abnormalities

THE PROBLEM of the genetic anomaly is something which all breeders should be aware. This is not to suggest that such anomalies are common, far from it. Yet, on the other hand, the cat must be expected to have its quota of defects as in other fancy and domestic animals. The distressing aspect is that these anomalies will recur in subsequent litters and in subsequent generations if no remedial action is taken. In most cases, in direct defiance of improvements in husbandry, diet or veterinary practice.

To appreciate the problem of genetic defects, it is necessary to view the situation in perspective. Against a background of deficiency disease, bacterial or viral infection or straightforward injury, the true nature of a genetic abnormality could pass unrecognized. Indeed, an afflicted animal could be one of the first to succumb to a non-genetic ailment since many anomalies either lower the resistance of the individual or render it less able to compete with its fellows. Now, the deficiency disease can be prevented and veterinary safeguards erected against infection but what of the genetic defect? The occurrence of the anomaly is distressing enough but the real problem is its ability to recur in future litters of either direct or collateral descent.

The situation could perhaps be put more explicitly. Take a cattery in which the general housing conditions border on the lamentable, the food inadequate (as a result of ignorance probably more than anything else) and the conditions of hygiene indifferent, if not actually deplorable is it small wonder that disease always seems to be lurking around the corner. Imagine, on the other hand, a cattery in which the housing is palatial, the food adequate and nutritious, and the hygiene attended to with scrupulous care. Here, most of the common ailments will be abolished and serious disease almost unknown. Yet, the breeder may find himself bothered with troubles of another sort. Those which seem peculiar to the individual and cannot be ascribed to bad husbandry, poor diet or neglect. These are the sort of ailments which could be due to genetic causes. Put another way, though genetic anomalies will occur in both bad and well-maintained catteries, it is in the latter that they will be most noticeable.

Genetic anomalies are usually grouped under the general term of "lethals" in genetic texts. However, various types of lethal action should be recognized. Firstly, there are genes which cause death prior to birth; this is the classical lethal. No homozygous anomalous kittens are even seen. However, the heterozygote usually differs from normal and is usually abnormal. It is the inter-breeding of these that will lead to the discovery of the lethality. Such a case exists in the cat in the form of the Manx. Manx cats have a deformed pelvic and caudal region and are almost tailless. The mating of Manx *inter se* results in a 2 : 1 ratio of Manx type and normal kittens (Fig. 22). The homozygote *M M* probably dies *in utero* and is absorbed. This fact reveals itself in a reduction in average litter size as well as in the kitten ratio.

Secondly, there is the teratological lethal which produces monstrous young at birth. Quite often the "monster" is still-born as a result of various gross defects. In other cases, death usually ensues within a short period. Thirdly, there is the delayed lethal.

Gametes from Manx *Mm*

		M	m
Gametes from Manx *Mm*	M	MM Dies	Mm Manx
	m	Mm Manx	mm Normal

FIG. 23. Expectations from mating two Manx cats: to illustrate the 2 : 1 ratio of Manx: normal tailed offspring. The homozygote *MM* probably dies *in utero*.

Here, the animal is normal at birth but eventually dies of a late developing affliction. The onset may be delayed for months or even years. Fourthly, there is the semilethal or partial lethal. As the name implies, death is not an inevitable accompaniment but the individual is always either mildly or severely abnormal. These latter are responsible for a wide variety of mild defects. Thus, to summarize, not all congenital defects are of genetic origin although it is a fair assumption in most cases until the facts disclose otherwise. Conversely, not all late developing afflictions are necessarily due to the environment.

Several of the anomalies to be described in following sections fall into the category of semi-lethals. In some, the partial lethality is obvious, in others, it is not. Examples of the former are the hairless, ataxic, hare-lip and cleft-palate conditions, while examples of the latter are four-ears and urolithiasis. Even the Manx heterozygote cannot be depicted as one hundred per cent healthy since their pre-natal death rate is higher than that for cats with normal tails. The heterozygote, therefore, could be regarded as semi-lethal, regardless of the fate of the homozygote.

A frequent question is: "How are genetic anomalies discovered?" Or, to rephrase the wording, how can one be sure that an anomaly is inherited? It is true that most disorders occur in isolated events and this can give no indication of a genetic influence. However, suppose that the disorder shows a pattern, such as appearing in successive litters from the same parents or in different litters from parents which share a common ancestor. This is usually the first evidence that an anomaly has a genetic basis. The incidence is then said to be "familial". At this stage, it might be thought that it should be easy to obtain some idea of the mode of inheritance. Sometimes this is so, but, only too often among mongrel cats, the matings are uncontrolled and no information is available for the male parent; nor for remoter ancestors such as grandparents or great grandparents. Even when several cases of a particular anomaly occur in one neighbourhood, it is often next to impossible to connect these up in a common family tree.

With pedigree cats, the situation is different. Here, parentage is important, the matings are controlled and accurate records are usually available. It is among this group that anomalies with a familial tendency are likely to be discovered. Generally, the mode of inheritance will emerge according to the recognized laws of heredity. If necessary, special matings can be arranged to provide decisive data. In general, the mode of inheritance can be due either to a single gene (monogenic) or to the combined action of polygenes, possibly showing the threshold effect. If the inheritance is monogenic, it is essential to determine whether the anomaly is caused by a dominant or a recessive gene.

An effort has been made to include all instances of abnormality which are either known or suspected to have a genetic basis. There are two reasons why this policy seems desirable. The first is that veterinarians who are consulted for advice on how to treat the anomaly should be aware that the condition could be heritable. This may be helpful for cases where the advisability of breeding from the animal is sought. Secondly, knowledge that the anomaly could be inherited may encourage the collection of relevant data. Such information as is available at present is so scanty that additional data would be welcomed. Any anomaly which shows signs of being familial deserves to be energetically followed up. With this in mind, reference has been made to the pertinent research articles which treat the anomaly under discussion.

Elimination of Anomalies

Everyone is agreed that it is desirable to eliminate genetic anomalies. Yet, they appear to persist tenaciously. Why should this be so? The reason is two-fold: firstly, the problem can be more complex than appears on the surface and, secondly, the remedy may demand more drastic action than is acceptable. Somewhat different problems arise and different procedures should be followed according to the known or assumed mode of inheritance. That is, whether the anomaly displays (1) dominant, (2) recessive monogenic heredity or (3) polygenic heredity.

With dominant monogenic heredity, there is no problem when the disorder is readily apparent or is regularly manifested. However, this is not always the situation. For example, the affliction may not be evident until late in life. Until after puberty and the animal has been breeding for some time. This latter aspect can only be tackled by means of clinical analysis designed for early diagnosis of onset of the disease. Also of course, the conscientious seeking and taking notice of such clinical reports. It is silly to ignore a positive report simply because an outstanding cat is apparently healthy. Eventually, it will not be and, meantime, the genetic damage it can do is considerable. The case of irregular manifestation is similar except that clinical diagnosis is excluded. Bodily, the animal is fully healthy and detection is probably best handled by the same methods as recommended for that of finding carriers of a recessive anomaly.

Theoretically, all dominant monogenic anomalies could be eliminated if all of the descendants of subsequently afflicted animals are prevented from breeding. This would be drastic action indeed when it is considered that about fifty per cent of the animal's descendants will be free of the anomaly. Unfortunately, the price to be paid is that the other fifty per cent will be handing on the anomaly until they are eventually detected. Fortunately, it is possible that the cat is not troubled with this sort of anomaly. It is to be hoped that this will always be so but, alas, this cannot be taken for granted. For instance, progressive retinal atrophy is a late developing genetic disease of the eye in the dog. In a few breeds, the disease is troublesome and the main factor for this is that the young dog can see perfectly but eventually becomes partially or totally blind. The late onset of the affliction means that the animal may have bred before the first symptoms are noticed. A similar disease could occur in the cat.

With recessive monogenic heredity, the problem is that of detection of the heterozygote or "carrier". It is not a question of clinical detection since these animals are fully normal. Their detection lies in another direction: that of test mating. This may be accomplished in one of two ways. If the anomaly is slight (undesirable, say, but not crippling) and does not interfere with reproduction, the animal to be tested can be mated to one or more affected animals. Provided sufficient normal kittens are produced, without the appearance of a *single* anomalous individual, the animal may be judged not to be a carrier. The number of kittens to be bred in each test will depend upon the level of acceptable error. It may be that a carrier animal could produce entirely normal young by chance. However, the chances of such an event become smaller as the number of kittens increases. This is, the error which must be made acceptably low by stipulating that a certain number of young be bred. Column A of the accompanying table gives the error for successive normal kittens examined. Two acceptable levels are 5 per cent (5 kittens or more) and 1 per cent (7 kittens). The latter is preferable to the former and there is a strong case for making if mandatory.

When the anomaly is severe, breeding from such individual may be either unethical or impracticable. A different procedure should be followed. This consists of mating the animal to be tested with known carriers. Again, the matter of acceptable error must be decided. Since this procedure is more roundabout, the number of kittens required must be increased. Column B of the table shows the error for successive normal kittens examined. The two levels of 5 per cent and 1 per cent require the rearing of 11 and 17 kittens, respectively. It should be apparent that the kittens produced by these test matings should not ordinarily be used or sold for breeding since all of them will be carriers in the first method of testing and 50 per cent at least in the second.

Now, for various reasons, it may not be convenient to keep known carriers, yet it may be felt desirable to test certain animals. This still can be done by a method which is practicable for males. The procedure is to mate the male to a number of his daughters (which need not necessarily be from the same mother). The error involved here is a two stage affair, (1) that of not mating the male to a carrier daughter (only half of the daughters will be expected to receive the suspected recessive gene) and (2) that of not breeding at least one anomalous kitten. To calculate the error, it is necessary firstly to find the value for each daughter according to the number of kittens she has produced. This is shown by column C of the table. Then the error for the male is derived by multiplying each of these values together. Thus, suppose it had been possible to mate a male with four daughters and the various litters result in totals of 3, 5, 6 and 7 young per daughter. The values of C from the table are 71, 62, 59 and 57, respectively. The error for the male, therefore, is the product of these, namely, 15 per cent. For totals of this average size, it would require 7 daughters to reduce the error to below the 5 per cent level.

This last test is often the one carried out in practice. In terms of numbers of kittens required to attain a certain minimum error, the test does not compare in efficiency with the two described earlier. However, it has an advantage not possessed by these, namely, that the test would reveal *any* recessive anomaly carried by the male, not one in particular. This fact gives the test an added appeal. It may be objected that the test could not be performed by a small breeder or possibly not repeatedly by medium or large breeders. In this case, it might be advisable for several breeders to band together and form a breeders' cooperative as far as testing-mating of outstanding males is concerned. If this is not practicable, a breed society could take matters in hand and arrange a scheme of test mating. Certified males should commend (and deserve) increased stud fees. Adequate means of independent assessment would have to be devised to avoid deceit and to assure the correct operation of the scheme.

In practice, it is rarely possible to test mate females. This is unimportant if a male can be properly tested and pronounced free of genetic anomaly. No matter how many carrier queens he may mate, none of the offspring will be anomalous. Some of the carrier queens will produce carrier offspring but this cannot be avoided. It means, however, that stud males must be test mated in each generation before being passed into general service. This testing will have to be continued until such time as the breed is judged to be free of the anomaly. It is difficult to be certain how many generations will be required. In part, it will depend upon the prevalence of the anomaly before the test mating was instigated.

The values in the table are for recessive genes whose occurrence are up to expectation. Not all anomalies behave in this manner. Some so weaken the individual that they die before (for example, *in utero*) they can be recorded. Also, certain individuals may have the gene for an anomaly yet fail to show it. In these circumstances, the values of the table are too optimistic. There are methods of tackling this complication but they are beyond the scope of this book. Whenever such a situation is encountered, or even suspected, the remedy is to either lower the level of acceptable error or to breed several more kittens than would otherwise be necessary.

The situation may arise that none of the above techniques of test mating can be carried out. In this event, the elimination will have to rely upon selective culling. All affected animals should be banished from the breeding pen, together with their parents and sibs as far as this is consistent with the overall breeding plan. Familial selection is more efficient than individual selection. The appearance of a single affected kitten means that each parent is a heterozygote and two-thirds of the sibs will be potential heterozygotes. These are the facts to be borne in mind in coming to a decision whether or not to test mate or how ruthlessly to cull.

TABLE 15. NUMBER OF KITTENS REQUIRED TO REDUCE THE ERROR PERCENTAGE
TO BELOW A CERTAIN VALUE
(e.g. below the 5 or 1 per cent)

No. of kittens	A	B	C
1	50	75	88
2	25	56	78
3	12·5	42	71
4	6·3	32	66
5	3·1	24	62
6	1·5	18	59
7	0·8	13	57
8	0·4	10	55
9	0·2	7·5	54
10	0·1	5·6	53
11	—	4·2	52
12	—	3·2	52
13	—	2·4	51
14	—	1·8	51
15	—	1·3	51
16	—	1·0	51
17	—	0·7	50
18	—	0·6	50
19	—	0·4	50
20	—	0·3	50

With polygenic heredity, the problem is that of detecting those animals which have a high propensity to produce anomalous kittens. Test mating is ruled out in any simple sense and even the determination of a high propensity for an individual means being wise after the event. If action is taken, it means being drastic because all of the healthy offspring will be potential "high producers", however excellent they may be in other respects. It is a question of balancing the quality of the individual offspring against the chances of passing on the anomaly.

There are two main types of anomaly with polygenic heredity. The first is that where the severity of the anomaly is variable and the severity is determined by polygenes. This implies that culling of the most affected animals will bring about a gradual improvement. The extent of the improvement and the rate at which it occurs will depend upon the level of culling. In general, the more ruthless the culling, the greater the relative improvement. There are various complicating factors, of course, of which the most important is that certain of the mildly affected animals (which are not culled) will be capable of producing severely affected offspring. Against this will be the fact that the average level of severity should decline per generation of selection.

The second type of polygenic trait is where the anomaly is due to a threshold effect. Despite the underlying polygenic inheritance, there is no real inter-grading as formerly, the animals are either normal or abnormal. The degree of abnormality may vary and this may be polygenically determined but the normals are, to all intents, fully normal in appearance. Test mating cannot be easily performed and the only remedy is that of selective culling of abnormals and, as far as practical, all those individuals with a high propensity to produce affected kittens.

To be really effective, the amount of selective culling should be ruthless. Ideally, once an anomaly has been assessed as genetic, no further young should be bred from either parent, none of the sibs should be used for breeding (regardless of their apparent healthiness or excellence), and the culling should extend into their immediate collateral relatives. In other words, a clean sweep is necessary. Doubtless, this is counsel of perfection and intolerably drastic. However, if the culling is less than this, a price must be paid in terms of breeding a small proportion of affected animals in future generations.

Persistence of Anomalies

It may be wondered how the odd genetic anomaly apparently persists in spite of everyone being on record as "agin" them and patient selection being the art of cat breeding. The answer must be sought among a variety of causes, several of which may combine to reinforce one another. Genes producing anomalies cannot multiply throughout a breed of their own volition but they are "opportunist" to the extreme in the sense that given favourable circumstances, they can spread surprisingly.

A major factor in the spread of an anomaly is a relaxation of culling. This can come about should a breed become exceptionally popular. Breeding stock is scarce and demand for kittens is high. The temptation is to breed from every animal, even from those which would normally be discarded. This means that inferior animals can pass on their inferior qualities, even if an effort is made to secure the services of a good sire. The practice of selling unneutered kittens to people who promise not to breed from them is scarcely sound long-term policy and it may suddenly short-circuit in present circumstances. Under pressure, the promise may be conveniently forgotten.

Instances are known (specially in animals other than the cat) where a much admired and widely used stud animal has subsequently been found to be a carrier of a recessive anomaly. This was unknown at the time of course, but becomes only too apparent after his offspring have multiplied and spread throughout the breed. Inter-breeding (not necessarily close inbreeding) will ultimately bring into being a rash of occurrences of the same anomaly. Breeders may suddenly find themselves confronted with the twin problems of preserving the reputation of the breed and of eliminating the gene causing the anomaly. It may be objected that this event must be uncommon. True, but this process is often behind the so-called mutant "epidemics".

A feature of this event is that the appearance of the first anomaly is usually delayed for several generations from the ancestral point of origin and that many years of effort is required to either eliminate the anomaly or to reduce it to such a low level that it is no longer a nuisance. Chance plays a major role in determining the type of defect which could be unwittingly spread in this manner, and the breed in which the process occurred. On the other hand, it may occur in any breed and at any time. The moral is perhaps not to place too much reliance upon one or a few exemplary sires. The process is usually mediated via the male since the female cannot produce enough offspring to influence the course of events.

Even in more normal periods of breeding where supply of kittens is roughly geared to demand, a particular defect may seem to strangely persist. Two possibilities may account for this. One is that the amount of culling may be reduced to a minimum because of a deliberate policy of not breeding more kittens than necessary to cover replacements and sales. The other is that of heterosis or hybrid vigour. Generalizing, there is a correlation between healthy vigour and the amount of genetic heterozygosity. It may be that when the amount of heterozygosity falls below a certain level, so-called "inbreeding depression" sets in. These animals appear sickly and "bad doers" and are culled. However, their more robust but heterozygous sibs are retained. Included among these may be carriers of a recessive anomaly; not because of the fact that they are carriers but because of their relatively high heterozygosity. Of course, should the gene producing the anomaly be associated with extra vigour when heterozygous (which is possible but not always likely), a ready answer is available for the persistence or even spread of the gene responsible.

A similar situation may arise in those circumstances where a breed standard encourages the breeding of a certain type of defective animal. The rise of the defect is inadvertent, of course, and quite rightly it is condemned. Yet the defect recurs because breeders are endeavouring to conform to the standard. A conflict situation may even come into being; as the breed moves closer to the standard, the incidence or severity of the defect may become greater. It has been suggested, for example, that the sinus ailment and running eyes of some long hairs is a consequence of selective breeding for a short nose.

Despite an avoidance of close inbreeding, many breeds of cats are inter-bred to some extent. Indeed it cannot be avoided if the breed is to be composed of a homogeneous group of animals of recognized breed conformation. In this sense, it is desirable. On the other hand, interbreeding is more conducive to bringing out the latent anomalies in comparison with a truly random breeding population. Therefore, while anomalies are likely to appear in both pure-bred and mongrel cats, their presence is more likely to be discovered in the former.

It is extremely unwise to breed from animals with inherited defects which have been surgically corrected. Even if the defect is relatively minor, it could reappear in later generations in an aggravated form. This aspect is probably diminishing in importance as it becomes more widely appreciated that, while such surgical intervention may be desirable for the individual cat, the genes for the defect are still transmitted in the gametes, surgery or no surgery.

Achondroplastic Dwarfism

A short-legged condition is regarded by Schwangart and Grau (1931) as being inherited. No details are given for the mode of inheritance. This is unfortunate for such conditions are known to be inherited in a variety of domestic animals and, if the cat is to be numbered among these, it would be desirable to have precise information. As a general statement, of course, this sort of deformity could easily be genetic in origin.

Amyloidosis

Amyloidosis is a disease in which an amyloid substance is deposited in many organs of the body, including the kidneys in which it is especially detrimental. The symptoms are listlessness, bedraggled coat, loss of weight and appetite, accompanied by excessive thirst and urination. The overall incidence of the ailment is rare but was relatively high in a strain of Abyssinians. DiBartola *et al.* (1986) found evidence of a familial propensity in the breed but were not able to determine the mode of inheritance.

Bent and Short Tails

Many cases of nodulated, kinked, bent or loss of the terminal portion of the tail are known to occur. In the majority, the defect is traceable to injury, possibly at parturition or at a later stage. Occasionally, however, the defect may occur in individuals of one particular strain or in blood lines. When this occurs, the likelihood of a genetic influence should be envisaged.

A form of partial tail loss is not uncommon in certain strains of Siamese. It has been thought for some time that the condition could be inherited although exactly how is unknown. However, Moutschen (1950) claims to have found that a shortened tail, observed in a strain of Siamese, is inherited as a simple recessive. There was variation in length for the affected animals but the tail was regularly shorter than normal. The gene is symbolised by *br* from brachyury (= "short tail").

In other strains, there may be little or no shortening of the tail. Instead, there are kinks or swellings such as would arise from a fusion of adjacent vertebrae. It is a debatable question whether these are an aspect of the same genetic situation which underlies the tail shortening or if an entirely different situation should be assumed. In the absence of critical experiments designed to probe this question, it is almost impossible to offer a worthwhile answer. The simpler explanation is that these are variable manifestations of the same genetic entity, the difference in expression being due to strain background. On the other hand, several different genetic tail anomalies may exist in the cat. At present, the only clue pointing in this direction would be differences of expression.

In most, and very probably in all, strains of exhibition-bred Siamese, there has been selection against deformed tails. The effect of this selection has been to reduce the frequency of occurrence and to alleviate the severity. Shortening of the tail is now rare but, not infrequently, the tail may be slightly kinked or firm nodules may be felt by palpation. When the manifestation of the deformity is slight it is conceivable that some impenetrance may occur. This could imply (1) that the descent of the deformity could be irregular and make accurate determination of the defect difficult, if not impossible, and (2) hamper elimination of the defect by means of simple culling of all affected animals.

The Japanese Bob-tail would seem to be an instance where a tail-shortening gene has been utilized to form the basis of a breed. The short tail may be viewed as a deformity but presumably of a minor character since the general health is not affected. Some preliminary breeding data imply that the trait is inherited monogenically, possibly as an incomplete dominant, since first-cross offspring from mating with normal tail cats have a twisted tail which falls short of being a true bob-tail.

Bite

Bite is a term used to denote the correct alignment of the teeth and is an important feature of the exhibition cat. More specifically, the term refers to the meeting of the upper and lower teeth, such that those of the upper jaw are in front of those of the lower (overshot) or are behind those of the lower (undershot) when the mouth is closed. Several grades of bite may be considered. The definite overshot is where a gap may be seen between the two sets of teeth—otherwise known as parrot mouth. When the upper teeth are immediate in front of the lower, with no gap, the bite is the scissor. When the teeth meet exactly edge to edge, the bite is said to be level or pincer. The reverse scissor is where the lower teeth are immediately in front of the upper, with no gap. When a gap is evident, the bite is truly undershot.

These differences arise from the relative lengths of the upper and lower jaws, and this pattern is due in part to accidents of growth and in part to genetic control of the growth processes. The genetic component of jaw formation is polygenic and is part of the overall growth of the skull. Nevertheless, there is sufficient genetic variation of the jaws for selection to influence the type of bite. Achievement of the perfect bite is a matter of careful selective breeding.

Incidentally, the jaw bones are subject to variation, apart from determining bite. It is not uncommon for the lower jaw to be slightly screwed or even twisted, or the jaw may be narrower than normal. Some of the variation is probably non-genetic but it is wise to assume for breeding purposes that it is genetic and to act accordingly.

Cardiac Stenosis

Clifford *et al.* (1971) refer to a congenital achasia of the aesophagus which appears to have a genetic basis. Affected kittens have difficulty in retaining food after weaning. There is intermittent vomiting and unproductive retching. Previous to the cardiac stenosis, the aesophagus is usually dilated. A recessive mode of inheritance is suggested by the breeding data but these are insufficient for this to be definitely established. Growth of the cat is severally retarded and there is some emaciation. Death may occur from a variety of causes.

Cataract

Rubin (1986) has described an inherited cataract in the Himalayan (Colourprint) breed. The cataract occurred in both eyes and was extensive when affected individuals were ophthalmologically examined at 12 weeks of age. The breeding data were scanty but suggestive of recessive monogenic heredity.

Chediak–Higashi syndrome

The most obvious feature of the syndrome is a lightening of the coat to produce a bluish colour. The iris tends to be yellow-green while the "eye-shine" is reddish instead of bright yellowish green. This is due to a marked reduction or absence of pigmentation of the tapetum. Photophobia is common in some individuals. The bleeding time is prolonged, even following minor surgery, and small haematomas may form in tissues. There is misrouting of optic ganglian in a similar manner to that described for Siamese and albino animals (Kramer *et al.*, 1977; Collier *et al.*, 1979; Prieur *et al.*, 1979, 1981a,b; Creel *et al.*, 1982a). The syndrome is inherited in a recessive manner and symbolized by *ch*.

Corneal mummification

Vawer (1981) has intimated that a corneal mummification which recurred in adult individuals of the Colourpoint breed could be inherited. The affected eye shows signs of a dark area in the cornea which was accompanied by chronic inflammation and ulceration. No breeding data were presented but it was stated that examination of relevant pedigrees revealed extensive inbreeding with common ancestors in both the maternal and paternal lines. This latter would follow from the inbreeding. These observations would certainly be indicative of a genetic predisposition but without necessarily revealing the mode of inheritance, in spite of Vawer's proposal that the condition is caused by a recessive gene.

Corneal oedema

An apparently inherited corneal oedema has been reported by Bistner *et al.* (1976). Fluid accumulates in the layers of the cornea to produce a haziness or cloudiness in the eyes of cats at about four months of age. The condition is progressive and leads to breakdown of corneal tissue, followed by bacterial infection. The condition is familial, possibly monogenic, but the exact mode of heredity could not be determined.

Cryptorchidism

A few people have surmised that the failure of either both testes to descend properly (bilateral cryptorchidism) or merely one (unilateral cryptorchidism; strictly, monorchidism is terminologically incorrect) could be genetically determined. Unfortunately, there is no evidence one way or the other. Perhaps this statement is not quite true, for there are rumours that certain breeds are more prone to the affliction than others. However, reliable data to support the rumours are scanty;

although such evidence could build up a preliminary case for genetic determination. Bilateral cryptorchidism can be a real misfortune since such animals are usually infertile. Unilateral cryptorchids are usually fertile but there should be great hesitation in placing these at stud.

The likelihood that cryptorchidism could have a genetic basis introduces an intriguing principle of causation. The defect is the outcome of failure of the testes to pass through the inguinal canal into the scrotum and, therefore, is a condition at least once removed from the primary cause. The inguinal canal may be imperfectly formed or not large enough to allow the passage of the testes or there may be a maladjustment of development, so that the testes are not ready to descend at the appropriate time. These are the factors which would be genetically determined, rather than the phenomenon of cryptorchidism. A thorough study would require a post mortem examination of all affected individuals and probably of the testes in normal brothers to ascertain if they are truly normal.

It may be wondered if there is a practical reason for distinguishing between the primary and secondary factors. There is, the reason is that while the primary defect may be present in every affected individual, the secondary defect (here, the cryptorchidism) may not be shown by every individual. Spuriously normal animals could have the primary defect and yet appear intact because testes descent had not been interfered with. The fact that the cryptorchidism can be unilateral could be an indication that something of this nature could be occurring. The cryptorchidism, therefore, would show impenetrance and anyone who was studying the heredity of the defect without recourse to autopsy would find the task more complicated. If such animals do exist, they would doubtless be used for breeding in the belief that they were perfectly normal. This is one means by which the anomaly could be passed on to future generations.

However, the main factor in the persistence of the defect is that cryptorchidism is an example of sex-limited inheritance. Only the male can have undescended testes. Whether, or not, the female may show a comparable primary defect to that presumed to occur in the male is something yet to be discovered. Externally, the female is normal although she may carry the propensity for cryptorchidism and be fully capable of transmitting the condition to her sons. In this respect, the carrier female is as big a menace as the unilateral cryptorchid. If a policy of selective culling is in progress, it would be wise to be wary of the apparently normal brothers and sisters of affected individuals. Other factors being equal, the sensible course would be to eliminate these.

Curl

A feature of the American Curl breed is the remarkable backward curve of the ear pinnae. However, although the ear shape is anomalous in the sense of being a departure from normality, it may be regarded as minor. The condition is due to a dominant gene Cu and a large number of heterozygotes have been bred which have shown no signs of other anomaly. Only the homozygote $CuCu$ may possibly turn out to possess undesirable defects but, at the time of writing, nothing of this nature has emerged (Robinson, 1989).

Cutaneous asthenia

The skin is excessively hyperextensile or loose, enabling folds of skin to be held away from the body. The skin is also fragile which results in lacerations and wounds from accidents and fighting. Even simple scratching by the animal can produce multiple laceration. The condition is due to defects in the collagen packing of both fibrils and fibres in the reticular layer of the dermis which determines the tensile strength of the skin. Breeding experiments have indicated that the anomaly is inherited in a dominant manner (Patterson and Minor, 1977). The causative gene may be symbolized by Cut.

Deafness

It is well known that white cats may be deaf but the association is not complete. Among a group of 240 white cats in which blue eye colour and deafness was recorded, 39 per cent had blue eyes and were deaf, 29 per cent were blue eyed with normal hearing, 7 per cent were yellow eyed and deaf, while 25 were yellow eyed with normal hearing. The association is clearly evident. In an independent study, the connection manifested as an association between blue eyes and deafness for either the same right or same left side of the head. However, it should be noted that individuals with yellow eyes can be deaf.

The genetic explanation for the association is that the W gene has several effects, of which only the white coat is constant. The gene also produces blue iris colour and deafness in 60 to 70 per cent and in 40 to 50 per cent, respectively, of cats. The eyes of white cats with orange or yellow irises are normally pigmented but those with blue irises had deficiencies. The tapetum may be regularly absent (Thibos et al., 1980).

Numerous studies have been carried out on the cause of the deafness. These have revealed that the onset of deafness is gradual and is due to degeneration of the organs of Corti and the spiral ganglion neurons. However, there is wide variation of time of onset and the extent to which the hearing structures are affected (Bosher and Hallpike, 1965; Mair and Elverland, 1977; Pujol et al., 1977; Elverland and Mair, 1980; Thibos et al., 1980; Rebillard et al., 1981a, 1981b).

Epibular dermoids

Fifteen cases of a similar epibular dermoid growth have been described in an inbred group of Birman kittens by Hendy-Ibbs (1985). The dermoids were hairy, pigmented and attached to the conjunctiva at the corner of the eye. In each case, the dermoid was unilateral and developed in the lateral corner of either the left or right eye. The dermoid hairs tended to be an irritant and gave rise to an early keratitis. Removal of the dermoid gave complete relief. From the similarity between cases and because the affected cats were related (some closely), a genetic predisposition may be assumed. The mode of inheritance could not be determined but it was speculated that the condition could be due to threshold heredity.

"Episodic weakness"

This is an abnormal behaviour pattern which manifested between four and 10 months of age, with an average of 7.4 months. Both sexes may be affected. The cat may appear normal until the attack is precipitated by various factors, such as excitement or mildly stressful situations. The head is held characteristically close to the chest when walking or at rest. When walking, the head position nods up and down, the fore legs are stiff, straight and high stepping, and the hind legs flex normally but are held more widespread. Afflicted individuals can only walk for short distances and if forced to jump cannot land properly. Pupil dilation and claw extension were seen. The condition was observed in the Burmese breed and was shown to be inherited recessively (Mason, 1988). The gene may be provisionally symbolized by *ew* until a precise cause of the condition has been ascertained.

Flat-chested kitten syndrome

The chest of afflicted young kittens appears compressed—"flat chested"—instead of being nicely rounded. Depending on the degree of compression, the kitten may show signs of breathing difficulties, distress and poor growth. Autopsy findings have revealed more or less severe dislocation of internal organs which can cause early death. On the other hand, kittens which are mildly affected can recover and appear to have normal chests. In the Burmese breed, there is good evidence that the condition is inherited in a recessive manner and the gene may be provisionally symbolized by *fck* (Robinson, unpublished observations).

Folded-ears

The ears of the normal cat are carried in a "pricked" position. The ears of the folded-eared animal, however, are bent forward in a characteristic manner. At birth, and until about 4 weeks of age, the ears appear to be normal. From 4 weeks, the tip of the ear tends to turn inwards and the fold is fully formed by approximately 3 months. When fully developed, the apexes of both ears are folded forward. The condition is inherited as an incomplete dominant (symbol *Fd*). The folded ear is a characteristic of the heterozygote *Fdfd*. Except for the ear tip, the majority of these animals are healthy but a few suffer from the same anomaly which besets the homozygote. The homozygote *FdFd* has the folded ear but it also afflicted with a crippling epiphyseal dysplasia which results in a short, thickened tail, swollen feet and a marked disinclination to indulge in normal activity (Jackson, 1975).

Four-ears

A curious head anomaly is described by Little (1957). It is termed "four-ears" because of the presence of a small extra pair of "ears" in affected animals. The eyes are reduced in size and the jaw is slightly undershot. In all, the head is said to be of a peculiar shape. Growth and size do not appear to be abnormal but the animal seems to be relatively inactive and lethargic. This latter could imply that the functioning of the brain is affected. The condition is inherited as a recessive and the responsible gene is symbolized by *dp*. The data show a deficiency of four-ears which implies that the gene could be a semi-lethal.

Gangliosidosis GM1

This is a degenerative disease of the brain and spinal cord. The clinical symptoms are a fine tremor of the head and hind limbs at about two to three months of age. This increases in severity until the cat cannot stand by some seven to eight months, followed by seizures by one year. Affected animals may suffer some loss of vision. The disease is due to an enzyme deficiency. Although the malady behaves as a recessive in heredity (symbol *ga-1*), noted that it must be the enzyme deficiency can be detected in heterozygotes should the need for an erradication programme arise (Baker *et al.*, 1971; Murray *et al.*, 1977).

Gangliosidosis GM2

This is another degenerative disease affecting the nervous system. A fine tremor of the head may be noticed at about six to ten weeks of age, and this progresses to ataxia and falling. The head has an unusual rounded appearance while the cornea of the eye is slightly opaque. The disease is inherited recessively (symbol *ga-2*) and is produced by an enzyme deficiency which may be detected in heterozygotes should the need arise for carriers to be identified (Cork, *et al.*, 1977, 1978).

Globoid leukodystrophy

Afflicted kittens show a tremor, weakness and lack of coordination of the back legs at about five to six weeks of age. Later, the condition becomes worse, the clumsy behaviour spreading to the front legs. The cause is due to degerative changes in the brain. The malady was shown to be familial but the data were too meagre to do more than hint at recessive heredity (Johnson, 1970).

Haemophilia A

This is the most well known of the "bleeding diseases"—protracted bleeding following injury and surgery. Haematomas are common at the joints or under the skin. The gene (*Hma*) is carried on the X chromosome and healthy, but carrier, queens transmit the gene to their sons, regardless of the male to which they may be mated. Haemophiliac males have heightened mortality but they can survive if the bleeding is of a mild character and if they are kept in a sheltered environment (Cotter *et al.*, 1978; Littlewood, 1986).

Haemophilia B

This is another bleeding disease following injury and surgery which is very similar to that described above. The gene (*Hmb*) is borne on the X chromosome and is transmitted to sons by carrier queens. The bleeding is prolonged but is somewhat milder than usually found for haemophilia A (Dodds, 1981).

Hageman factor deficiency

Deficiency of one of the factors involved in blood clotting can result in a bleeding disease, but it is unusual for the malady to result in prolonged bleeding. The deficiency is inherited as an incompletely dominant trait, with the symbol *Hag* for the mutant gene (Kier *et al.*, 1980).

Hairlessness

Every so often an account of a hairless cat appears in the literature. These odd, if not bizarre, looking creatures cannot avoid attracting attention, for the condition is rarely lethal. The loss of hair is not usually total. More often than not, various parts of the body may be nude while the remainder (e.g. muzzle, feet) is covered by fine down or fuzzy hair. Quite often the condition worsens with age, the fine covering of the young adult giving way to bare wrinkled skin and complete hairlessness over much of the body. This progressive loss usually distinguishes the true hairless animal from a temporary loss which may be due to a variety of factors. No improvement of feeding or nursing can produce a normal coat on the true hairless cat.

Hairless individuals may turn up spontaneously in any part of the world. Reports have come in as far apart as Australia, Canada, France and Morocco. There is even a description of a "Mexican hairless cat", given as if these curious animals were a breed in their own right. Anyone, of course, is at liberty to take this view since the condition is presumably inherited.

Three of the hairless conditions have been investigated, those occurring in France (Letard, 1938), Canada (Robinson, 1973) and England (Robinson, 1981; Hendy-Ibbs, 1984). In each case, it was evident that the hypotrichosis was due to a recessive gene (symbolized by *h*, *hr* and *hd*, respectively. The Canadian hairless is currently being bred under the name of "Sphinx." It is difficult to ascertain if the same or different mutant alleles are producing the various hairless conditions, mainly because the alleles are being expressed against different genetic backgrounds. However, Hendy-Ibbs is of the opinion that the various hairless conditions can be explained in terms of two distinct alleles, on the basis of absence or presence of short and curled vibrissae. There are breeding data to suggest that the *hr* gene is either closely linked to, or is an allele of, the Devon rex gene *re*.

It is a disputable point whether hairless cats should be kept. The lack of hair could mean that they will suffer from debilitating heat loss during cold weather. It would seem humane to have them destroyed at an early age. However, if this seems unnecessarily heartless, they should certainly be kept in a warm environment and be provided with a knitted woollen "over-coat" in very cold spells.

Rex cats have a tendency to lose their fur, sometimes in the form of a premature moult or sometimes more permanently in old individuals. This may be represented as a hairless condition, although it is not a true independent loss of hair. The condition is part of the rex syndrome, for the rex coat itself is anomalous. The guard hairs are abortive and the down hairs are thin. In some animals, the anomaly is possibly intensified to cause a deficiency of the down hairs or to produce a baldness where the thin hairs either break off or are pulled from a weakly gripping hair follicle by the habitual incessant grooming of the cat. The Devon rex is the more prone of the two English rexes to baldness and the reason seems to be that the Devon rex hair fibres are particularly fragile. The loss of hair in the rex is termed baldness to distinguish it from the hairless condition due to the *h* gene.

Hare-lip and Cleft-palate

These two often associated anomalies are mentioned by Schwangart and Grau (1931) as being probably inherited. The basis for this statement seems to be that of a female cat with a slight hare-lip which produced kittens with a similar defect. One kitten was undersized and possessed a cleft-palate. The animals' ability to suckle was impaired and it eventually died. This information is interesting but scarcely sufficient in itself to more than hint at a genetic basis. As an isolated observation, little more can be expected but if a number of such familial associations are reported, perhaps a more positive conclusion can be reached.

Hydrocephalus

Hydrocephalus is a morbid condition associated with a swelled oedamatous head region, often with other defects. Such animals occur at odd intervals, usually as a result of development mishaps. However, such conditions can be inherited and a case has been reported for the cat (Silson and Robinson, 1969). The breeding evidence indicates that a single recessive gene is involved. The mutant gene has been symbolized by *hy*.

The abnormality is readily identifiable at birth. The affected kitten is always very large and bloated in appearance around the head and limbs. It may also have various degrees of hare-lip, cleft-palate or talipes. However, it is uncertain if these abnormalities are strictly a part of the hydrocephalus condition.

Hyperoxaluria

Cats with this disease succumb to acute renal failure at between five and nine months of age. They become anorexic, dehydrated and exceedingly weak, death occurring within a few days. Palpation of the stomach reveals painful kidneys. Kidney failure is due to the disposition of oxalate crystals in the tubules. The condition was shown to be inherited in a recessive manner (McKerrell *et al.*, 1989). The gene is symbolized by *ho*.

Hyperchylomicronaemia

Although growth is more or less normal, affected kittens show a persistent lipaemia—excess of fatty substances in the blood. At approximately eight to nine months of age, an inability to move the eyelids, chew food properly and to extend the toes, makes an appearance, together with loss of the patella reflex. Clinically, the occurrence of multiple haematomas appears to compress the peripheral nerves, resulting in loss of sensation. The malady is inherited recessively and is symbolized by *hce* (Jones *et al.*, 1986a, b).

"Kangaroo" Cat

A number of extraordinary animals are described by William-Jones (1944). These possessed unusually short front legs but otherwise appear to be normal. The gait of these creatures tends to resemble that of a ferret in their smooth but hunched-up movements. When induced to sit back, the posture is that, if anything, of a miniature kangaroo. The peculiarity is said to be inherited in that affected animals are observed in at least four litters. Unfortunately, precise details are lacking which might have established the mode of inheritance. This curiosity has occurred at least twice in widely separated localities, hence it is possible that it may turn up again.

Mannosidosis

The majority of affected kittens with this disease are either stillborn or die at birth. For those which survive, the initial signs develop during the first few days or weeks as a general apathy and diarrhoea, followed by tremor and ataxic behaviour. The individual appears unable to stand properly. The voice becomes weaker and the stomach appears swollen due to an enlarged liver. The anomaly is induced by an enzyme deficiency which adversely affects the central nervous system (Vandevelde *et al.*, (1982). The anomaly manifests recessive inheritance (symbol *man*).

Manx Taillessness

It has been known for some time that Manx taillessness is inherited as a dominant trait, with the symbol *M*. This has been confirmed and, what is more important, the accumulation of breeding data has shown that individuals homozygous for the Manx gene die prior to birth. The evidence for this is: (1) an apparent absence of pure-breeding strains of Manx and (2) a decrease of the average number of young per litter for matings of Manx to Manx. The reduction is from an average of about four to three living offspring per litter.

Thus, the Manx seems to be lethal when homozygous and, apparently, semi-lethal at all times. One aspect of this is a preponderance of females among the viable Manx offspring, as if the males are less likely to survive. Also, examination of Manx still-born kittens, and those which died before the age of twelve months, revealed a greater number of both skeleton and organ anomalies than was shown by those Manx cats which lived beyond the twelve months.

The absence of a tail is readily apparent although careful examination has shown that the loss can be relative. In all, four types of Manx taillessness have been distinguished. The true Manx is known as "rumpy", in which no tail vertebrae can be observed. Indeed, there is often a small dimple where the vertebrae would normally issue. A second type is "rumpy-riser", in which an extremely small number of tail vertebrae can either be seen or felt as an upright projection, usually immovable. The third type is "stumpy". Here, the tail is longer and usually moveable although often deformed, nobbly and kinked. The fourth type is the "longie" and possibly is the rarer of the four. The tail is longer than many of the above (though shorter than normal) and is of more normal appearance. One series of experiments are suggestive that the various expressions of the Manx taillessness are controlled in part by modifying polygenes.

The influence of the Manx may be observed for the whole length of the vertebral column. In the fore-part of the column, this seems to be little more than a slight decrease in the length of the individual vertebrae but, in the hind-part, there is also a decrease in number and, particularly, fusion of vertebrae. The sacral and pelvic bones are also drawn into the general fusion and maldevelopment. In a number of cases, variable degrees of spinal bifida has been found upon autopsy. Occasional or recurrent bowel stoppage may occur because of a narrowing of the anal opening. This may be observed when the kitten takes to solid food. The spinal cord frequently terminates prematurely. This could lead to a failure of innervation of certain organs and their proper functioning, such as loss of control of the hind legs (Howell and Siegel, 1966; James *et al.*, 1969; Leipold *et al.*, 1974; DeForest and Basrur, 1979).

It is well known that the homozygous Manx is a prenatal lethal condition but it is only comparatively recently that the moribund fetuses have been identified. These have been detected at as early as five weeks gestation as abnormally small and globoid foetuses with gross malformation of the central nervous system (Basrur and DeForest, 1979).

Meningoencephalocele

This is a congenital defect of the cranium which allows fatal herniation of meninges and brain tissues in the newborn kitten. Externally, the anomaly manifests as soft swellings on the forehead and face of the newborn. A study of the incidence in a strain of Burmese revealed that the condition was inherited as a recessive trait, with the mutant gene being symbolized by *mc*. It was thought that the selection for a short nose and rounded skull for the American Burmese may have been conducive for the presence of the gene in the breed but this does not seem to be so. Defective kittens have been bred from Burmese cats with relatively long skulls (Zook *et al.*, 1983; Noden and Evans, 1986; Sponenberg and Graf-Webster, 1986).

Mucopolysaccharidosis I

The profile of cats with disease is subtly altered; the nose is short and broad, with a depressed nasal bridge, prominent forehead, small ears and opacity of the cornea. The afflicted cat sits in a crouching position, with spread forelegs. The cervical vertebrae are wider than normal, asymmetrical and frequently fused, while the sternum is unusually concave. The stomach may be swollen because of enlarged liver and spleen. The neurons of the brain and spinal cord are grossly abnormal. Phenotypically, the anomaly behaves as a recessive trait (symbol *mps-1*) but the malady arises from an enzyme deficiency which can be detected in heterozygotes as well as homozygotes (Haskins *et al.*, 1979, 1982).

Mucopolysaccharidosis VI

Cats with this disease tend to resemble those described above. The nose is short and broad and the nasal bridge is depressed, giving the face a flattened appearance. The eyelids appear to be narrow, with the upper lid swollen and drooping. The cornea of the eye is slightly opaque. The vertebral column is deformed, especially the cervical, thoractic and lumbar regions. Clinically, the anomaly is inherited as a recessive trait (symbol *mps-6*). However, the affliction has been traced to an enzyme deficiency which may be detected in both heterozygotes and homozygotes. Interestingly, two different mutant *mps-6* alleles have been discovered. These produced very similar or identical diseases but were found to be biochemically distinct (Haskins *et al.*, 1979, 1982; McGovern *et al.*, 1981, 1985). The progress of the malady can be corrected by bone marrow transplantation (Gasper *et al.*, 1984).

Neuroaxonal Dystrophy

This behavioural disorder is peculiar as it is associated with a pale coat colour. The colour is described as similar to "lilac" on a non-agouti background. Affected kittens display a progressive ataxia: by five weeks of age, nodding of the head is apparent; by 6 weeks, the head is definitely shaking and these symptoms steadily worsen; by 8 weeks, the gait shows signs of incoordination. There is probably an impairment of vision and some deafness. Body size is reduced. The cause of the disease is a degeneration of the main neurones of the brain stem and is due to a recessive gene *no* (Woodward, Collins and Hessler, 1974).

Onion hair

The whiskers and guard hairs normally taper to a fine point but this anomaly is characterized by "onion-like" swellings to the hairs. The swelling usually occurs at the tip of the hair but may arise at sites along the hair shaft. The swelling is just visible to the naked eye. The coat appears lustreless and feels rough when stroked. In one cat, the anomaly was confined to the whiskers. The swelling is due to an enlargement of the inner core of medulla cells. Examination of the skin revealed that the hair follicles and appendages were apparently normal.

The anomaly was observed in the Abyssinian breed. Although no breeding data are reported, cats with the abnormal coat were produced by normal-coated parents. The implication is that the anomaly could be inherited as a monogenic recessive trait.

Patella luxation

Patella luxation is displacement of the patella from its normal position in the trochlear groove, either by force or spontaneously. The condition may recur if the groove is unusually shallow or incorrectly formed. A survey of breeds of cats for the anomaly revealed that the Devon rex showed a notably high incidence (Flecknell and Gruffydd-Jones, 1979). The condition may rectify itself with but temporary discomfort to the individual. However, in a minority of cases, the condition can lead to lameness. The breed incidence implies a genetic predisposition but without indicating the mode of inheritance nor the precipitating factors. It is possible that the condition is inherited in a polygenic manner, perhaps as a threshold character, affecting the form of growth of the trochlear groove.

Pelger–Huet anomaly

This curious defect is an abnormal segmentation of the nuclei of granulocytes, one of the several forms of leucocyte (white blood cell). The trait is inherited in a dominant way (symbol *Ph*) but, as far as can be ascertained, the defect does not have any adverse effects on the health of the cat (Latimer *et al.*, (1985).

Polycystic renal disease

Kittens with this disease have greatly enlarged abdomens; death ensues at about six to seven weeks of age. Affected kittens were shown to have enlarged kidneys, composed of dilated cystic channels, and cystic bile ducts of the liver. It is possible that the lesions are congenital. The anomaly was observed in a closely inbred group of farm cats, and was clearly familial, although the mode of heredity could not be ascertained (Crowell *et al.*, 1979).

Polydactyly

If the number of separate reports is anything to judge by, the presence of extra toes on the foot is something that attracts attention. This anomaly has been noted as early as 1868, if not earlier, and on many occasions since that date. The distinguishing feature is, of course, the presence of extra toes, most noticeably on the front feet. There is considerable variation from animal to animal in the number of extra toes and how perfectly formed they may be.

The variation in this respect may range from an enlargement of the inside digit to resemble a thumb to the formation of three apparently well formed extra toes. Making a total of seven toes on one foot! This variation in expression may occur between different feet on the same cat. In fact, the hind feet are never, or rarely, affected unless the front are abnormal. Despite the marked variation, it seems to be rather rare for a genetic polydactylous cat to be normal, as could so well happen with anomalies of this nature. Different cases may vary in this respect, however.

Reviewing the various reports of polydactyly, it is remarkable how many give either direct or indirect evidence of a dominant mode of heredity. This aspect is remarkable since not all of the separate cases need be due to the same mutant gene. It is possible, of course, for the same gene to have arisen by mutation in different localities, and at different times, and this is an explanation which could account for the similar heredity. However, doubtless it would be wise to remember that other cases of polydactyly might behave somewhat differently. At the moment, only one polydactyly gene is recognized which is symbolized by *Pd*. Those who wish for details of the anatomical aspects of the anomaly should consult the reports of Danforth (1947a,b) and Chapman and Zeiner (1961).

Porphyria

Porphyrins are precursor substances for the production of haem, a major component of haemoglobin. These substances arise in the bone marrow and, should they be produced in excessive amounts, are deposited in the body tissues such as the skin, bones and teeth, as well as being void in the urine. When this occurs, the teeth may appear to be unusually discoloured and the urine turns bloody. These symptoms are usually expressed from an early age. The diagnosis of the porphyric cat may be easily accomplished by examination of the teeth or bones under ultra-violet light. The impregnated teeth and bones exhibit a bright pinkish-red fluorescence (Glenn *et al.*, 1968). The condition is inherited as a dominant trait which is symbolized by *Po*.

A different form of porphyria has been reported (Desnick *et al.*, 1982). The symptoms were similar to those described above but were accompanied by noticeable lethargy and anaemia. The data were consistent with monogenic transmission of the malady but the precise mode of heredity could not be determined.

Progressive retinal atrophy

A number of accounts may be found in the literature of the occurrence of this degenerative disease of the retina. The age of onset may vary and the degeneration may take various forms, but the outcome is invariably loss of vision. The typical signs are a dilation of the iris, increased tapetal reflectability, cautious behaviour, especially in leaping from heights, and blundering into obstacles which a cat with normal vision would easily avoid.

Two early studies were indicative that the anomaly is inherited. That of West-Hyde and Buyukmihci (1982) showed that the condition was transmitted to the offspring in a possible dominant manner but the breeding data were too few to establish this with certainty. Somewhat better data were reported by Rubin and Lipton (1973) but here the inheritance was recessive. The anomaly could be detected at between 12 to 15 weeks of age by pupil dilation and hesitant behaviour.

Two cases which coincidentally occurred in the Abyssinian breed have been investigated in detail. The first was found in Swedish Abyssinian cats and was determined to be inherited in a recessive way (symbol *rdg*). Early stages of the defect could be diagnosed in many affected individuals by 18 to 24 months of age, but the advanced stages of retinal degeneration were not reached until three to four years (Narfström, 1983, 1985).

The second case was found in English Abyssinian cats and was inherited as a dominant trait (symbol *Rdy*). In these cats the onset could be seen as early as four to five weeks and the advanced stages were reached by 12 weeks of age (Barnett and Curtis, 1985; Curtis *et al.*, 1987). The differing ages of onset and progression of the disease, as well as modes of heredity, would seem to indicate two independent mutant genes, despite their occurrence in the same breed of cats.

Pyloric Stenosis

Pyloric stenosis or pylorospasm is a malfunction of the lower opening of the stomach. The condition can be diagnosed by X-ray analysis following barium feeding. The symptoms are persistent vomiting after weaning, often quite violently. The vomiting occurs usually after a meal but not necessarily. The inability to retain food leads to a slow-down of growth. The observations of Pearson and others (1974) imply that the defect could be inherited, although it was not possible to decide on the manner of the inheritance.

Sparse-fur

Sparse-fur is a marked alopecia which results in a thin straggly coat that is rough to the hand. All guard hairs are short and deformed, with few down hairs, while the whiskers are bent and curled. A reddish-brown exudate leading to encrustation forms along the rim of the eyelids, about the nostrils and mouth, frequently affecting the hairs of the chest and stomach. The eyelids become thickened and inflamed, and the bulbus shows signs of sepsis if left untreated. The condition is inherited as a recessive trait (symbol *sp;* Robinson, unpublished observations).

Spasticity

This is a name given to a muscular disorder which has been found in the Devon rex. The symptoms usually develop between four and seven weeks of age but may be delayed until 12 to 14 weeks. The kitten is active but displays an unusual posture, with the shoulder blades held high and the neck arched downwards. At rest, the body lies flat with the head held to one side. Feeding presents a problem for the kitten since the arched neck interferes with the normal feeding action of extending the neck. When drinking, the nose may be plunged below the surface of the liquid. These symptoms are usually interspersed with short periods, measured in days, of apparent normality. As the kitten matures, the condition becomes worse. The cat remains active but rests more often, either by lying flat with the head to one side or by leaning against an upright object. An analysis of the frequency of normal and spastic kittens born to normal parents indicated that the condition is inherited as a recessive trait, symbolized as *spt* (Robinson, unpublished observations).

Spheroid lysosomal disease

The initial symptoms arise at about eight to twelve weeks of age as a tremor which progresses to nodding of the head and swaying of the body. Movement is slow, with ataxia and much falling. The sense of direction is impaired and seizures may occur when the cat is handled. The appetite is not disturbed but the actual feeding is a messy affair. The cause was traced to anomalous inclusions in the tissues of the brain and spinal cord. The anomaly occurred in the Ayssinian and is due to a recessive gene *sl* (Berg *et al.*, 1977; Lange *et al.*, 1977).

Sphingomyelinosis

Kittens with this nervous disease display a loss of interest in their surroundings and develop a tremor, followed by ataxic behaviour. The appetite is impaired or lost. The disease is due to an enzyme deficiency which is inherited as a recessive trait (symbol *spl*) as regards clinical manifestation. The heterozygotes can be detected by biochemical analysis (Wenger *et al.*, 1980).

Split-foot

The typical manifestation is that of a central cleft of either one or both fore feet. Other disturbances may be present, however, such as an absence of toes or fusion to produce double claws and abnormal foot-pads. X-ray photographs disclose considerable disorder of the bones, particularly the metacarpals and carpals. The defect did not appear to interfere with normal activity except that of climbing. The hind feet did not appear to be involved in those animals studied (Searle, 1953).

The split-foot condition is inherited as a dominant trait and the responsible gene is symbolized by *Sh*. The number of defective animals is observed to be less than expected and it is suggested that this may mean that a proportion of the genetically split-food individuals may appear normal footed. This could easily occur as a result of the variability of expression of the gene.

Squint

The Siamese breed is sometimes regarded as possessing a convergent squint as a breed characteristic. This may be true for some strains of Siamese but it does not seem correct as a general statement. Whatever may have happened in the past, there are many strains in existence at the present time which do not show this affliction. It will be appreciated, of course, that a squint may occur in any individual or breed in addition to that of Siamese.

The situation is complicated to some extent by the fact that a kitten may display a mild squint while young which is slowly corrected as it becomes older. This means that genetically squint animals may appear as normal if the early life of the cat is unknown. Only one report on the condition in Siamese has made any attempt to interpret the mode of inheritance (Moutschen, 1950). However, the results of a number of crosses have not yielded clear-cut results. The condition seems to be inherited but seemingly as the outcome of the interaction of two or more genes. It seems possible that the squint is inherited as a polygenically controlled threshold character; alternatively, of course, it could be determined monogenetically but with impenetrance.

Testicular Feminization

Although only one case has been reported in the cat, the anomaly so resembles comparable inherited conditions in other mammals that an account is warranted. The adult cat was an apparently normal female but with no signs of oestrus behaviour. Upon examination, it was found that the sex chromosomes were male (XY) and that the sex organs had been incompletely developed as female (Meyers-Wallen et al., 1989). In general, the condition is due to a mutant gene (adopted symbol tfm) on the X chromosome which disrupts development of normal male secondary sex structures. The feminized male will come to notice because of the accompanying sterility. Female sterility may arise from numerous causes and testicular feminization must now be added to the list.

Tremor

This disease is characterized by a continuous, whole body, tremble which commences at about 2 to 4 weeks of age. The kitten rolls and bobs in an undulating fashion while the tail weaves in circles. The trembling only ceases when the animal is completely at rest or is held firmly. Even when held by the nape of the neck, the tremble is still obvious. A single recessive gene tr is postulated for the anomalous behaviour (Norby and Thuline, 1970). There is no sign of underdeveloped cerebellum which typifies the virus-induced ataxia.

Umbilical Hernia

Two research veterinarians (Henricson and Bornstein, 1965) have observed a particularly high incidence of umbilical hernia among the Abyssinian breed in Sweden. The precise mode of inheritance could not be determined but the influence of heredity is unmistakable in their data. For example, the chances of the offspring being herniated is about 75 per cent when one parent is known to have an hernia, against 3 per cent for the offspring of parents which are known to be normal or are unknown. These figures are cited merely as a guide and must not be taken too literally.

The fact of the high incidence among the progeny, when one parent is known to be herniated, prompted the suggestion that the predisposition towards the occurrence of an hernia might be inherited as a dominant. This may be the case, and the data is certainly suggestive in this respect, but it may be wise to be cautious. When the breeding data are closely examined, too many individuals are marked as "unknown" for positive conclusions to be drawn.

Umbilical hernia is usually due to an inherent defect in the umbilical ring. A weakness can result in a part of the abdominal contents being extrude as a soft bulge. However, even if the musculature is defective, a hernia need not always develop or the development may be so slight as to escape notice. This means that if attention is focussed entirely upon the presence or absence of hernia the fundamental or primary defect will not be detected in some cases. The hernia condition is a "secondary" manifestation of a probable anomaly of the umbilical region. The descent of the hernia from one generation to the next could appear to be irregular, in spite of the probability that the primary defect is inherited along regular lines. However, it must be admitted that the problem is complex. The simplest hypothesis is that the incidence of hernia is a threshold character. (Robinson, 1976).

Urolithiasis

Livingston (1965) has outlined a case of urolithiasis which reveals a familial tendency. A male cat showed the disease and so did three kittens out of four from matings with his sister. Full details of the urolithiasis are not given except the statement that the disease failed to respond to any treatment, including surgery. The affected animals are otherwise healthy and no other cats in the neighbourhood have developed obvious symptoms. It is proposed that a hereditary influence may be involved.

Though intriguing, these observations would carry little weight, standing alone, but they are the sort that could contribute towards

something tangible should a number of similar reports come in over
the years. For this reason, if no other, Livingston's note deserves to
be cited. It is quite likely that a predisposition towards the formation
of urinary calculi could be determined to some extent by heredity. A
genetic propensity towards urolithiasis is suspected in the dog.

Visual pathways

True albino animals are completely without pigment, hence the
coat is white and the pupil of the eye is pink or red, surrounded by
a translucent iris. In the cat, the Siamese allele is a form of partial
albinism with a limited amount of pigment to create a blue iris.

A curious feature of albinotic animals is a misrouting of the visual
ganglion axons from the retina to the brain. An unusual number pass
to the wrong side of the brain. However, this may not seriously impair
vision since the cat's brain is apparently able to compensate. Both
albino and Siamese cats are affected, the latter to a lesser extent
than the former. It is of interest that, while white coat colour is
recessive to fully coloured (C), the heterozygotes Cc^s and Cc have
misrouted pathways although to a lesser degree than the homozygotes
$c^s c^s$ or cc.

Cats with the Chediak–Higashi syndrome also show misrouting
of the pathways but to a lesser extent than the albino. Incidentally,
neither Burmese of the albino series of alleles nor dominant white
exhibit signs of visual misrouting. There are many reports on the
anomaly but only the more revealing and recent are cited: Guillery
(1974); Cooper and Blasdel (1980); Guillery et al. (1981); Creel et
al., 1982a, Leventhal (1982), Leventhal et al. (1985).

Weeping Eye

A perpetually weeping or running eye could be due to several
causes, such as injury to the eyelid, entropion or inward turning of
the eyelid, so that hairs irritate the eyeball, or to blockage of either
the naso-lacrinal canal or the lacrinal duct which are responsible for
draining excess tears. The blockage could result from a foreign body
in the canal or duct. It is advisable to consult a veterinary surgeon if
the condition persists.

However, it should be noted that the condition may arise as a
consequence of selective breeding for an excessively short nose in

TABLE 16. CHECK LIST OF GENETIC ANOMALIES AND SYMBOLS

Symbol	Name	Page
br	Brachyury	191
ch	Chediak–Higashi syndrome	193
Cu	American curl	196
Cut	Cutaneous asthenia	196
dp	Duplicate pinnae	199
ew	Episodic weakness	197
fck	Flat-chested kitten syndrome	198
Fd	Folded ears	198
ga-1	Gangliosidosis GM1	199
ga-2	Gangliosidosis GM2	199
h	French hairless	201
Hag	Hageman factor	200
hce	Hyperchylomicronaemia	203
hd	Redcar hairless	201
Hma	Haemophilia A	200
Hmb	Haemophilia B	200
ho	Hyperoxaluria	203
hr	Canadian hairless	201
hy	Hydrocephalus	202
M	Manx taillessness	204
man	Mannosidosis	203
mc	Meningoencephalocele	205
no	Neuroaxonal dystrophy	206
Pd	Polydactyly	208
Ph	Pelger–Huet anomaly	208
Po	Porphyria	209
rdg	Progressive retinal atrophy	210
Rdy	Progressive retinal atrophy	210
rt	Retinal degeneration	210
Sh	Split-foot	212
sl	Spheroid lysosomal disease	211
sp	Sparse fur	210
spl	Sphingomyelinosis	212
spt	Spasticity	211
tr	Tremor	213

some breeds. This leads to distortion, narrowing or even blockage of the naso-lacrinal canal or lacrinal duct. The eyes overflow with tears which trickle down the side of the nose. In this case, the condition may be held to be genetic, probably polygenically, as a result of changes in skull shape. If affected animals recur in related litters or over several generations, the breeding policy should be reviewed. It would be foolish to breed from afflicted cats even if surgically corrected. It would also be wise to retire from breeding any animal which produces such offspring.

8

Record Keeping

A SIMPLE yet efficient system of record keeping is a vital adjunct of animal breeding. Indeed, it might not be too much to say that the art of successful breeding derives from the possession of reliable records and the use to which these are put. Alas, to some people, the writing up of breeding results and notes on the appearance of each kitten is a chore to be put off to a later date. Such an attitude is understandable when there is work to be done with the animals but it would be idle to pretend that it is good enough for well organized breeding. Fortunately, the majority of breeders appreciate the value of records—even those of the most simple kind—as a log of past achievement and as an aid to future breeding.

Record keeping in animal breeding is required to fulfil three functions: (1) to present an accurate record of familial relationship, (2) to provide information upon the phenotype characteristics and breeding performance of every animal and (3) to be a source of data from which to make future decisions. Accordingly, it is easy to sketch out the minimum of data which ought to be kept but less easy to set an upper limit. Clearly, if record keeping is not to be a burden, the chosen method should be simple to operate. On the other hand, the amount of information it is desirous to collect will depend upon the breeding programme which the breeder has set himself. It will also depend upon the temperament of the breeder. People's opinions differ on the relevancy of information for a given task. In general, however, it is advisable to record as much data as possible, provided it appears to have potential value and it does not make the whole business too onerous. It is convenient if all of the information can be brought together in one place: the stud book.

It is essential that each cat should be individually and readily

217

identifiable once it has been entered in the stud book. When only a few breeding queens are kept and all of the animals receive regular attendance, it may be wondered if a means of individual identification is worthwhile. Possibly not, if mistakes can be definitely ruled out. With a large colony and new litters of kittens arriving at frequent intervals during the peak of a breeding season, a reliable method may be desirable. A simple method is to have metal or durable plastic tags attached to collars. Two sizes of collar may be necessary, one for kittens and one for adults, the tag being transferred from collar to collar. Frayed collars should always be promptly replaced and a careful watch kept for animals which develop a habit of worrying or slipping their collars. Metal tags may have to be engraved while plastic tags could be written upon in water-proof ink. With latter, it would be wise to be on the *qui vive* for rubbing or straining which could lead to illegibility of the wording.

A day-to-day record for breeding queens may be kept in the form of ordinary small filing cards. A supply of these, together with specially made boxes to contain them, can usually be bought quite cheaply from stationers. These cards are for dates of visits to the stud cat, parturitions and preliminary details of the litter. A separate card is made out for each female. The name and/or reference number in the stud book (see later) should be written at the head of the card. Every visit to the male should be listed, giving name and reference number of male, not forgetting the date. Should the mating fail, this should be noted and, if a reason can be adduced for the failure, this can be entered.

When the female conceives, the date of birth of litter and the number of kittens should be written down. Brief details should be given whether the kittens look fully healthy and if the queen had an easy parturition. These cards are a check on the reproductive history of the queen. Whether or not she conceives readily and produces the average number of kittens per litter can be seen at a glance. When the time arrives for the kittens to be examined and be entered in the stud book, the details of the litter are transferred at the same time. The litter reference number in the stud book can be written on the card for purposes of cross-reference. All of the cards should be preserved even after the queen has ceased to breed.

The stud book should be made the permanent repository for all information and most systems of recording revolve around it. The book may range from an ordinary note book, with a board cover for greater durability, to a spring-back binder. A loose-leaf binder permits the insertion of extra pages and the need for these can recur with surprising frequency when the breeding programme is going well and new aspects are subsequently found to merit consideration. A recommended system of recording rests upon the successive numbering of litters. Commencing with the first page of the stud book, a number should be prominently written in the top right hand corner, beginning with 1, 2, 3, . . . , etc. It may be found convenient to always have the number at the top right-hand corner of the next available blank page, according to the amount of space required. This could be as little as a page or could extend over several pages depending upon the amount of information to be entered. Each succeeding litter is assigned the next unused number in the book.

Since certain details will be the same for all litters, a number of headings could be written in beforehand or, if practicable, the pages could be obtained already mimeographed. An illustration of the possible arrangement of the basic details are shown by Fig. 24. The main headings are those on the left and consist of Queen, Male, Number of Matings to conception, Date of Mating and so on. The figure shows an example for a litter designated as 42 (the number at top right). This litter is produced by a mating of a queen with stud book reference 17d with a male of reference 9a (their stud names are also given in parenthesis). She was mated on the 12th of February and gave birth to five young on the 18th of April after a normal parturition.

One of the kittens died at birth but the other four were successfully reared. The kittens were weaned and recorded for coat colour and length. Two were normal coated self black, one a normal blue and the last a long-haired black. Each kitten is given one of the first few lower case letters of the alphabet and the above details listed for each one; together with the sex and genotype as shown. Each kitten has now been precisely designated by a number (42) and a letter. At this stage, a note may be added whether the mother has or has not nursed the litter satisfactorily. Finally, space may be left for subsequent history of the kittens. That is to say, whether they were sold (if so, to whom), died from disease (if so, state the disease) or from senility (if so, give date). After a while, the procedure soon becomes a matter of routine.

42

Queen	**17d**	(Abigal)		
Male	**9a**	(Racine)		

NO. OF MATINGS TO CONCEPTION   One

DATE OF MATING   February 12th 1968

DATE OF BIRTH   April 18th 1968

PARTURITION   Uneventful

No. of YOUNG BORN

     LIVE   4

     DEAD   1

DETAILS OF LITTER

    a   Male black   *aaD–L–*

    b   Female black   *aaD–L–*

    c   Male blue   *aaddL–*

    d   Female blue LH   *aaddll*

CONDITION at WEANING   Excellent

GRADING OF CHARACTERS

KITTEN	H	CC	CT	BB	HS	F	T
a	10	9	9	6	6	4	4
b	10	8	8	7	4	5	4
c	10	–	7	6	5	6	4
d	5	5	–	5	6	3	3

FIG. 24. A specimen page from the stud book, showing the basic data which should be recorded for each litter and a proposed layout of the entries.

The main genotype can usually be appended to the colour description of the kittens similarly to that shown. However, it will also be highly desirable to record variation of polygenic characteristics, either by description or by grading on a suitable scale. On earlier occasions, the advantages (if not the necessity) of employing a suitable scale has been emphasized. These were for analysing a polygenic character and for the calculation of a total score. If the total score method of selection is being employed, there is no reason why this should not be used as a succinct method of describing the variation. Additional supplementary notes can always be given, though this ought not to be necessary, since every effort should be made to ensure that the scoring is as accurate and relevant as possible.

The figure shows how the grading of the four kittens could be arranged for the same seven characters as defined in the section on the construction of a total score. Suppose that the breeder is interested in the self blacks. Though the blue SH and the black LH will be discarded, all of the other characteristics for these cats should be graded as conscientiously as possible. These will vary independently (with the possible exception of CC because of the long hair in kitten d could interfere with accurate grading) of each other and no opportunity should be neglected to obtain data on the variation.

The nature and amount of data which is recorded will depend entirely upon the interests of the breeder. For instance, it may be that the breeder is seeking to create a particular form of spotted tabby which cannot be easily graded. In which case, the pattern for each kitten may have to be described in some detail if the breeder is to have an adequate record. Photographs would be useful, especially if the posture of each kitten can be standardized in order to minimize distortion. The employment of sketches should not be despised, particularly if outlines can be prepared beforehand and it is simply a matter of filling in details.

The advantage of having a reference system based upon consecutive numbering of litters is that it facilitates cross-reference. All the information on litters and individual cats are to be found in one book. At any time it is desired to check on any animal, it is only necessary to turn to the appropriate page number (viz. litter number) and consult the pertinent letter. For example, the mother is 17d, indicating she is the fourth kitten of litter 17. The composition of litter 42 might provide additional data on her genotype. Suppose she is a normal haired black; hence the colours of the kittens show that she must be heterozygous for blue dilution and long hair. If the heterozygosity was unknown (or only suspected) at the time of writing up of litter 17, the pages may be turned back and the relevant data added to that already entered for kitten d. Similarly, any new information on the male 9a can be added. In this respect, the comprehensiveness of the stud book will increase as the entries mount up. After a number of years, the stud book may consist of a number of volumes. However, the principle of consecutive litter numbering still applies, the numbers being carried on from one volume to the next. The numbers contained in a volume could be written on the spine for easy location.

The incorporation of purchased stock into the system can be accomplished by either of two methods. One is to treat the animal as a "litter" and assign a number to it at the time of purchase (but recording that it had in fact been purchased). Or, to designate those animals by simple numbers or capital letters (or group of capital letters which may be so composed as to act as a mnemonic for the origin of the cat). If the second procedure has been adopted, a whole page should be given over to each animal for recording any data which may be available. The seller would no doubt be pleased to supply such basic details as date of birth, parentage and litter sibs. These pages may be inserted in the stud book at any convenient position, such as in serial order prior to the home-bred litters.

It will be appreciated that the use of the rather impersonal combination of litter number and lower case letter in no manner replaces either pet names or formal names under which cats are usually registered. The reference numbers are primarily for quick and easy location of individual animals in the stud book and for tracing parentages or ancestral lineages extending through successive generations. The system has been proven to function very well in this respect. When this is linked up with records of reproduction of the individual and the quality of the kittens produced, it forms a serviceable system of permanently recording breeding data.

References

BAKER, H. J., LINDSEY, J. R., McKHANN, G. M. AND FARRELL, D. F. (1971) Neuronal GM1 gangliosidosis in a Siamese cat. *Science,* **174:** 838–9.

BAMBER, R. C. AND HERDMAN, E. C. (1931) Two new colour types in cats. *Nature,* **127:** 558.

BARNETT, K. C. AND CURTIS, R. (1985) Autosomal dominant progressive retinal atrophy in Abyssinian cats. *J. Hered.,* **76:** 168–70.

BASRUR, P. K. AND DEFOREST, M. E. (1979) Embryological impact of the Manx gene. *Carnivor. Genet. Newsl.,* **3:** 378–84.

BERG, P. B. V., BAKER, M. K. AND LANGE, A. L. (1977) A suspected lysosomal storage disease in Abyssinian cats. *J. S. Afr. Vet. Assoc.,* **48:** 195–9.

BERGSMA, D. R. AND BROWN, K. S. (1971) White fur, blue eyes and deafness in the domestic cat. *J. Hered.,* **62:** 171–85.

BISTNER, S. I., AGUIRRE, G. AND SHIVELY, J. N. (1976) Hereditary corneal dystrophy in the Manx cat. *Invest. Ophthalmol.,* **15:** 15–26.

BOGART, R. (1959) *Improvement of Livestock.* New York: MacMillan.

BOSHER, S. K. AND HALLPIKE, C. S. (1965) Observation on the histological features, development and pathogenesis of the inner ear degeneration of the deaf white cat. *Proc. Roy. Soc. B.,* **162:** 147–62.

CENTERWALL, W. R. AND BENIRSCHKE, K. (1973) Male tortoiseshell and calico cats. *J. Hered.,* **62:** 272–8.

CHAPMAN, V. A. AND ZEINER, F. N. (1961) The anatomy of polydactylism in cats with observations on genetic control. *Anat. Rec.,* **141:** 105–27.

CLIFFORD, D. H., SOIFOR, F. K., WILSON, C. F., WADDELL, E. D. and GUILLAND, G. L. (1971) Congenital achasia of the esophagus in four cats of common ancestry. *J. Amer. Vet. Med. Assoc.,* **158:** 1554–60.

COLLIER, L. L., BRYAN, G. M. AND PRIER, D. J. (1979) Ocular manifestation of the Chediak–Higashi syndrome in four species of animals. *J. Amer. Vet. Med. Assoc.,* **175:** 587–90.

COOPER, M. L. AND BLASDEL, G. G. (1980) Regional variation in the representation of the visual field in the visual cortex of the Siamese cat. *J. Comp. Neurol.*, **193**: 237–53.

CORK, L. C., MUNNELL, J. F. AND LORENZ, M. D. (1978) The pathology of feline GM2 gangliosidosis. *Amer. J. Pathol.*, **90**: 723–30.

CORK, L. C., MUNNELL, J. F., LORENZ, M. D., MURTHY, J. V., BAKER, H. J. (1977) Gm2 ganglioside lysosomal storage disease in cats. *Science*, **196**, 1014–17.

COTTER, S. M., BRENNER, R. M. AND DODDS, W. J. (1978) Haemophilia A in three unrelated cats. *J. Amer. Vet. Med. Assoc.*, **172**: 166–8.

CREEL, D., COLLIER, L. L., LEVENTHAL, A. G., CONLEE, J. L. AND PRIER, D. J. (1982a) Abnormal retinal projections in cats with the Chediak–Higashi syndrome. *Invest. Ophthalmol. Vis. Sci.*, **23**: 798–801.

CREEL, D., HENDRICKSON, A. E., LEVENTHAL, A. (1982b) Retinal projections in tyrosinase negative albino cats. *J. Neurosci.*, **2**: 907–11.

CROWELL, W. A., HUBBELL, J. J. AND RILEY, J. C. (1979) Polycystic renal disease in related cats. *J. Amer. Vet. Med. Assoc.*, **175**: 286–8.

CURTIS, R., BARNETT, K. C. AND LEON, A. (1987) An early onset retinal dystrophy with dominant inheritance in the Abyssinian cat. *Invest. Ophthalmol. Vis. Sci.*, **28**: 131–9.

DANFORTH, C. H. (1947a) Heredity of polydactyly in the cat. *J. Hered.*, **38**: 107–12.

DANFORTH, C. H. (1947b) Morphology of the feet in polydactyl cats. *Amer. J. Anat.*, **80**: 143–71.

DEFOREST, M. E. AND BASUR, P. K. (1979) Malformation and the Manx syndrome in cats. *Canad. Vet. J.*, **20**: 304–14.

DESNICK, R. J., MCGOVERN, M. M., SCHUCH, E. H., HASKINS, M. E. (1982). Animal analogues of human inherited metabolic diseases. In Desnick, R. J., Pattison, D. F., and Scarpelli, D. G. (Eeditors) *Animal Models of Inherited Metabolic Diseases.* New York: Alan R. Liss Inc.

DIBARTOLA, S. P., HILL, R. L., FECHHEIMER, N. S. AND POWERS, J. D. (1986) Pedigree analysis of Abyssinian cats with familial amyloidosis. *Amer. J. Vet. Res.*, **47**: 2666–8.

DODDS, W. J. (1981) Haemophilia B. *ILAR News*, **24**(4):R8

DORN, C. R., TAYLOR, D. O. N. AND SCHNEIDER, R. (1971) Sunlight exposure and risk of developing cutaneous and oral squamous cell carcinomas in white cats. *J. Nat. Cancer. Inst.*, **46**: 1073–8.

ELVERLAND, H. H. AND MAIR, I. W. S. (1980) Hereditary deafness in the cat. *Acta Otolaryngol.*, **90**: 360–9.

FALCONER, D. S. (1981) *Introduction to Quantitative Genetics.* London: Longman.

FLECKNELL, P. A. AND GRUFFYDD-JONES, T. J. (1979) Congenital luxation of the patella in the cat. *Feline Pract.*, **9**: 18–20.

GASPER, P. W., THRALL, M. A. AND WENGER, D. A. (1984) Correction of feline mucopolysaccharidosis VI by bone marrow transplantation. *Nature*, 312: 467–9.

GEORGES, M., HILBERT, P., LEQUARRE, A. S., LECLERC, V., HANSET, R., AND VASSART, G. (1988) Use of DNA bar codes to resolve a canine paternity dispute. *J. Amer. Vet. Med. Assoc.*, 193: 1095–8.

GILLESPIE, T. H. (1954) Cats – wild and domestic. *Scotsman*, 27 November 1954.

GLENN, B. L., GLENN, H. G. AND OMTVEDT, I. T. (1968) Congenital porphyria in the domestic cat. *Amer. J. Vet. Res.*, 29: 1653–7.

GUILLERY R. W. (1974) Visual pathways in albinos. *Sci. Amer.*, 230: 44–54.

GUILLERY, R. W., HICKER, T. L. AND SPEAR, P. D. (1981) Do blue eyed white cats have normal or abnormal retinofugal pathways? *Invest. Ophthalmol. Vis. Sci.*, 21: 27–33.

HAMILTON, E. 1986. *The Wild Cat of Europe*. London: Porter.

HASKINS, M. E., JEZYK, P. F., DESNICK, R. J., MCDONOUGH, S. K. AND PATTERSON, D. F. (1979) Alpha-L-iduronidase deficiency in a cat. *Pediat. Res.*, 13: 1294–7.

HASKINS, M. E., JEZYK, P. F., DESNICK, R. J., MCGOVERN, M. M., VINE, D. T. AND PATTERSON, D. F. (1982) In DESNICK, R. J. (Ed.) *Animal Models of Inherited Metabolic Diseases*. New York: Alan R. Liss Inc.

HASKINS, M. E., JEZYK, P. F. AND PATTERSON, D. F. (1979) Mucopolysaccharide storage disease in three families of cats. *Pediat. Res.*, 13: 1203–10.

HENDY-IBBS, P. M. (1984) Hairless cats in Great Britain. *J. Hered.*, 75: 506–7.

HENDY-IBBS, P. M. (1985) Familial feline epibulbar dermoids. *Vet. Rec.*, 116: 13–14.

HENRICSON, B. AND BORNSTEIN, S. (1965) Hereditary umbilical hernia in cats. *Svensk. Vet. Tid.*, 17: 95–7.

HOWELL, J. M. AND SIEGEL, P. B. (1966) Morphological effects of the Manx factor in cats. *J. Hered.*, 57: 100–4.

HUTT, F. B. (1964) *Animal Genetics*. New York: Ronald Press.

ILJIN, N. A. AND ILJIN, V. N. (1930) Temperature effects on the color of the Siamese cat. *J. Hered.*, 21: 309–18.

JACKSON, J. M. AND JACKSON, J. (1967) The hybrid jungle cat. *Newsl. Long Island Ocelot Club*, 11: 45.

JACKSON, O. F. (1975) Congenital bone lesions in cats with folded ears. *Bull. Feline Advisory Bur.*, 14(4); 2–4.

JAMES, C. C., LASSMAN, L. P. AND TOMLINSON, B. E. (1969) Congenital anomalies of the lower spine and spinal cord in Manx cats. *J. Pathol.*, 97; 269–76.

226 GENETICS FOR CAT BREEDERS

JEFFREYS, A. J. AND MORTON, D. B. (1987) DNA fingerprints of dogs and cats. *Anim. Genet.*, **18**: 1–15.

JOHNSON, K. H. (1970) Globoid leukodystrophy in the cat. *J. Amer. Vet. Med. Assoc.*, **157**: 2057–64.

JOHNSTON, S. D., BOUEN, L. C., MADL, J. E., WEBER, A. F. AND SMITH, F. O. (1983) X chromosome monosomy (37,XO) in a Burmese cat with gonadal dysgenesis. *J. Amer. Vet. Med. Assoc.*, **182**: 986–9.

JONES, B. R., JOHNSTONE, A. C., HANCOCK, W. S. AND WALLACE, A. (1986a) Inherited hyperchylomicronemia in the cat. *Feline Pract.*, **16**: 7–12.

JONES, G. R., JOHNSTONE, A. C., CAHILL, J. I., AND HANCOCK, W. S. (1986b) Peripheral neuropathy in cats with inherited primary hyperchylomicronaemia. *Vet. Rec.*, **119**: 268–72.

KIER, A. B., BRESNAHAN, J. F., WHITE, F. J., AND WAGNER, J. E. (1980) The inheritance pattern of factor XII (Hageman) deficiency in domestic cats. *Canad. J. Comp. Med.*, **44**: 309–14.

KRAMER, J. W., DAVIS, W. C. AND PRIEUR, D. J. (1977) The Chediak-Higashi syndrome of cats. *Lab. Invest.*, **36**: 554–62.

KUHN, A. AND KRONING, F. (1928) Ueber der vererbung der weisezchung bei der hauskatze. *Zuchtungskunde*, **3**: 448–54.

LANGE, A. L., BERG, P. B. V. AND BAKER, M. (1977) A suspected lysosomal storage disease in Abyssinian cats. *J. S. Afr. Vet. Assoc.*, **48**: 201–9.

LATIMER, K. S., RAKICH, P. M. AND THOMPSON, D. F. (1985) Pelger-Huet anomaly in cats. *Vet. Pathol.*, **22**: 370–4.

LEIPOLD, H. W., HUSTON, K., BLAUCH, B. AND GUFFY, M. M. (1974) Congenital defects of the caudal vertebral column and spinal cord in Manx cats. *J. Amer. Vet. Med. Assoc.*, **164**: 520–623.

LETARD, E. (1938) Hairless Siamese cats. *J. Hered.*, **29**: 173–5.

LEVENTHAL, A. G. (1982) Morphology and distribution of retinal ganglion cells projecting to different layers of the dorsal lateral geniculate nucleus in normal and Siamese cats. *J. Neurosci.*, **8**: 1024–42.

LEVENTHAL, A. G., VITEK, D. J. AND CREEL, D. J. (1985) Abnormal visual pathways in normally pigmented cats that are heterozygous for albinism. *Science*, **229**: 1395–7.

LITTLE, C. C. (1957) Four ears, a recessive mutation in the cat. *J. Hered.*, **48**: 57.

LITTLEWOOD, J. D. (1986) Haemophilia A (factor VIII deficiency) in the cat. *J. Small Anim. Pract.*, **27**: 541–6.

LIVINGSTON, M. L. (1965) A possible hereditary influence in feline urolithiasis. *Vet. Med. Small Anim. Clin.*, **60**: 705.

LOMAX, T. D. AND ROBINSON, R. (1988) Tabby alleles of the domestic cat. *J. Hered.*, **79**: 21–3.

LUSH, J. L. (1945) *Animal Breeding Plans*. Ames: Iowa State College Press.

MAIR, I. W. S. AND ELVERLAND, H. H. (1977) Hereditary deafness in the cat. *Arch. Oto-Rhino-Laryngol.*, **217**: 199–217.

MASON, K. (1988) A hereditary disease in Burmese cats manifested as an episodic weakness with head nodding and neck ventroflexion. *J. Amer. Anim. Hosp. Assoc.*, **24**: 147–51.

MATHER, K. (1977) *Introduction to Biometrical Genetics*. London: Chapman and Hall.

MCGOVERN, M. M., MANDELL, N., HASKINS, S. AND DESNICK, R. J. (1985) Animal model studies on allelism, *Genetics*, **110**: 733–49.

MCGOVERN, M. M., VINE, D. T., HASKINS, M. E. AND DESNICK, R. J. (1981) An improved method for heterozygous identification in feline and human mucopolysaccharidosis VI. *Enzyme*, **26**: 206–10.

MCKERRELL, R. E., BLAKEMORE, W. F., HEATH, M. F., PLUMB, J., BENNETT, M. J., POLLITT, R. J. AND DANPURE, C. J. (1989) Primary hyperoxaluria in the cat. *Vet. Rec.*, **125**: 31–4.

MEYERS-WALLEN, V. N., WILSON, J. D., GRIFFIN, J. E., FISHER, S., MOORHEAD, P. H., GOLDSCHMIDT, M. H., HASKINS, M. E. AND PATTERSON, D. F. (1989) Testicular feminization in a cat. *J. Amer. Vet. Med. Assoc.*, **195**: 631–4.

MORAN, C., GILLIES, C. B. AND NICHOLAS, F. W. (1984) Fertile male tortoiseshell cats. *J. Hered.*, **75**: 397–402.

MORRISON-SCOTT, T. C. S. (1952) The mummified cats of ancient Egypt. *Proc. Zool. Soc. Lond.*, **121**: 861–7.

MOUTSCHEN, J. (1950) Quelques particularités héréditaires du chat siamois. *Nat. Belges*, **31**: 200–3.

MURRAY, J. A., BLAKEMORE, W. J. AND BARNETT, K. C. (1977) Ocular lesions in cats with GM1 gangliosidosis with visceral involvement. *J. Small Anim. Pract.*, **18**: 1–10.

NARFSTRÖM, K. (1983) Hereditary progressive retinal atrophy in the Abyssinian cat. *J. Hered.*, **74**: 273–6.

NARFSTRÖM K. (1985) Progressive retinal atrophy in the Abyssinian cat. *Invest. Ophthalmol. Vis. Sci.*, **26**: 193–200.

NODEN, D. M. AND EVANS, H. (1986) Inherited homeotic midfacial malformations in Burmese cats. *J. Craniof. Genet. Devel. Biol. (Suppl.)*, **2**: 249–66.

NORBY, D. E. AND THULINE, H. C. (1965) Gene action in the X chromosome of the cat. *Cytogenetics*, **4**: 240–4.

NORBY, D. E. AND THULINE, H. C. (1970) Inherited tremor in the domestic cat. *Nature*, **227**: 1262–3.

PATTERSON, D. F. AND MINOR, R. F. (1977) Hereditary fragility and hyperextensibility of the skin of cats. *Lab. Invest.*, **37**: 170–9.

PEARSON, H., GASKELL, C. J., GIBBS, C. AND WATERMAN, A. (1974) Pyloric and oesophageal dysfunction in the cat. *J. Small Anim. Pract.*, 15: 487–501.

POCOCK, R. I. (1907) Crosses between *Felis silvestris* and *Felis acreata ugandae. Proc. Zool. Soc. Lond.*, 1907: 749–50.

PRIEUR, D. J. AND COLLIER, L. L. (1981a) Inheritance of the Chediak–Higashi syndrome in cats. *J. Hered.*, 72: 175–7.

PRIEUR, D. J. AND COLLIER, L. L. (1981b) Morphologic basis of inherited coat colour dilutions of cats. *J. Hered.*, 72: 178–82.

PRIEUR, D. J. AND COLLIER, L. L. (1984) Maltese dilution of domestic cats. *J. Hered.*, 75: 41–4.

PRIEUR, D. J., COLLIER, L. L., BRYAN, G. M. AND MEYERS, K. M. (1979) The diagnosis of feline Chediak–Higashi syndrome. *Feline Pract.*, 9: 26–32.

PUJOL, R., REBILLARD, M. AND REBILLARD, G. (1977) Primary neural disorders in the deaf white cat cochlea. *Acta Otolaryngol.*, 83: 59–64.

REBILLARD, M., PUJOL, R. AND REBILLARD, G. (1981a) Variability of hereditary deafness in the white cat. II. Histology. *Hear. Res.*, 5: 189–200.

REBILLARD, M., REBILLARD, G. AND PUJOL, R. (1981b) Variability of the hereditary deafness in the white cat. I. Physiology. *Hear, Res.*, 5: 179–87.

ROBINSON, R. (1959) Genetics of the domestic cat. *Bibliogr. Genet.*, 18: 273–362.

ROBINSON, R. (1973) The Canadian hairless or sphinx cat. *J. Hered.*, 64: 47–9.

ROBINSON, R. (1976) Genetic aspects of umbilical hernia incidence in cats and dogs. *Vet. Rec.*, 100: 9–10.

ROBINSON, R. (1981) A third hypotrichosis in the domestic cat. *Genetica*, 55: 39–40.

ROBINSON, R. (1985) Fertile male tortoiseshell cats. *J. Hered.*, 76: 137–8.

ROBINSON, R. (1989) The American curl cat. *J. Hered.*, 80: 474–5.

RUBIN, L. F. (1986) Hereditary cataract in Himalayan cats. *Feline Pract.*, 26: 14–15.

RUBIN, L. F. AND LIPTON, D. E. (1937) Retinal degeneration in kittens. *J. Amer. Vet. Med. Assoc.*, 162: 467–9.

SCHWANGART, F. AND GRAU, H. (1931) Ueber entformung, besonders die vererbbaren Schwangmissbildungen bei des Hauskatze. *Z. Tierz. Zuchtsbiol.*, 21: 203–49.

SEARLE, A. G. (1953) Hereditary "split-hand" in the domestic cat. *Ann. Eugen.*, 17: 279–82.

SEARLE, A. G. (1968) *Comparative Genetics of Coat Colour in Mammals*. London: Logos Press.

SILSON, M. AND ROBINSON, R. (1969) Hereditary hydrocephalus in the cat. *Vet. Rec.*, **84**: 477.

SPONENBERG, D. P. AND GRAF-WEBSTER, E. (1986) Hereditary meningoencephalocele in Burmese cats. *J. Hered.*, **77**: 60.

THIBOS, L. N., LEVICK, W. R. AND MORSTYN, R. (1980) Ocular pigmentation in white and Siamese cats. *Invest. Ophthalmol. Vis. Sci.*, **19**: 475–82.

THOMPSON, J. C., COBB, V. C., KEELER, C. V. AND DMYTRYK, M. (1943) Genetics of the Burmese cat. *J. Hered.*, **34**: 119–23.

TJEBBES, K. (1924) Crosses with Siamese cats. *J. Genet.*, **14**: 355–66.

TODD, N. B. (1951) A pink eyed dilution in the cat. *J. Hered.*, **52**: 202.

TURNER, P. AND ROBINSON, R. (1973) Melanin inhibitor: a dominant gene in the cat. *J. Hered.*, **71**: 427–8.

TURNER, P., ROBINSON, R. AND DYTE, C. E. (1981) Blue eyed albino: a new albino allele in the domestic cat. *Genetica*, **56**: 71–3.

ULLMAN, E. AND HARGREAVES, A. (1958) New coat colours in domestic cats. *Proc. Zool. Soc. Lond.*, **130**: 606–9.

VANDEVELDE, M., FRANKHAUSER, R., WIESMANN, U. AND HERSCHKOWITZ, N. (1982) Hereditary neurovisceral mannosidosis associated with alpha-mannosidase deficiency in a family of Persian cats. *Acta Neuropathol.*, **58**: 64–5.

VAWER, G. D. (1981) Corneal mummification in colourpoint cats. *Vet. Rec.*, **109**: 413.

WEIGEL, L. (1961) Das Fellmuster der wildebenden Katzenarten und der Hauskatze in wergleichender und stammesgeschtlicher Hinsicht. *Saugetierk. Mitt.*, (*Suppl.*), **9**, 120pp.

WENGER, D. A., SATTLER, M., KUDOH, T., SNYDER, S. P. AND KINGSTON, R. S. (1980) Niemann-Pick disease: a genetic model in Siamese cats. *Science*, **208**: 1471–3.

WEST-HYDE, L. AND BUYUKMIHCI, N. (1982) Photoreceptor degeneration in a family of cats. *J. Amer. Vet. Med. Assoc.*, **181**: 243–5.

WHITING, P. W. (1919) Inheritance of white spotting and other coat characters in cats. *Amer. Nat.*, **53**: 433–82.

WILKINSON, G. T. AND KRISTENSEN, T. S. (1989) A hair abnormality in Abyssinian cats. *J. Small Anim. Pract.*, **30**: 27–8.

WILLIAM-JONES, H. E. (1944) Arrested development of the long bones of the fore limbs in a female cat. *Vet. Rec.*, **56**: 449.

WOODARD, J. C., COLLINS, G. H. AND HESSLER, J. R. (1974) Feline hereditary neuroaxonal dystrophy. *Amer. J. Pathol.*, **74**: 551–66.

ZEUNER, F. E. (1963) *A History of Domestic Animals*. London: Hutchinson.

ZOOK, B. C., SOSTARIC, B. R., DRAPER, D. J. AND GRAF-WEBSTER, E. (1983) Encephalocele and other congenital craniofacial anomalies in Burmese cats. *Vet. Med. Small Anim. Pract.*, **75**: 675–701.

Index

The entries may be used as a glossary for genetic terms by referring to the cited page(s).

Impenetrance 55
Inbreeding 87
Inbreeding depression 101
Inbreeding version selection 108
Incomplete dominance 43
Individual merit section 76
Inhibitor allele 116, 166

Japanese bob-tail 179, 192

Kangaroo cat 203
Kinked tail 191
Korat 141

Lactation period 15
Lethal genes 181
Level bite 192
Like-to-like mating 98
Lilac colour 141
Lilac tabby 151
Linkage 57
Lipaemia 203
Litter size 15
Litters 14
Locus 29
Long hair 129, 132
Long haired breeds 174
Longevity 16
Longie Manx 204

Mackerel tabby 110, 142
Maine coon 176
Mannosidosis 203
Manx 16, 178, 204
Masking 48
Maternal impression 11
Meiosis 21
Melanin inhibitor 116
Meningoencephalocele 205
Mimic genes 52
Mitosis 20
Modifiers 67
Modifying genes 67
Mosaics 26
Mucopolysaccharidosis I 206
Mucopolysaccharidosis VI 206
Multiple alleles 44

Neuroaxonal dystrophy 206
Nicking 82
Non-agouti allele 112, 140
Normal overlaps 55
Norwegian forest cat 176

Ocicat 112, 156
Odd eyed white 125, 173
Oestrus 14
Onion hair 207
Orange 118
Orange eyed white 173
Oregon rex 131, 135
Overshot jaw 192

Parental generation (P) 31
Parrot mouth 192
Patella luxation 207
Pelger-Huet anomaly 208
Penetrance 55
Phenotype 33
Piebald spotting 122
Pink-eyed albino allele 113
Pink-eyed dilution 116
Pleiotropism 56
Polycystic renal disease 208
Polydactyly 208
Polygenes 64
Polygenic inheritance 66, 70
Porphyria 209
Prepotency 97
Progeny testing 83
Progressive retinal atrophy 209
Puberty 13
Pyloric stenosis 210

Ragdoll 172
Random assortment 33
Random mating 86
Recessive 33
Red tabby 153
Repulsion linkage 58
Rex breeds 52, 176
Rex coat 129
Rufism 126
Rumpy Manx 204
Rumpy-riser Manx 204
Russian blue 141